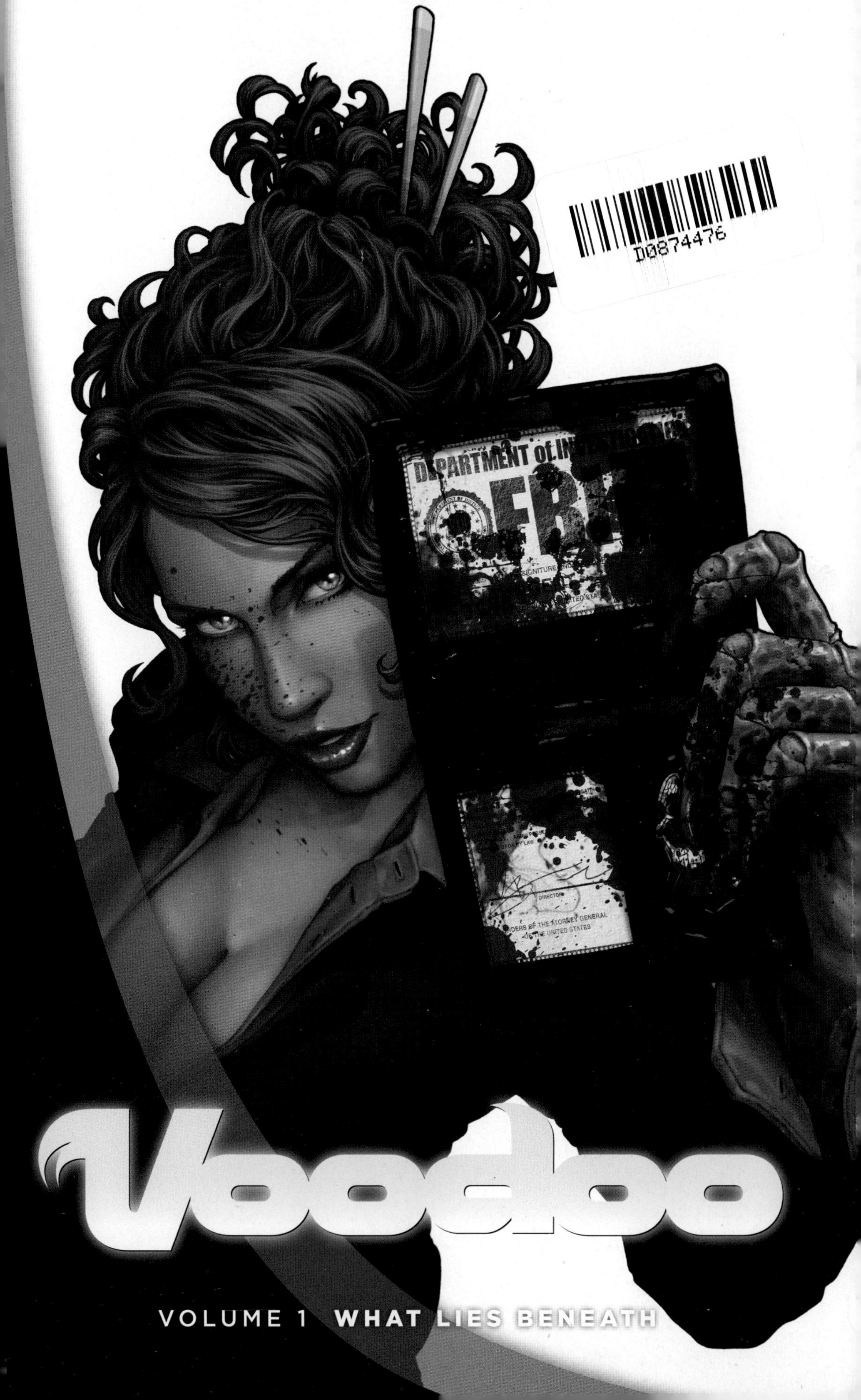

Voodoo

VOLUME 1 WHAT LIES BENEATH

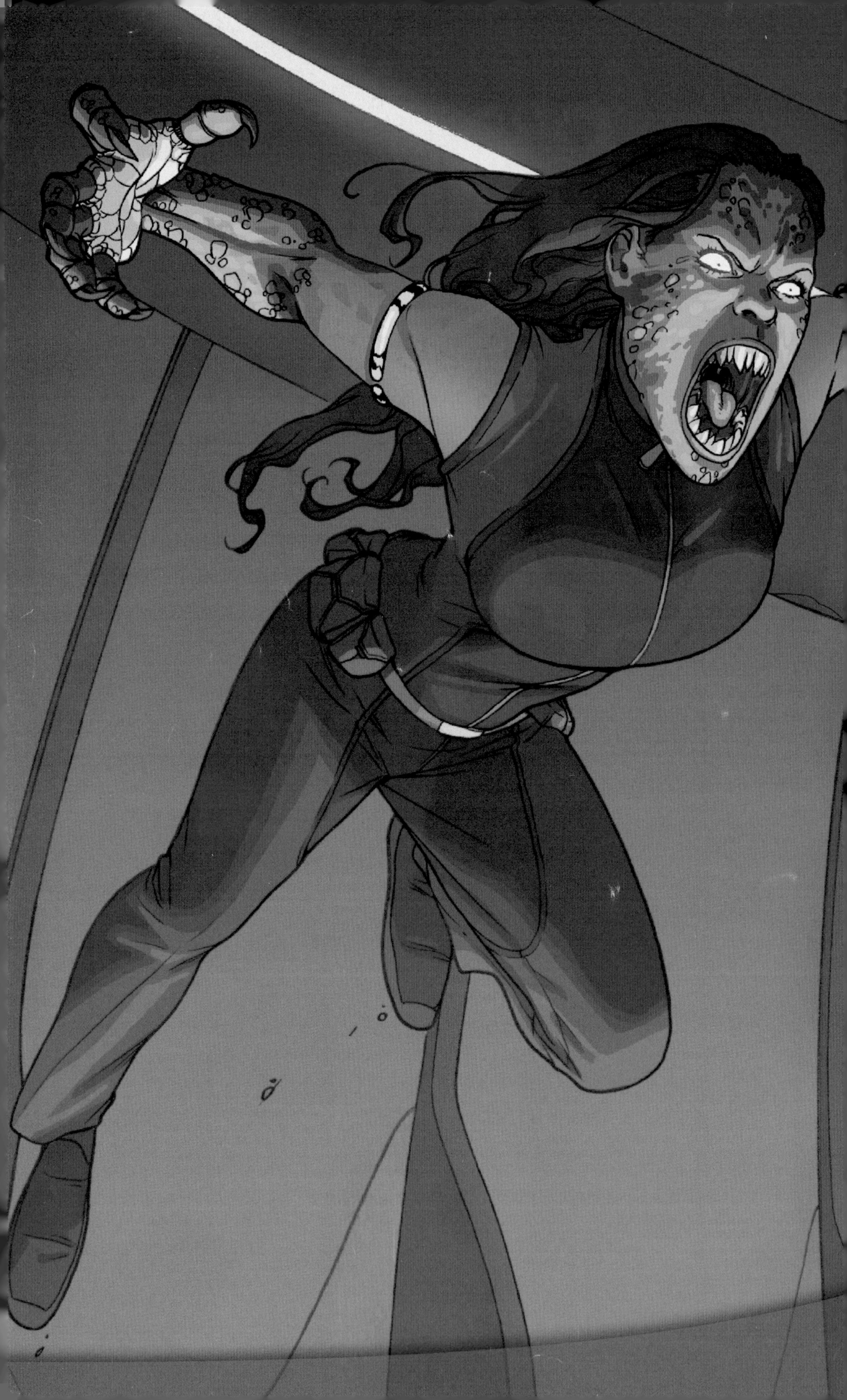

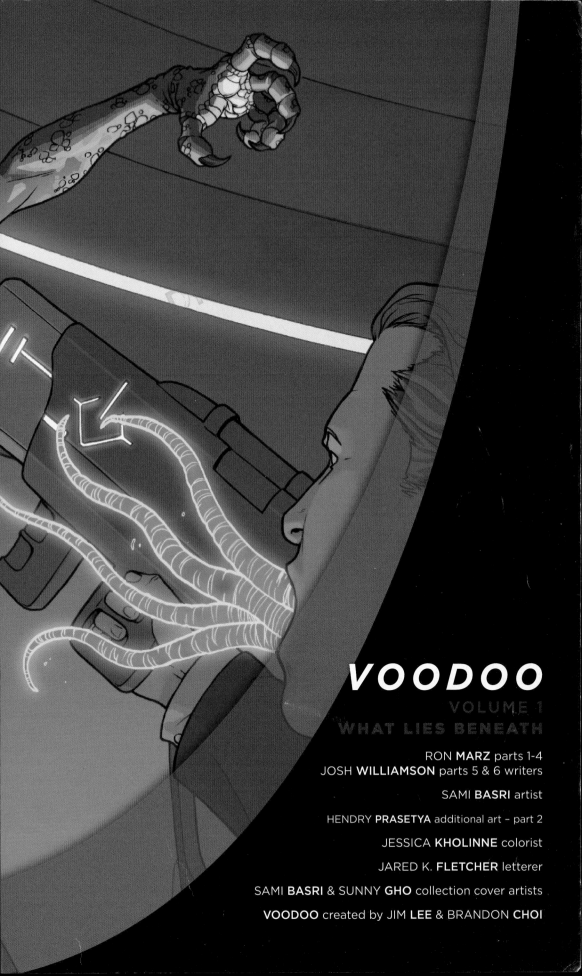

VOODOO

VOLUME 1
WHAT LIES BENEATH

RON **MARZ** parts 1-4
JOSH **WILLIAMSON** parts 5 & 6 writers

SAMI **BASRI** artist

HENDRY **PRASETYA** additional art – part 2

JESSICA **KHOLINNE** colorist

JARED K. **FLETCHER** letterer

SAMI **BASRI** & SUNNY **GHO** collection cover artists

VOODOO created by JIM **LEE** & BRANDON **CHOI**

BRIAN CUNNINGHAM BOBBIE CHASE REX OGLE Editors – Original Series DARREN SHAN KATIE KUBERT Assistant Editors – Original Series
ROWENA YOW Editor ROBBIN BROSTERMAN Design Director – Books ROBBIE BIEDERMAN Publication Design

BOB HARRAS VP – Editor-in-Chief

DIANE NELSON President DAN DIDIO and JIM LEE Co-Publishers GEOFF JOHNS Chief Creative Officer
JOHN ROOD Executive VP – Sales, Marketing and Business Development AMY GENKINS Senior VP – Business and Legal Affairs
NAIRI GARDINER Senior VP – Finance JEFF BOISON VP – Publishing Operations MARK CHIARELLO VP – Art Direction and Design
JOHN CUNNINGHAM VP – Marketing TERRI CUNNINGHAM VP – Talent Relations and Services
ALISON GILL Senior VP – Manufacturing and Operations HANK KANALZ Senior VP – Digital
JAY KOGAN VP – Business and Legal Affairs, Publishing JACK MAHAN VP – Business Affairs, Talent
NICK NAPOLITANO VP – Manufacturing Administration SUE POHJA VP – Book Sales
COURTNEY SIMMONS Senior VP – Publicity BOB WAYNE Senior VP – Sales

VOODOO VOLUME 1: WHAT LIES BENEATH

DC Comics, 1700 Broadway, New York, NY 10019
A Warner Bros. Entertainment Company.
Printed by RR Donnelley, Salem, VA, USA. 8/24/12. First Printing.
ISBN: 978-1-4012-3561-1

Library of Congress Cataloging-in-Publication Data

Marz, Ron.
Voodoo. Volume 1, What lies beneath / Ron Marz, Josh Williamson, Sami
Basri.
p. cm.
"Originally published in single magazine form in VOODOO 1-6."
ISBN 978-1-4012-3561-1
1. Graphic novels. I. Williamson, Joshua. II. Basri, Sami. III. Title.
IV. Title: What lies beneath.
PN6728.V66M37 2012
741.5'973—dc23
2012018775   2012015217

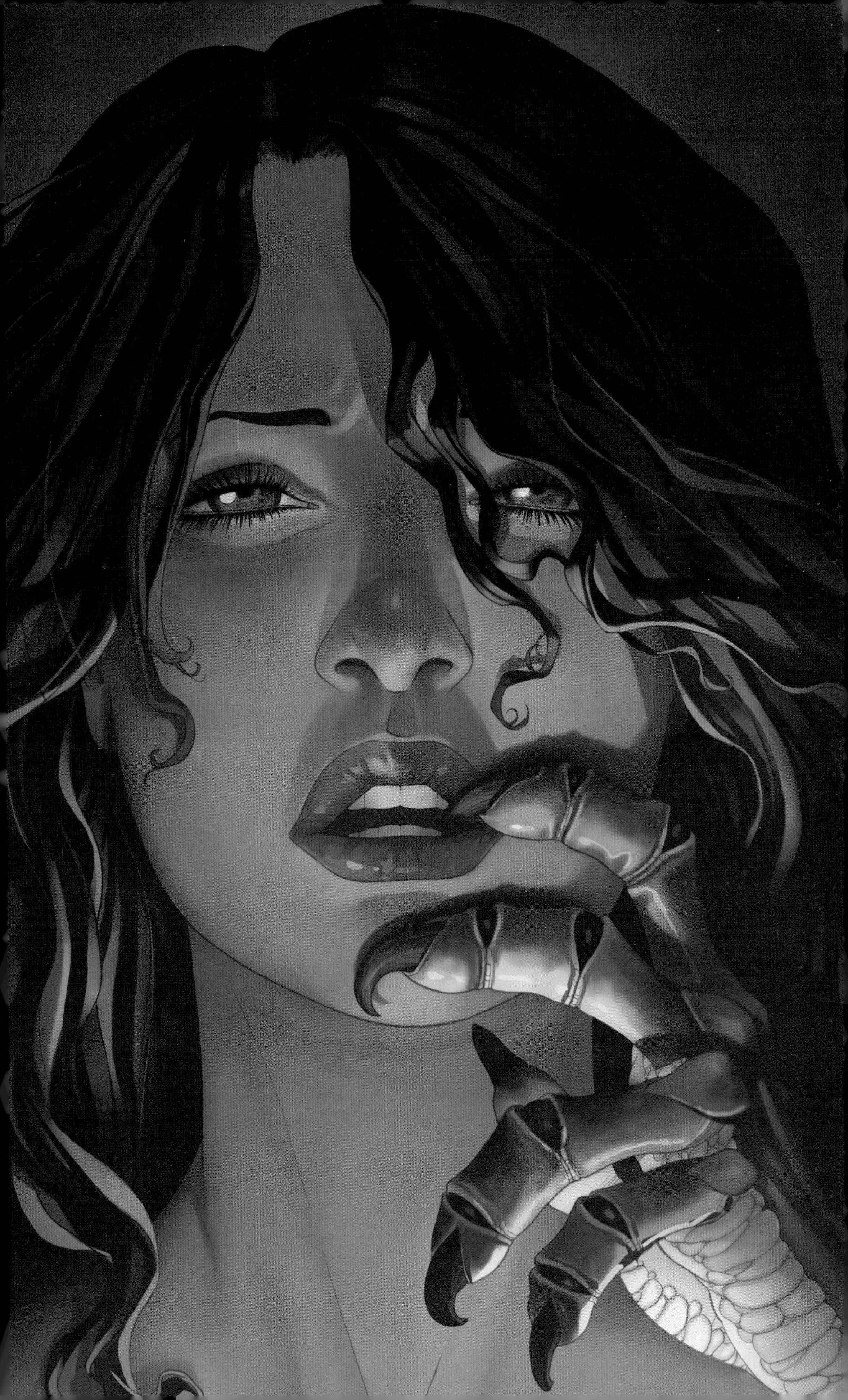

cover art by
SAMI BASRI & SUNNY GHO

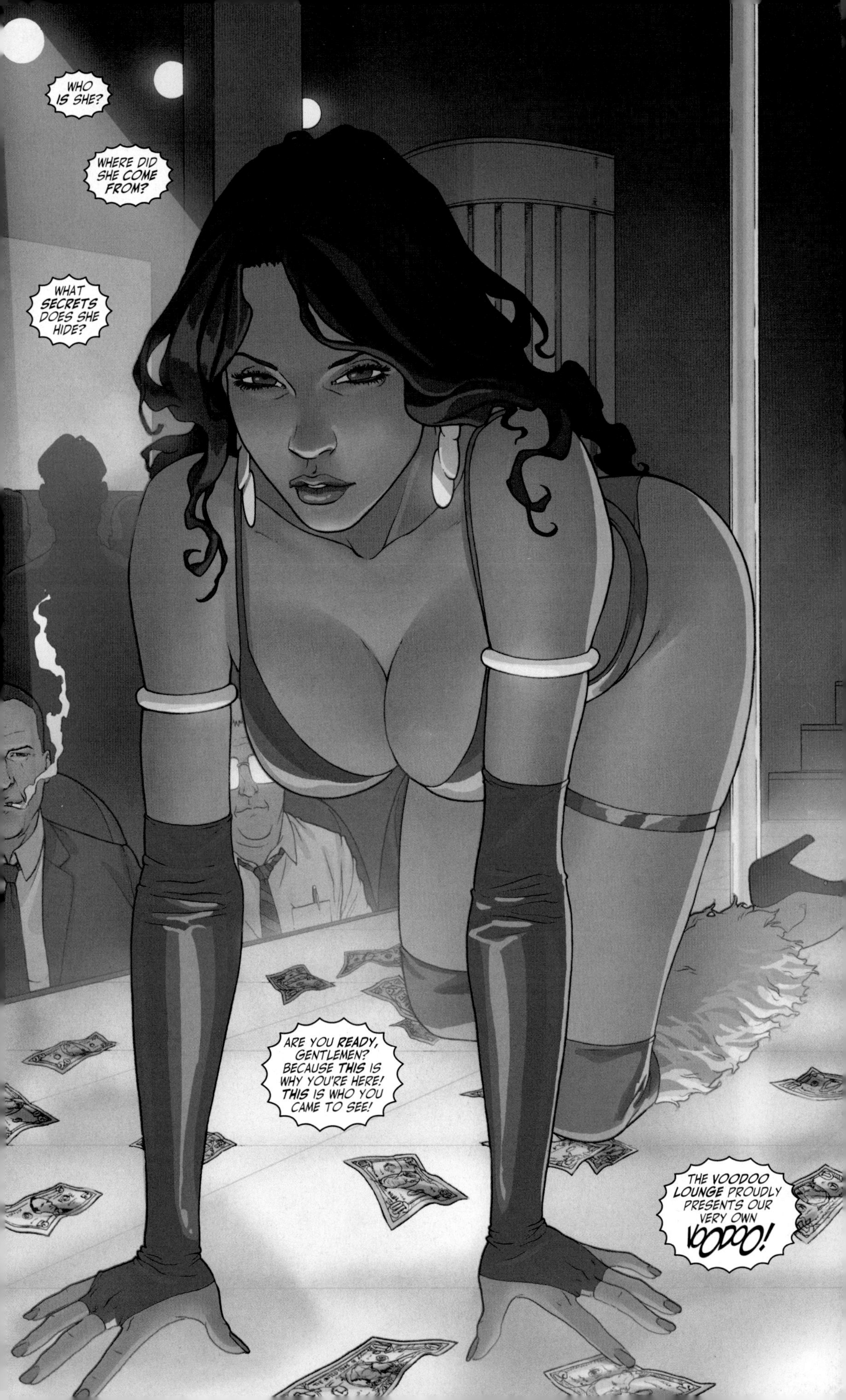
WHO IS SHE?
WHERE DID SHE COME FROM?
WHAT SECRETS DOES SHE HIDE?
ARE YOU READY, GENTLEMEN? BECAUSE THIS IS WHY YOU'RE HERE! THIS IS WHO YOU CAME TO SEE!
THE VOODOO LOUNGE PROUDLY PRESENTS OUR VERY OWN VOODOO!

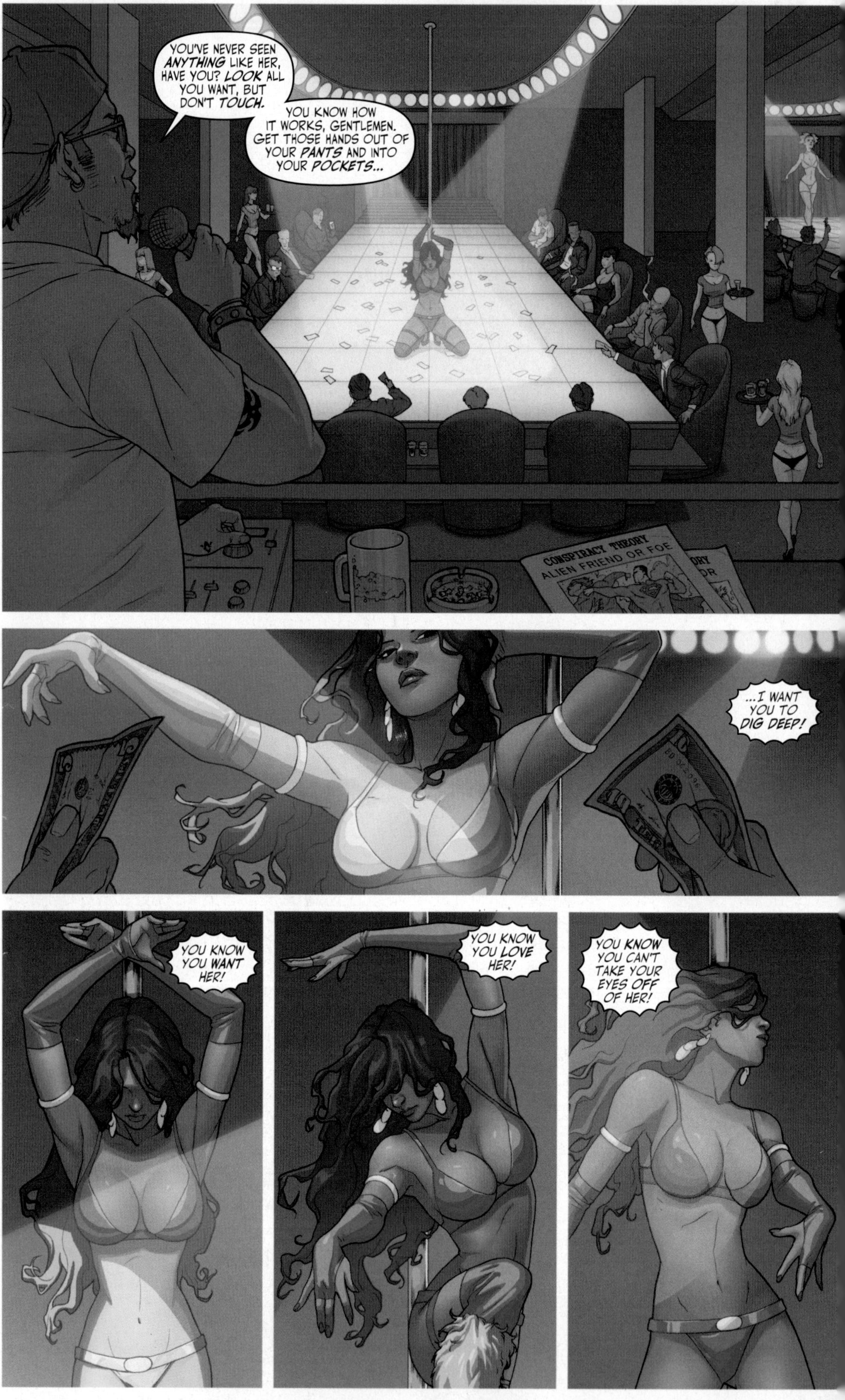
YOU'VE NEVER SEEN ANYTHING LIKE HER, HAVE YOU? LOOK ALL YOU WANT, BUT DON'T TOUCH.
YOU KNOW HOW IT WORKS, GENTLEMEN. GET THOSE HANDS OUT OF YOUR PANTS AND INTO YOUR POCKETS...
CONSPIRACY THEORY
ALIEN FRIEND OR FOE
...I WANT YOU TO DIG DEEP!
YOU KNOW YOU WANT HER!
YOU KNOW YOU LOVE HER!
YOU KNOW YOU CAN'T TAKE YOUR EYES OFF OF HER!

HOW LONG YOU PLANNING ON SITTING HERE, EVANS?

WHAT'S THE PROBLEM? WE'RE GETTING *PAID.* ENJOY THE SHOW.

NOT MY FLAVOR. WHICH I THINK YOU *KNOW.*

WE'RE SUPPOSED TO BE KEEPING AN EYE ON HER, RIGHT? THAT'S WHAT I'M DOING, FALLON.

WE DON'T NEED TO BE DOING IT FROM A RINGSIDE SEAT.

IT'S NOT LIKE WE CAN *MOVE* ON HER WITHOUT EXEC ORDERS ANYWAY.

WELL, I'D BETTER STICK CLOSE TO THE TARGET JUST IN CASE.

YOU'RE AN ASS.

I'M GOING BACK TO MY ROOM.

SUIT YOURSELF.

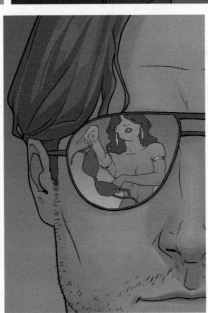

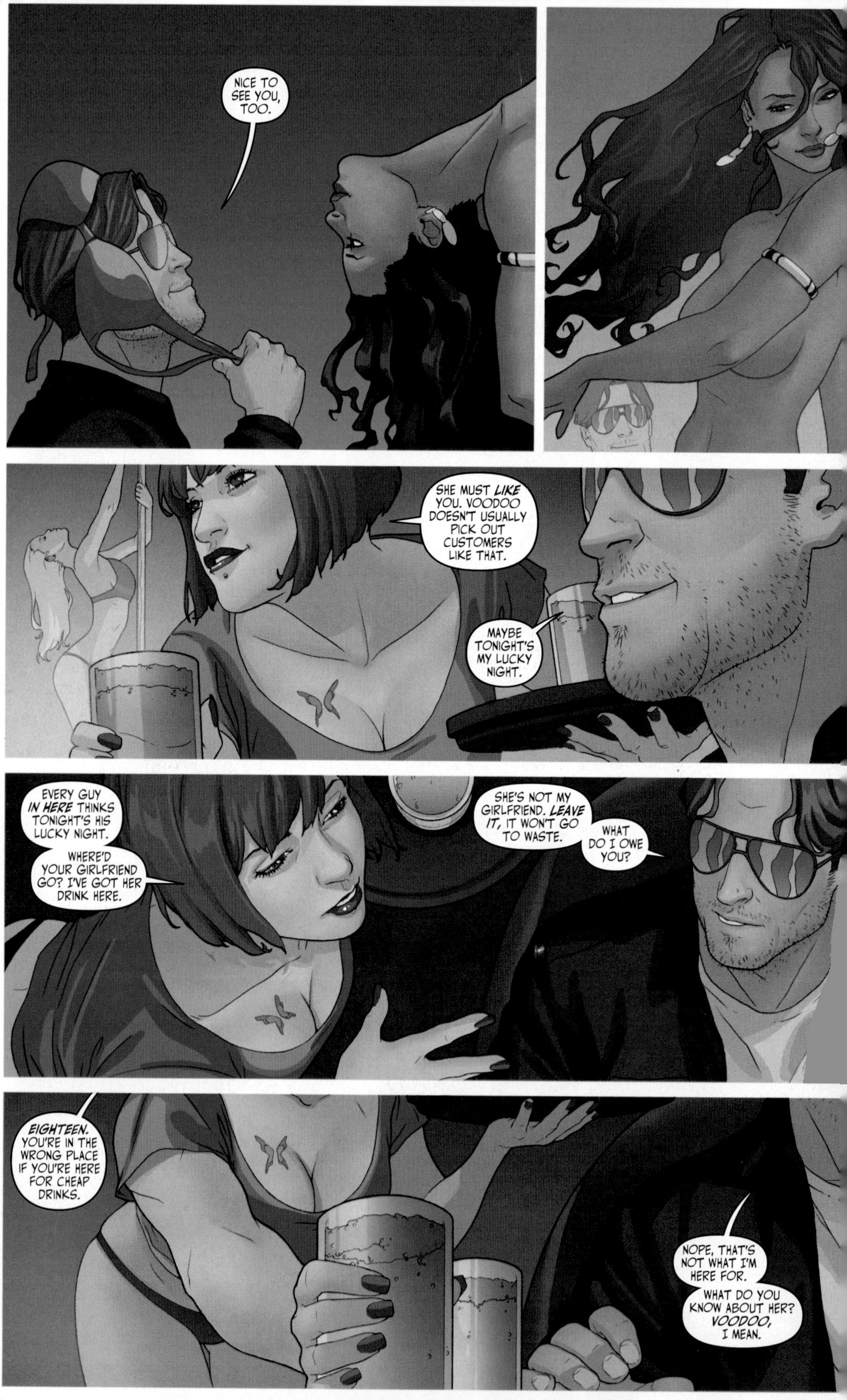
NICE TO SEE YOU, TOO.
SHE MUST LIKE YOU. VOODOO DOESN'T USUALLY PICK OUT CUSTOMERS LIKE THAT.
MAYBE TONIGHT'S MY LUCKY NIGHT.
EVERY GUY IN HERE THINKS TONIGHT'S HIS LUCKY NIGHT.
WHERE'D YOUR GIRLFRIEND GO? I'VE GOT HER DRINK HERE.
SHE'S NOT MY GIRLFRIEND. LEAVE IT, IT WON'T GO TO WASTE.
WHAT DO I OWE YOU?
EIGHTEEN. YOU'RE IN THE WRONG PLACE IF YOU'RE HERE FOR CHEAP DRINKS.
NOPE, THAT'S NOT WHAT I'M HERE FOR.
WHAT DO YOU KNOW ABOUT HER? VOODOO, I MEAN.

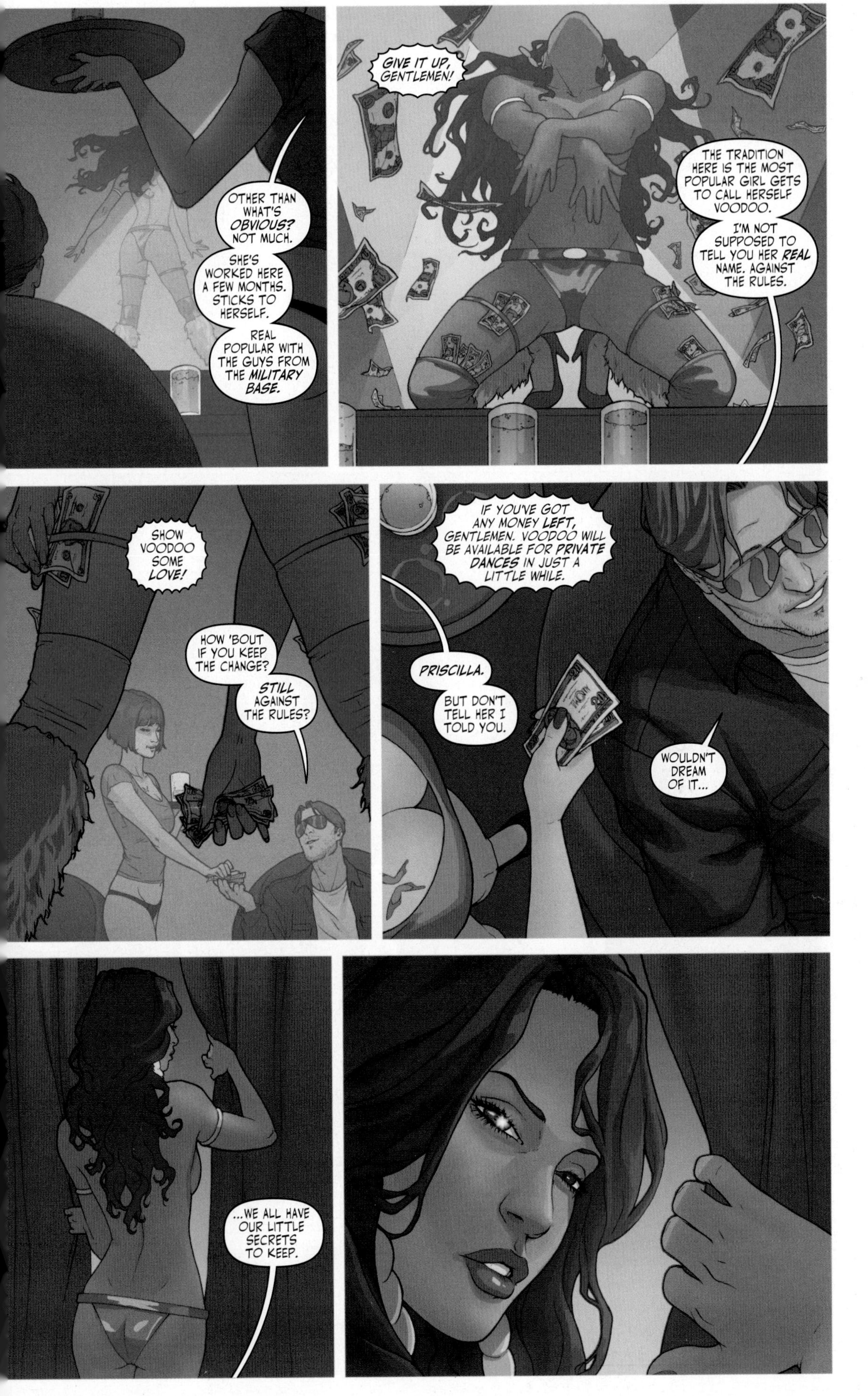

OTHER THAN WHAT'S OBVIOUS? NOT MUCH.
SHE'S WORKED HERE A FEW MONTHS. STICKS TO HERSELF.
REAL POPULAR WITH THE GUYS FROM THE MILITARY BASE.
GIVE IT UP, GENTLEMEN!
THE TRADITION HERE IS THE MOST POPULAR GIRL GETS TO CALL HERSELF VOODOO.
I'M NOT SUPPOSED TO TELL YOU HER REAL NAME. AGAINST THE RULES.
SHOW VOODOO SOME LOVE!
HOW 'BOUT IF YOU KEEP THE CHANGE?
STILL AGAINST THE RULES?
IF YOU'VE GOT ANY MONEY LEFT, GENTLEMEN. VOODOO WILL BE AVAILABLE FOR PRIVATE DANCES IN JUST A LITTLE WHILE.
PRISCILLA.
BUT DON'T TELL HER I TOLD YOU.
WOULDN'T DREAM OF IT...
...WE ALL HAVE OUR LITTLE SECRETS TO KEEP.

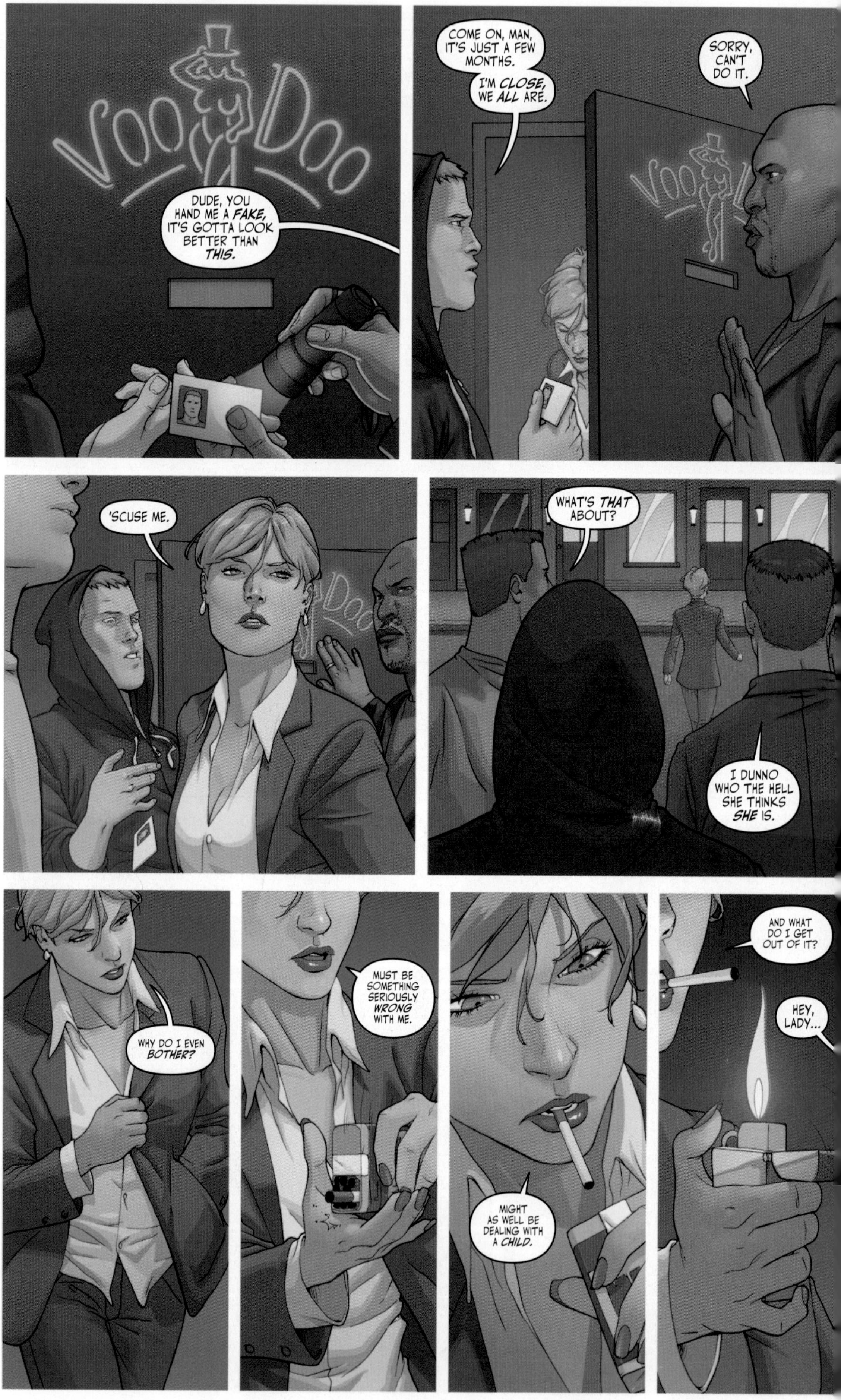
DUDE, YOU HAND ME A FAKE, IT'S GOTTA LOOK BETTER THAN THIS.
COME ON, MAN, IT'S JUST A FEW MONTHS.
I'M CLOSE, WE ALL ARE.
SORRY, CAN'T DO IT.
'SCUSE ME.
WHAT'S THAT ABOUT?
I DUNNO WHO THE HELL SHE THINKS SHE IS.
WHY DO I EVEN BOTHER?
MUST BE SOMETHING SERIOUSLY WRONG WITH ME.
MIGHT AS WELL BE DEALING WITH A CHILD.
AND WHAT DO I GET OUT OF IT?
HEY, LADY...

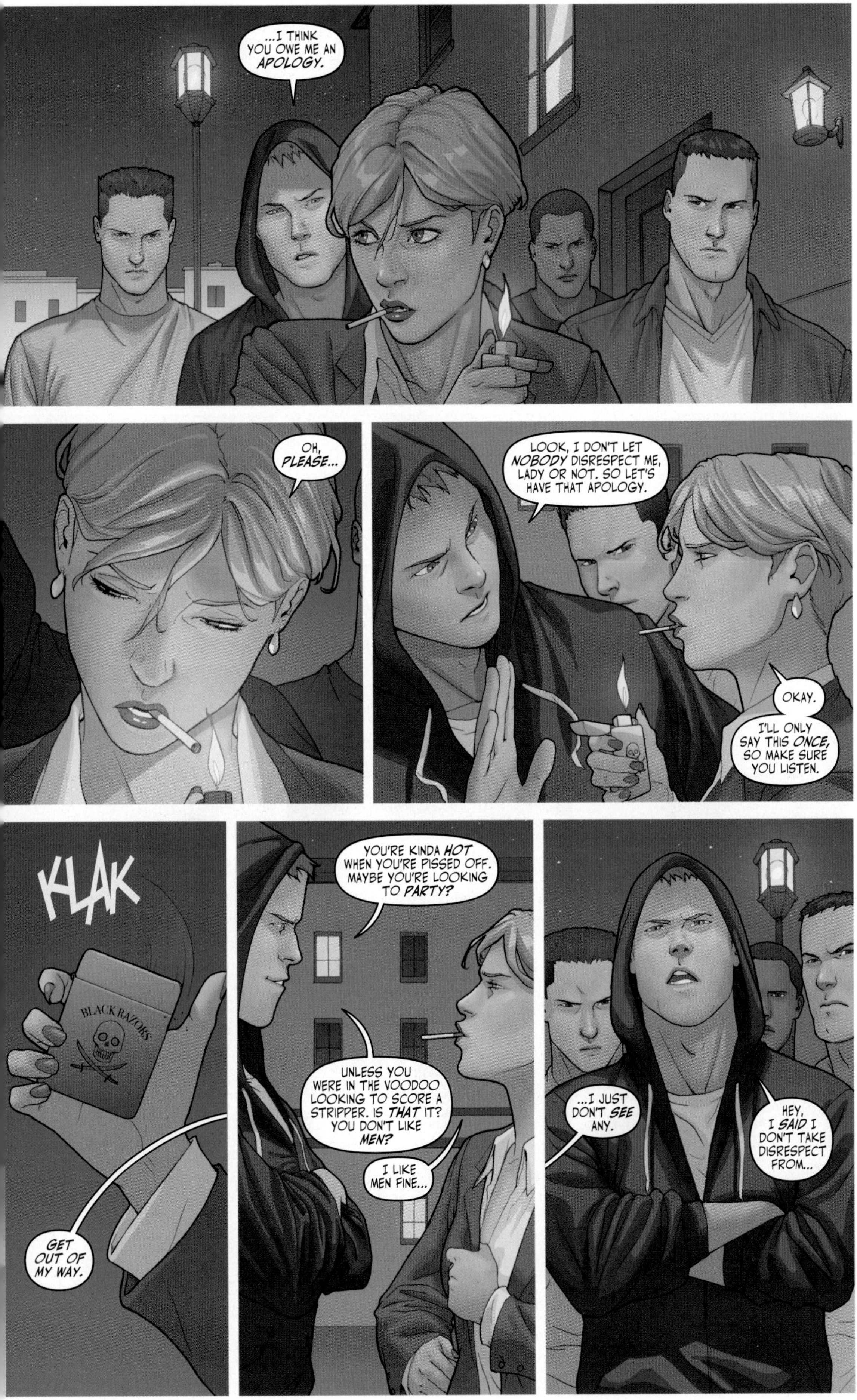
...I THINK YOU OWE ME AN APOLOGY.
OH, PLEASE...
LOOK, I DON'T LET NOBODY DISRESPECT ME, LADY OR NOT. SO LET'S HAVE THAT APOLOGY.
OKAY.
I'LL ONLY SAY THIS ONCE, SO MAKE SURE YOU LISTEN.
KLAK
BLACK RAZORS
GET OUT OF MY WAY.
YOU'RE KINDA HOT WHEN YOU'RE PISSED OFF. MAYBE YOU'RE LOOKING TO PARTY?
UNLESS YOU WERE IN THE VOODOO LOOKING TO SCORE A STRIPPER. IS THAT IT? YOU DON'T LIKE MEN?
I LIKE MEN FINE...
...I JUST DON'T SEE ANY.
HEY, I SAID I DON'T TAKE DISRESPECT FROM...

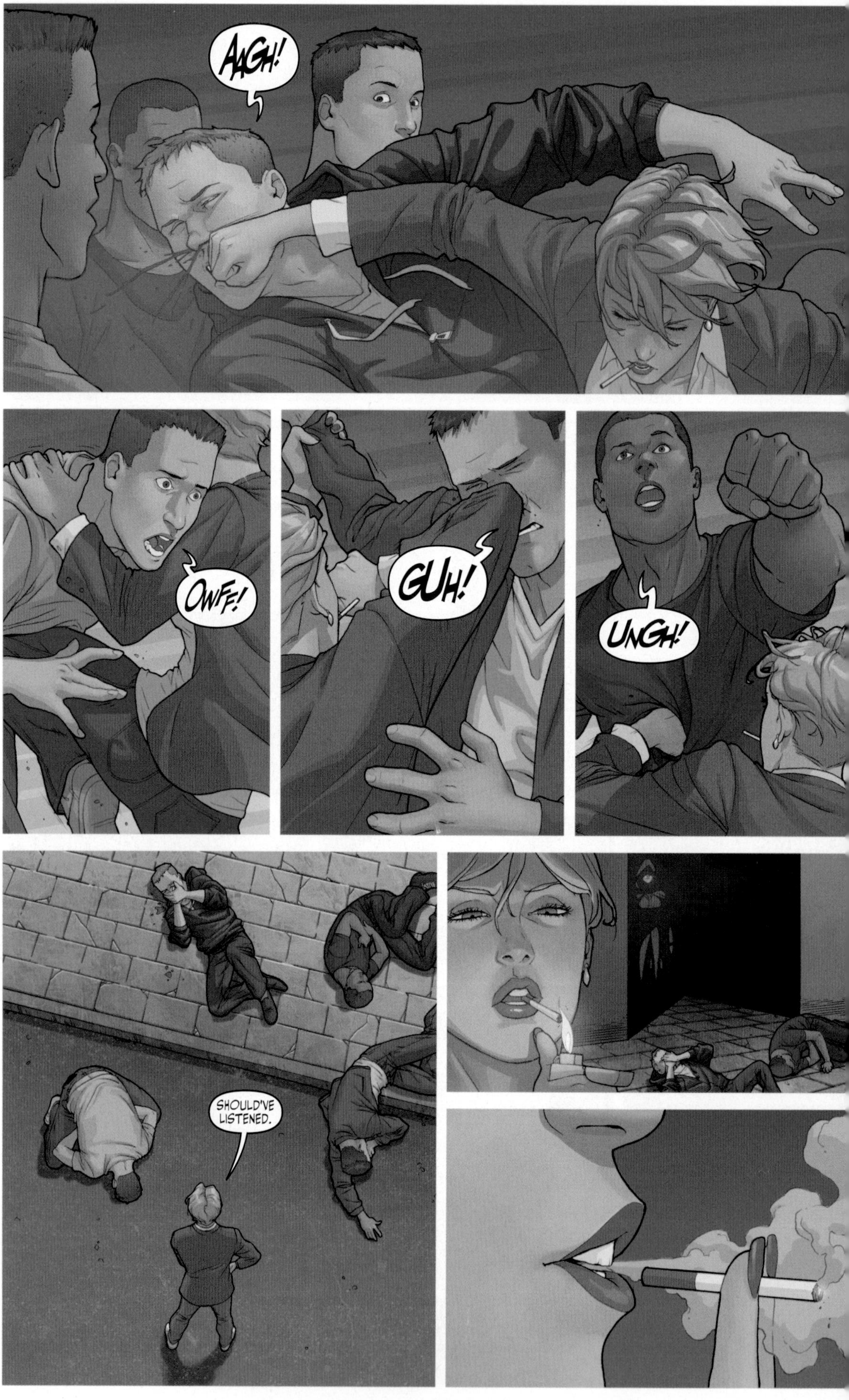
AAGH!
OWFF!
GUH!
UNGH!
SHOULD'VE LISTENED.

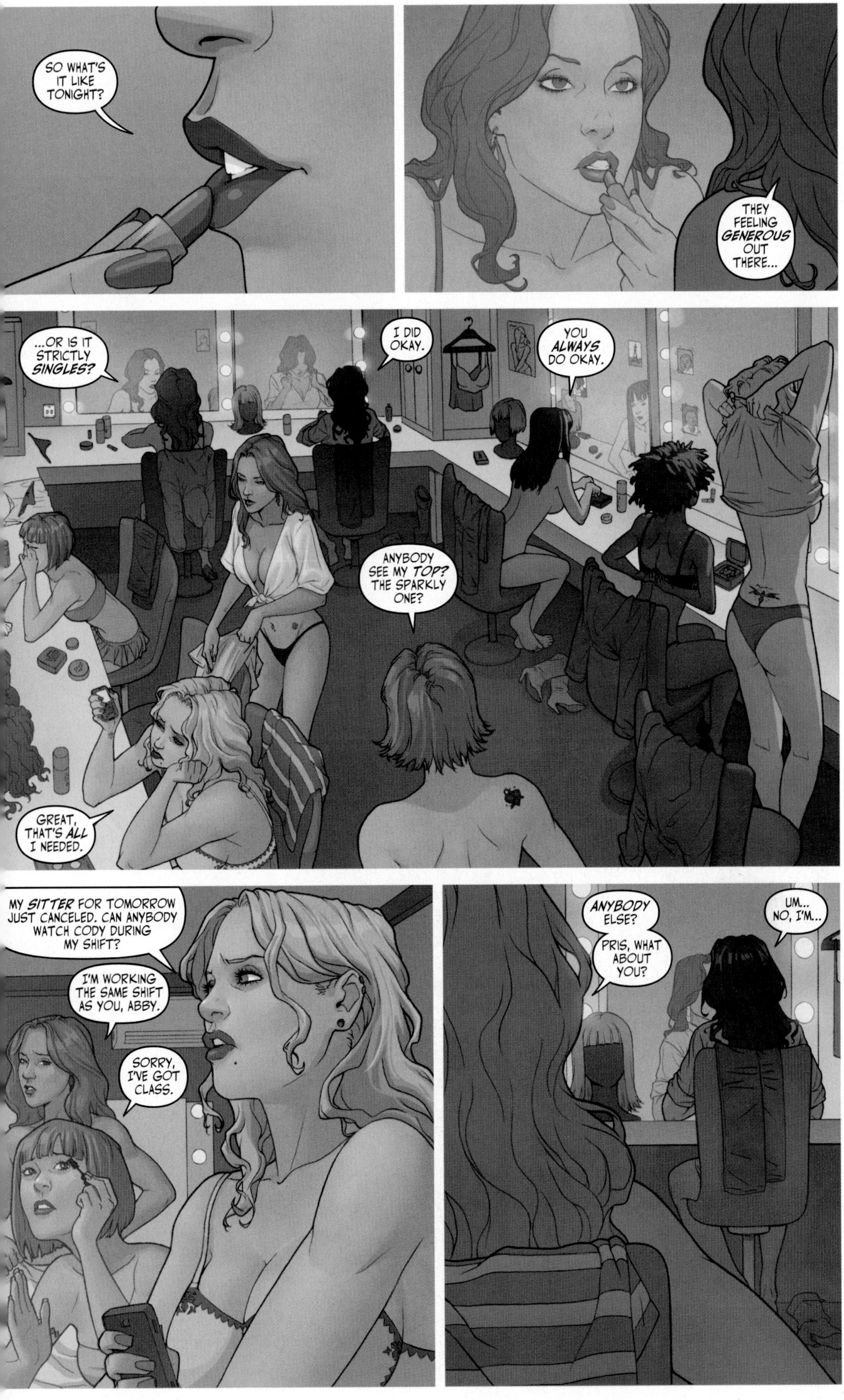
SO WHAT'S IT LIKE TONIGHT?
THEY FEELING GENEROUS OUT THERE...
...OR IS IT STRICTLY SINGLES?
I DID OKAY.
YOU ALWAYS DO OKAY.
ANYBODY SEE MY TOP? THE SPARKLY ONE?
GREAT, THAT'S ALL I NEEDED.
MY SITTER FOR TOMORROW JUST CANCELED. CAN ANYBODY WATCH CODY DURING MY SHIFT?
I'M WORKING THE SAME SHIFT AS YOU, ABBY.
SORRY, I'VE GOT CLASS.
ANYBODY ELSE?
PRIS, WHAT ABOUT YOU?
UM... NO, I'M...

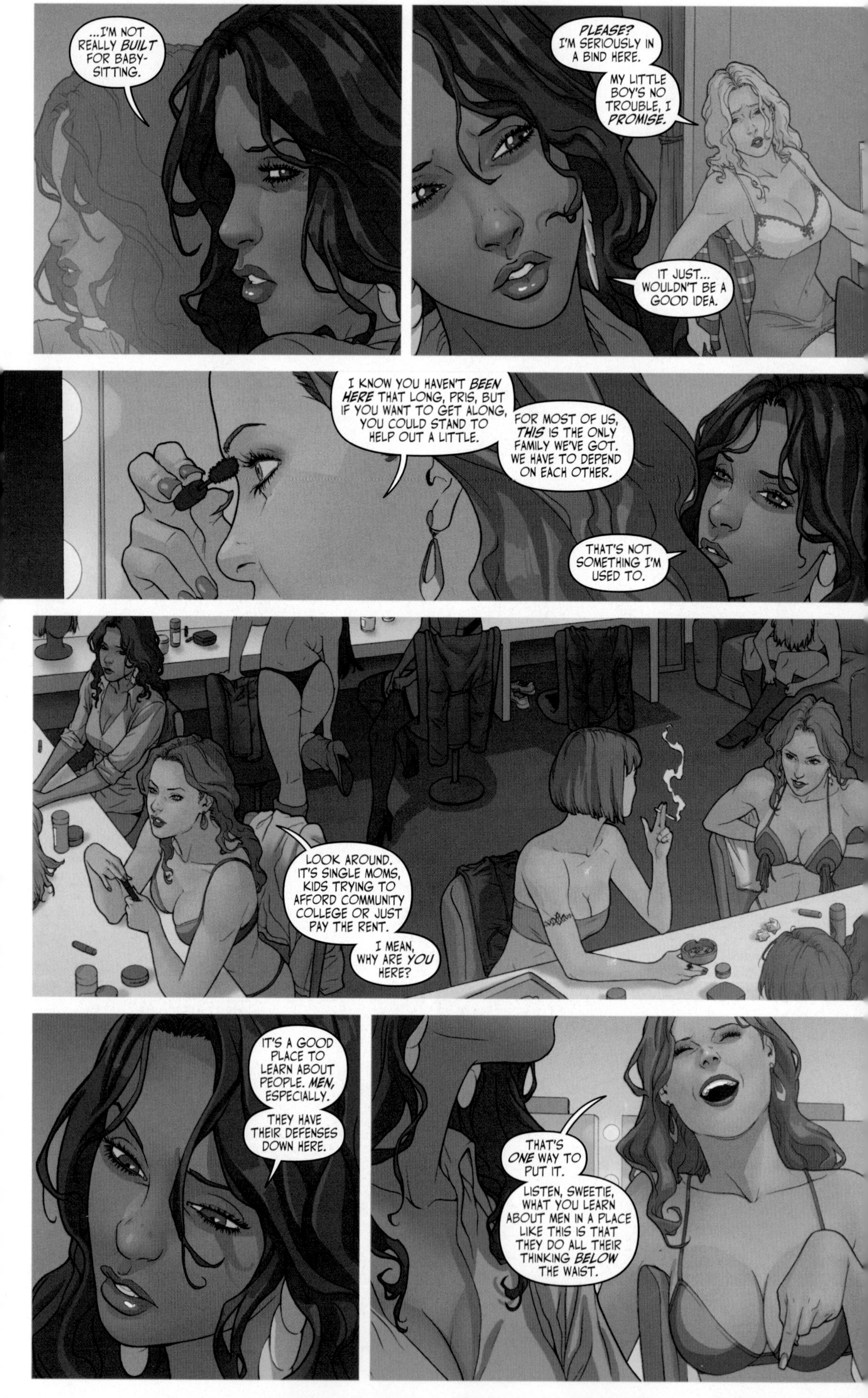
...I'M NOT REALLY BUILT FOR BABY-SITTING.
PLEASE? I'M SERIOUSLY IN A BIND HERE.
MY LITTLE BOY'S NO TROUBLE, I PROMISE.
IT JUST... WOULDN'T BE A GOOD IDEA.
I KNOW YOU HAVEN'T BEEN HERE THAT LONG, PRIS, BUT IF YOU WANT TO GET ALONG, YOU COULD STAND TO HELP OUT A LITTLE.
FOR MOST OF US, THIS IS THE ONLY FAMILY WE'VE GOT. WE HAVE TO DEPEND ON EACH OTHER.
THAT'S NOT SOMETHING I'M USED TO.
LOOK AROUND. IT'S SINGLE MOMS, KIDS TRYING TO AFFORD COMMUNITY COLLEGE OR JUST PAY THE RENT.
I MEAN, WHY ARE YOU HERE?
IT'S A GOOD PLACE TO LEARN ABOUT PEOPLE. MEN, ESPECIALLY.
THEY HAVE THEIR DEFENSES DOWN HERE.
THAT'S ONE WAY TO PUT IT.
LISTEN, SWEETIE, WHAT YOU LEARN ABOUT MEN IN A PLACE LIKE THIS IS THAT THEY DO ALL THEIR THINKING BELOW THE WAIST.

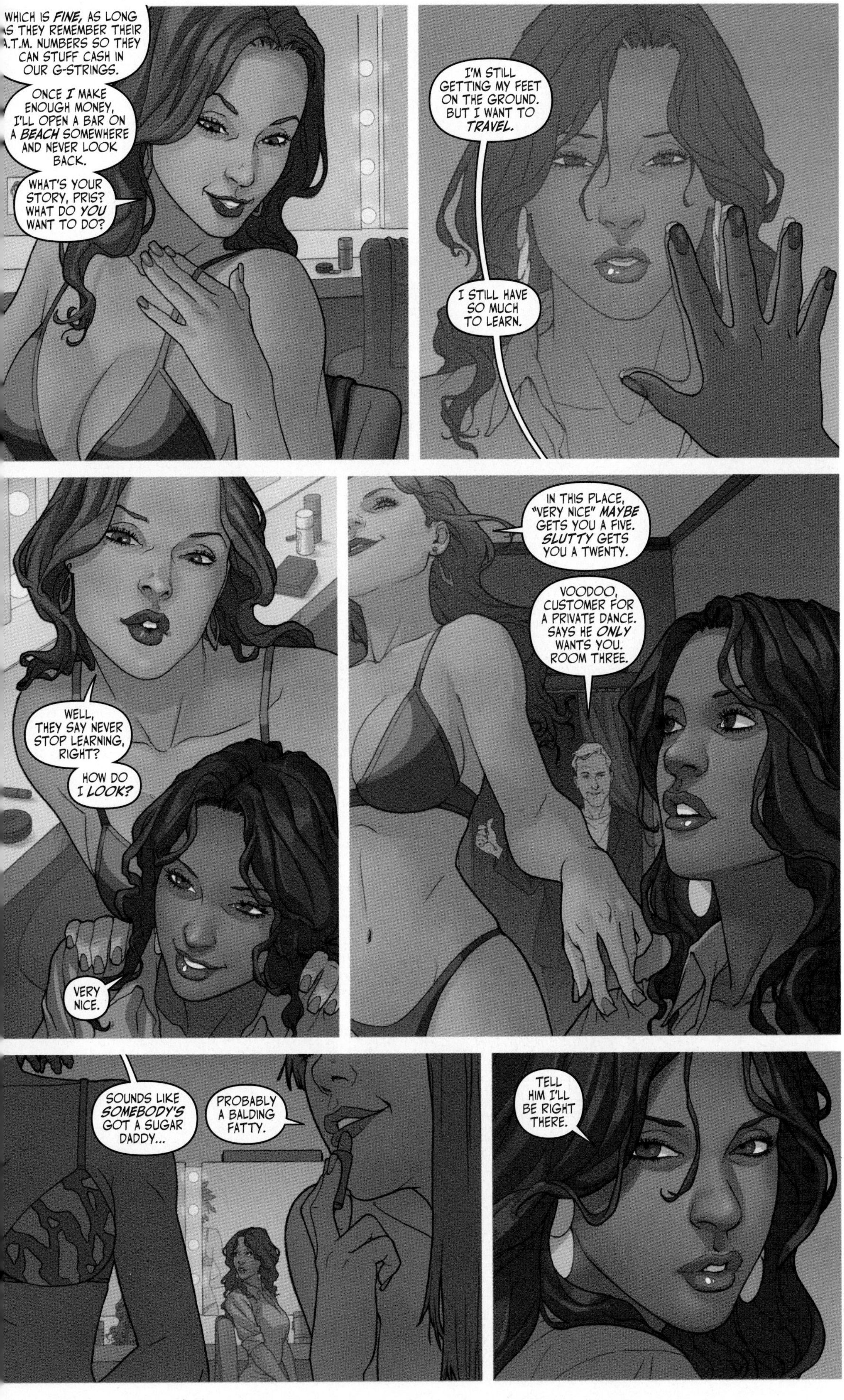
WHICH IS FINE, AS LONG AS THEY REMEMBER THEIR A.T.M. NUMBERS SO THEY CAN STUFF CASH IN OUR G-STRINGS.
ONCE I MAKE ENOUGH MONEY, I'LL OPEN A BAR ON A BEACH SOMEWHERE AND NEVER LOOK BACK.
WHAT'S YOUR STORY, PRIS? WHAT DO YOU WANT TO DO?
I'M STILL GETTING MY FEET ON THE GROUND. BUT I WANT TO TRAVEL.
I STILL HAVE SO MUCH TO LEARN.
WELL, THEY SAY NEVER STOP LEARNING, RIGHT?
HOW DO I LOOK?
VERY NICE.
IN THIS PLACE, "VERY NICE" MAYBE GETS YOU A FIVE. SLUTTY GETS YOU A TWENTY.
VOODOO, CUSTOMER FOR A PRIVATE DANCE. SAYS HE ONLY WANTS YOU. ROOM THREE.
SOUNDS LIKE SOMEBODY'S GOT A SUGAR DADDY...
PROBABLY A BALDING FATTY.
TELL HIM I'LL BE RIGHT THERE.

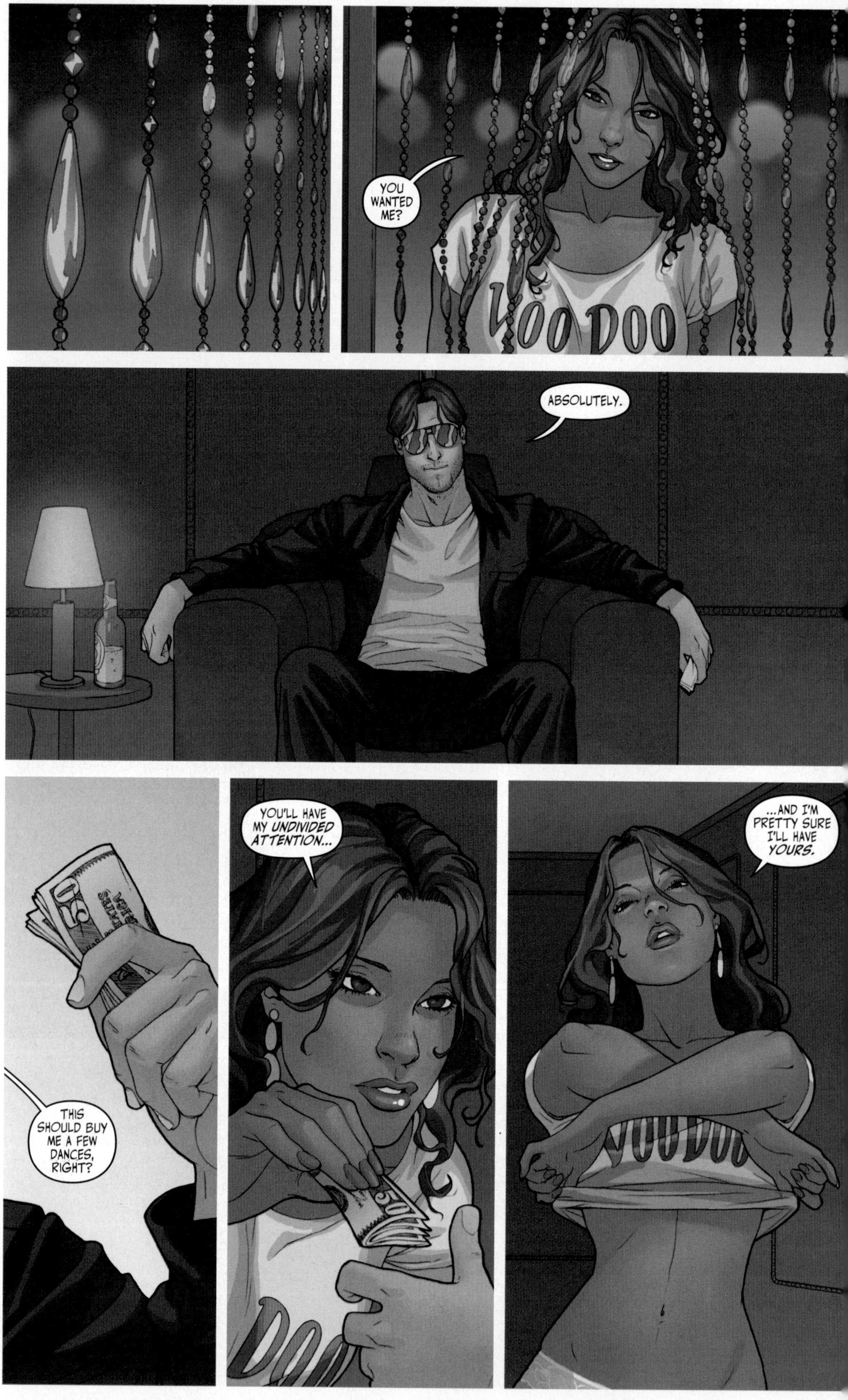
YOU WANTED ME?
ABSOLUTELY.
THIS SHOULD BUY ME A FEW DANCES, RIGHT?
YOU'LL HAVE MY *UNDIVIDED ATTENTION*...
...AND I'M PRETTY SURE I'LL HAVE *YOURS*.

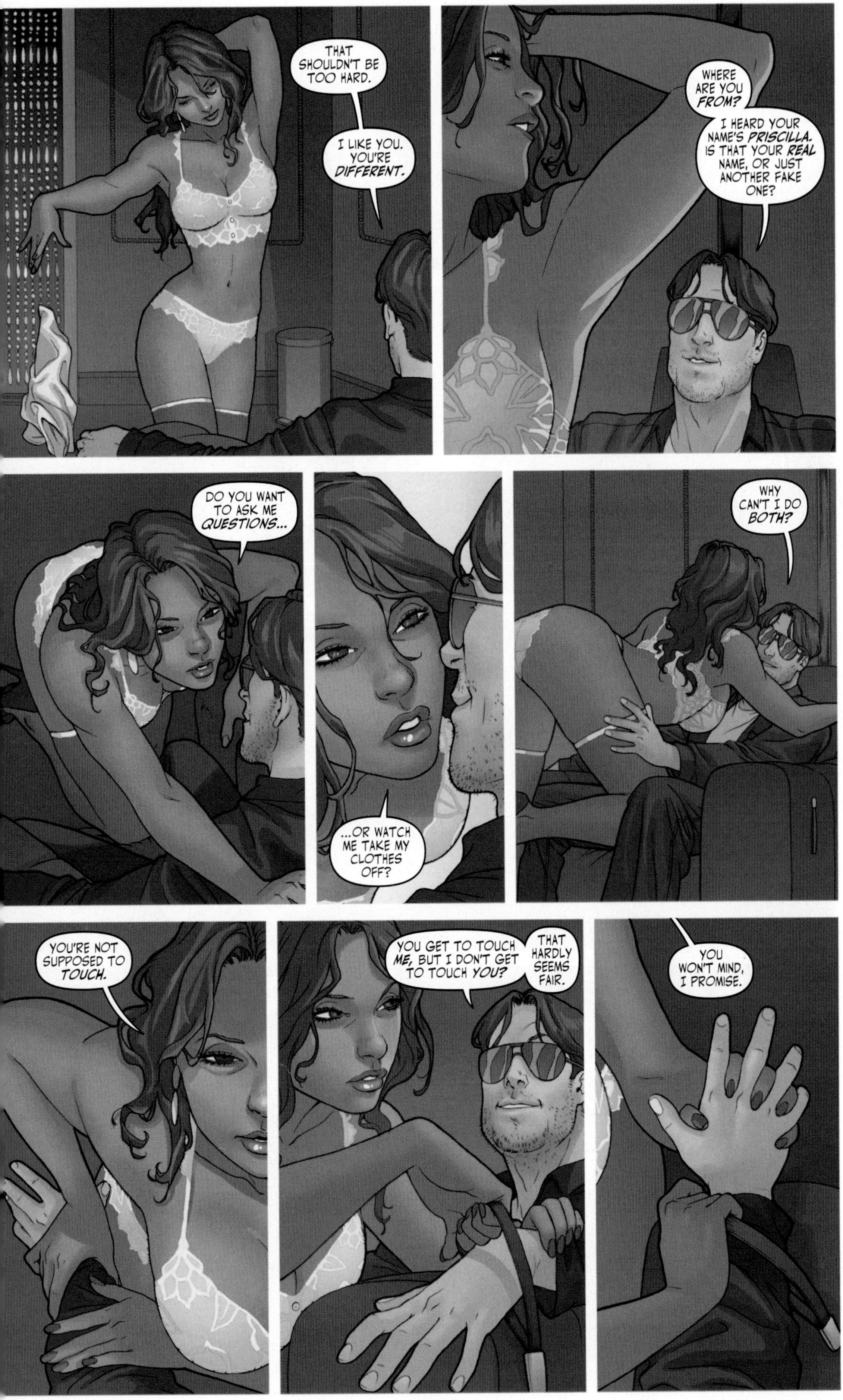
THAT SHOULDN'T BE TOO HARD.
I LIKE YOU. YOU'RE *DIFFERENT*.
WHERE ARE YOU *FROM?*
I HEARD YOUR NAME'S *PRISCILLA*. IS THAT YOUR *REAL* NAME, OR JUST ANOTHER FAKE ONE?
DO YOU WANT TO ASK ME *QUESTIONS*...
...OR WATCH ME TAKE MY CLOTHES OFF?
WHY CAN'T I DO *BOTH?*
YOU'RE NOT SUPPOSED TO *TOUCH*.
YOU GET TO TOUCH *ME*, BUT I DON'T GET TO TOUCH *YOU?*
THAT HARDLY SEEMS FAIR.
YOU WON'T MIND, I PROMISE.

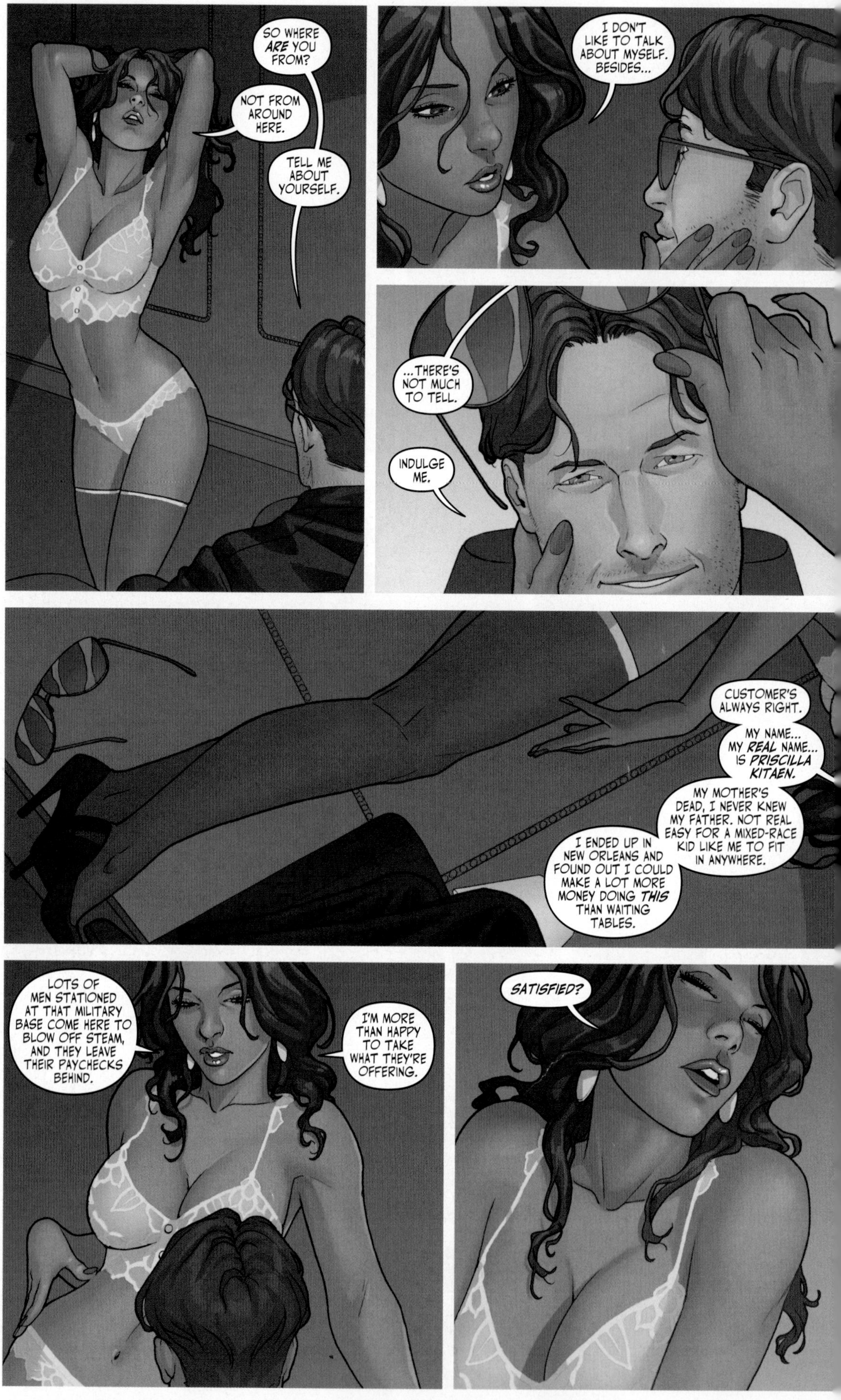

SO WHERE ARE YOU FROM?
NOT FROM AROUND HERE.
TELL ME ABOUT YOURSELF.
I DON'T LIKE TO TALK ABOUT MYSELF. BESIDES...
...THERE'S NOT MUCH TO TELL.
INDULGE ME.
CUSTOMER'S ALWAYS RIGHT.
MY NAME... MY REAL NAME... IS PRISCILLA KITAEN.
MY MOTHER'S DEAD, I NEVER KNEW MY FATHER. NOT REAL EASY FOR A MIXED-RACE KID LIKE ME TO FIT IN ANYWHERE.
I ENDED UP IN NEW ORLEANS AND FOUND OUT I COULD MAKE A LOT MORE MONEY DOING THIS THAN WAITING TABLES.
LOTS OF MEN STATIONED AT THAT MILITARY BASE COME HERE TO BLOW OFF STEAM, AND THEY LEAVE THEIR PAYCHECKS BEHIND.
I'M MORE THAN HAPPY TO TAKE WHAT THEY'RE OFFERING.
SATISFIED?

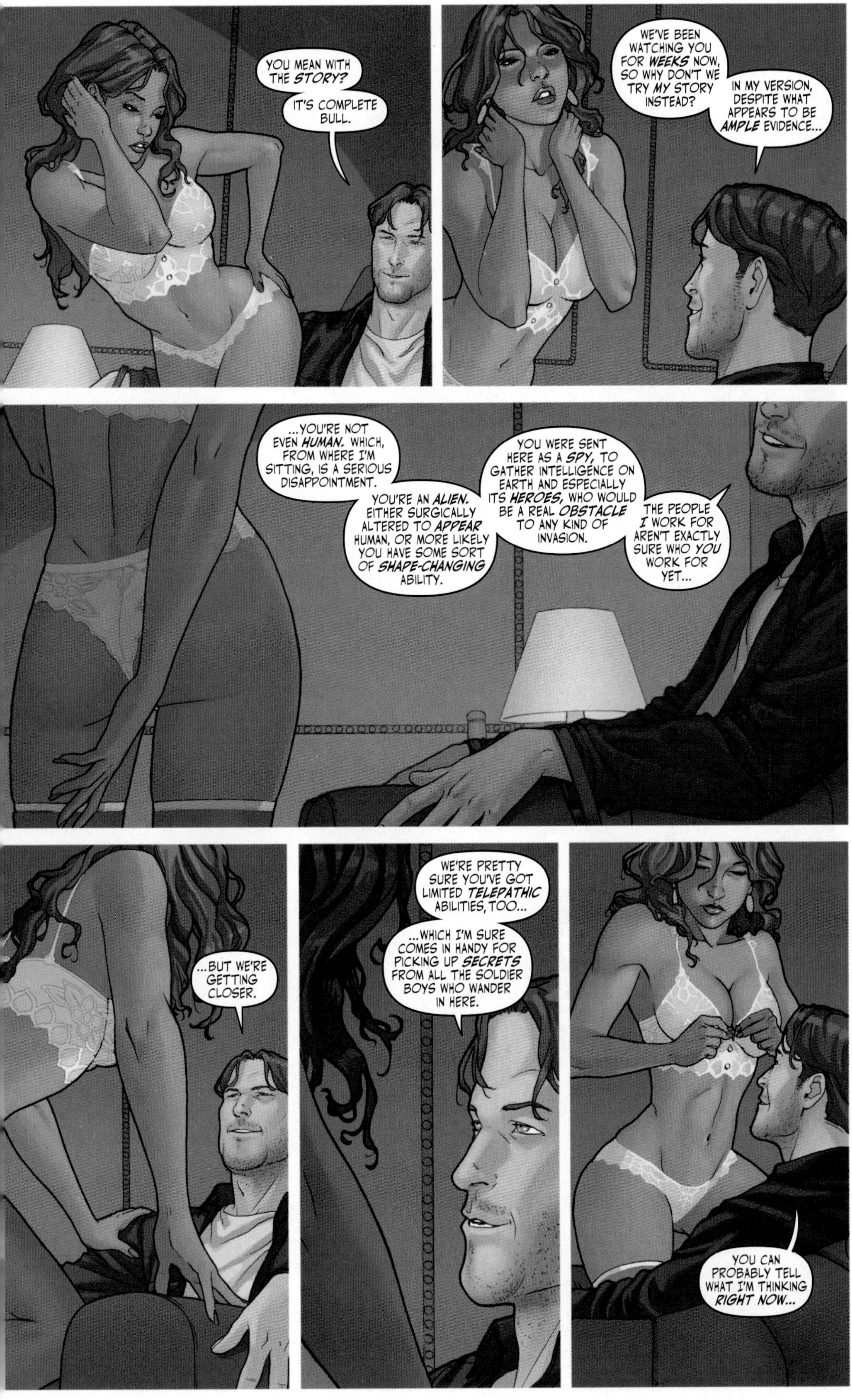
YOU MEAN WITH THE STORY?
IT'S COMPLETE BULL.
WE'VE BEEN WATCHING YOU FOR WEEKS NOW, SO WHY DON'T WE TRY MY STORY INSTEAD?
IN MY VERSION, DESPITE WHAT APPEARS TO BE AMPLE EVIDENCE...
...YOU'RE NOT EVEN HUMAN. WHICH, FROM WHERE I'M SITTING, IS A SERIOUS DISAPPOINTMENT.
YOU'RE AN ALIEN. EITHER SURGICALLY ALTERED TO APPEAR HUMAN, OR MORE LIKELY YOU HAVE SOME SORT OF SHAPE-CHANGING ABILITY.
YOU WERE SENT HERE AS A SPY, TO GATHER INTELLIGENCE ON EARTH AND ESPECIALLY ITS HEROES, WHO WOULD BE A REAL OBSTACLE TO ANY KIND OF INVASION.
THE PEOPLE I WORK FOR AREN'T EXACTLY SURE WHO YOU WORK FOR YET...
...BUT WE'RE GETTING CLOSER.
WE'RE PRETTY SURE YOU'VE GOT LIMITED TELEPATHIC ABILITIES, TOO...
...WHICH I'M SURE COMES IN HANDY FOR PICKING UP SECRETS FROM ALL THE SOLDIER BOYS WHO WANDER IN HERE.
YOU CAN PROBABLY TELL WHAT I'M THINKING RIGHT NOW...

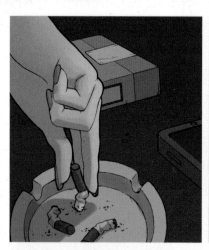

Calling
Tyler Evans

bdeep

COME ON, YOU JERK, PICK UP...

TYLER, IT'S JESS. I DON'T EVEN WANT TO *THINK* ABOUT WHY YOU'RE NOT ANSWERING, BUT... LOOK, I SHOULDN'T HAVE WALKED OUT.

I SHOULDN'T DO THAT TO *ANY* FELLOW AGENT, MUCH LESS MY *PARTNER.* IT WASN'T PROFESSIONAL...

...NOT THAT WHAT *WE'RE* DOING IS PROFESSIONAL, BUT YOU GET WHAT I'M SAYING.

I JUST...DON'T DO ANYTHING *STUPID.* AND "STUPID" COVERS A WHOLE *RANGE* OF BEHAVIOR.

I'D RATHER NOT SPEND MY NIGHT DRINKING ALONE IN A CHEAP MOTEL ROOM.

CALL ME BACK, OKAY?

YOU KNOW WHERE TO FIND ME.

bdeep

Call Ended

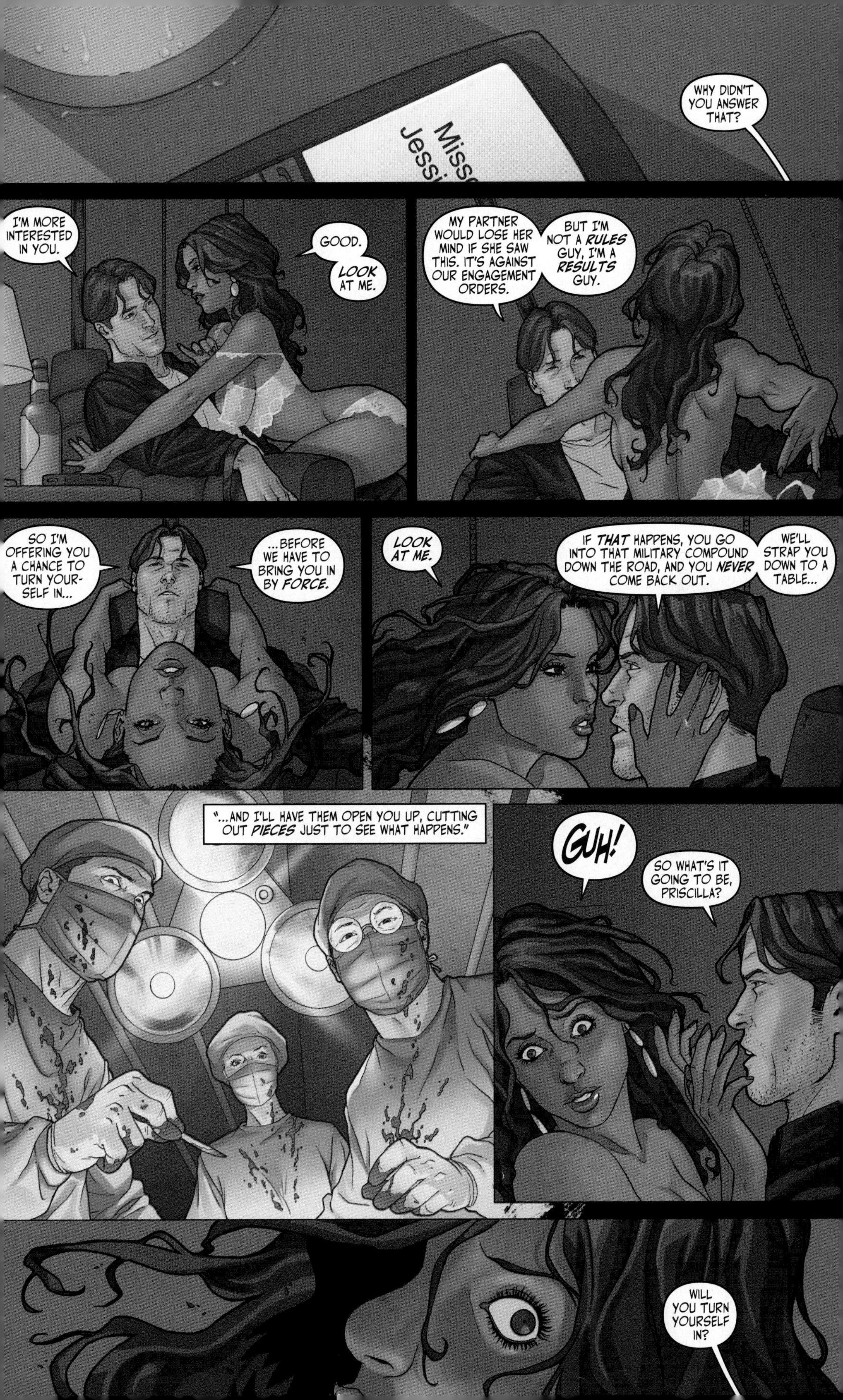
Miss
Jess
WHY DIDN'T YOU ANSWER THAT?
I'M MORE INTERESTED IN YOU.
GOOD.
LOOK AT ME.
MY PARTNER WOULD LOSE HER MIND IF SHE SAW THIS. IT'S AGAINST OUR ENGAGEMENT ORDERS.
BUT I'M NOT A RULES GUY, I'M A RESULTS GUY.
SO I'M OFFERING YOU A CHANCE TO TURN YOURSELF IN...
...BEFORE WE HAVE TO BRING YOU IN BY FORCE.
LOOK AT ME.
IF THAT HAPPENS, YOU GO INTO THAT MILITARY COMPOUND DOWN THE ROAD, AND YOU NEVER COME BACK OUT.
WE'LL STRAP YOU DOWN TO A TABLE...
"...AND I'LL HAVE THEM OPEN YOU UP, CUTTING OUT PIECES JUST TO SEE WHAT HAPPENS."
GUH!
SO WHAT'S IT GOING TO BE, PRISCILLA?
WILL YOU TURN YOURSELF IN?

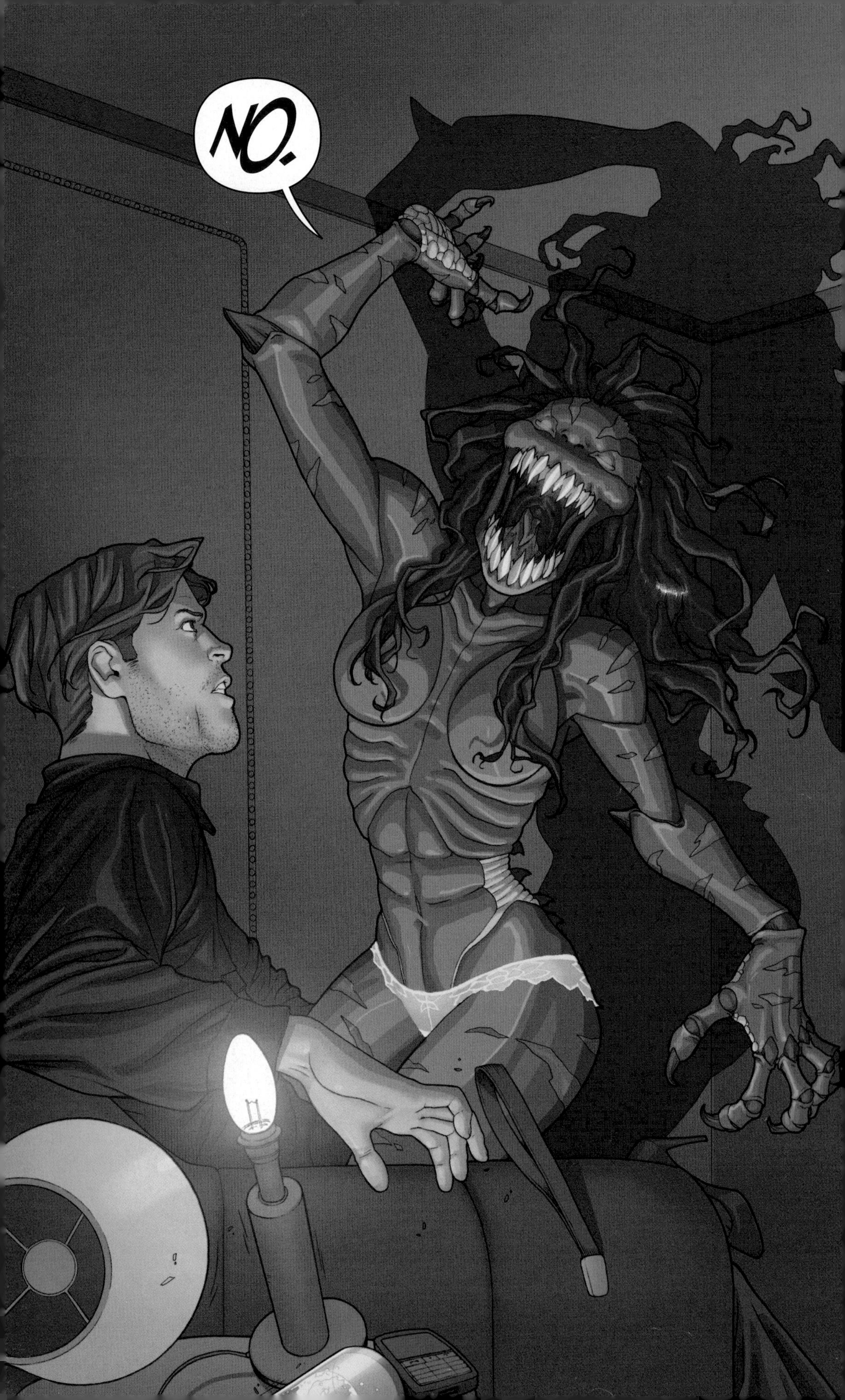
NO.

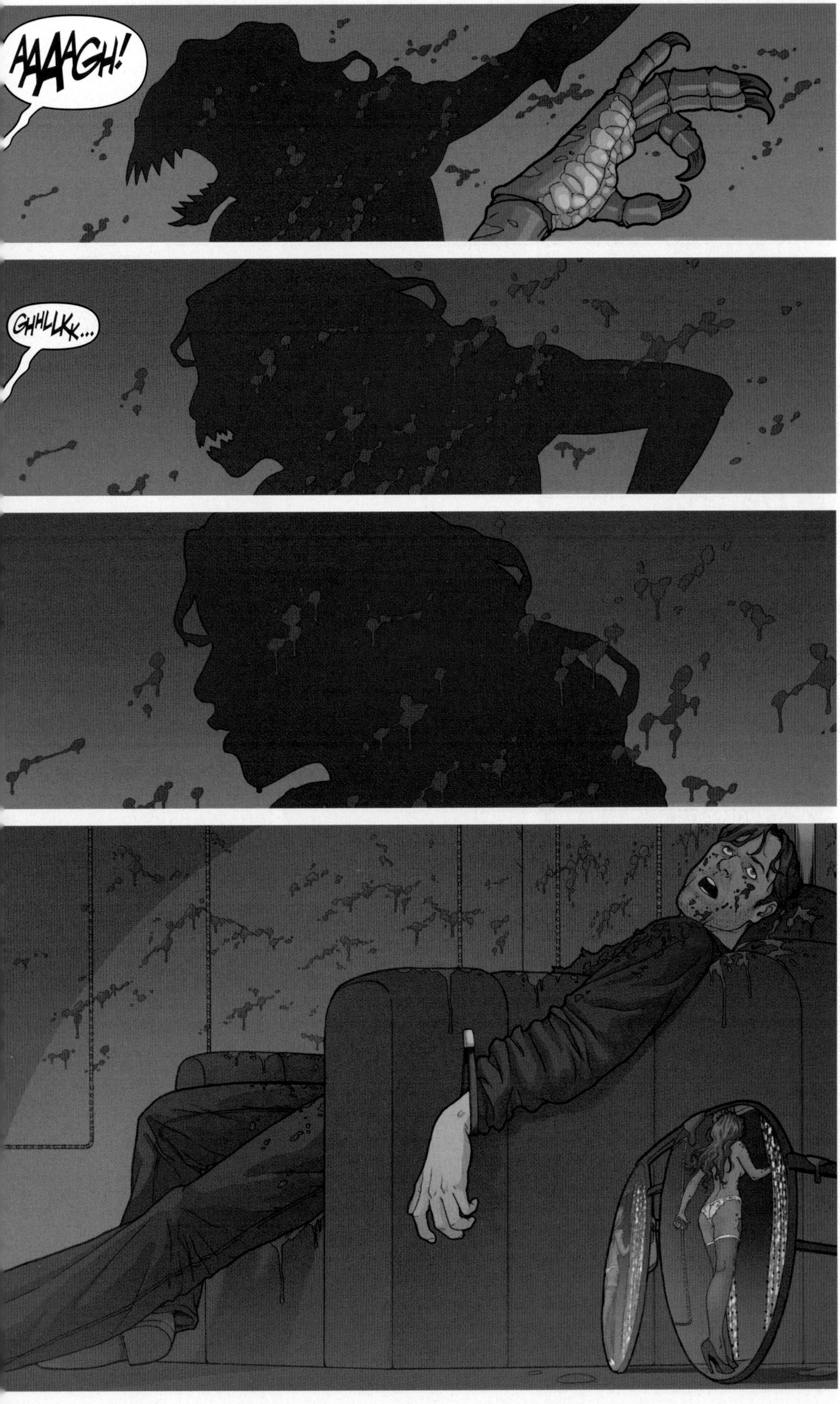
AAAAGH!
GHHLLKK...

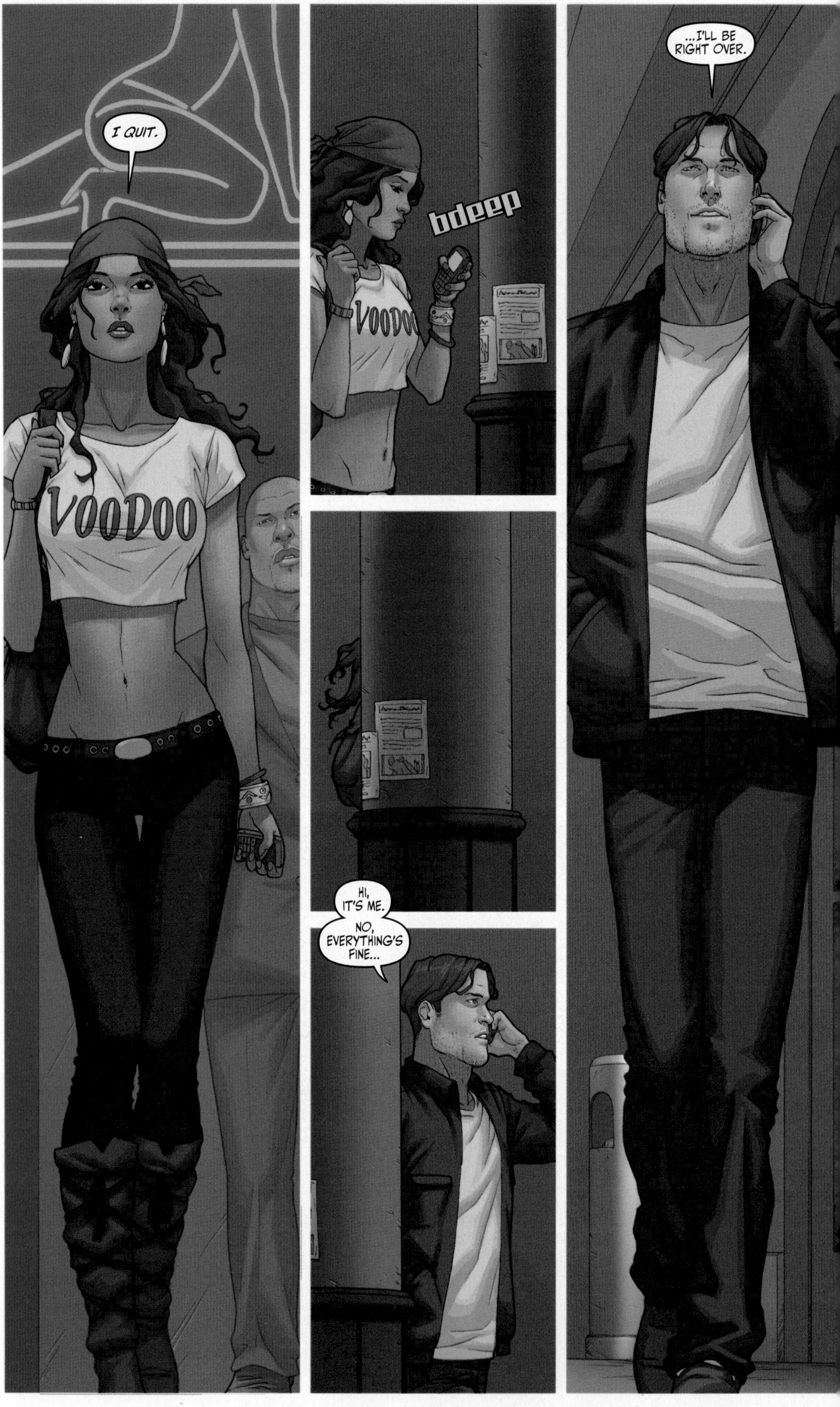
I QUIT.
bdeep
HI, IT'S ME.
NO, EVERYTHING'S FINE...
...I'LL BE RIGHT OVER.

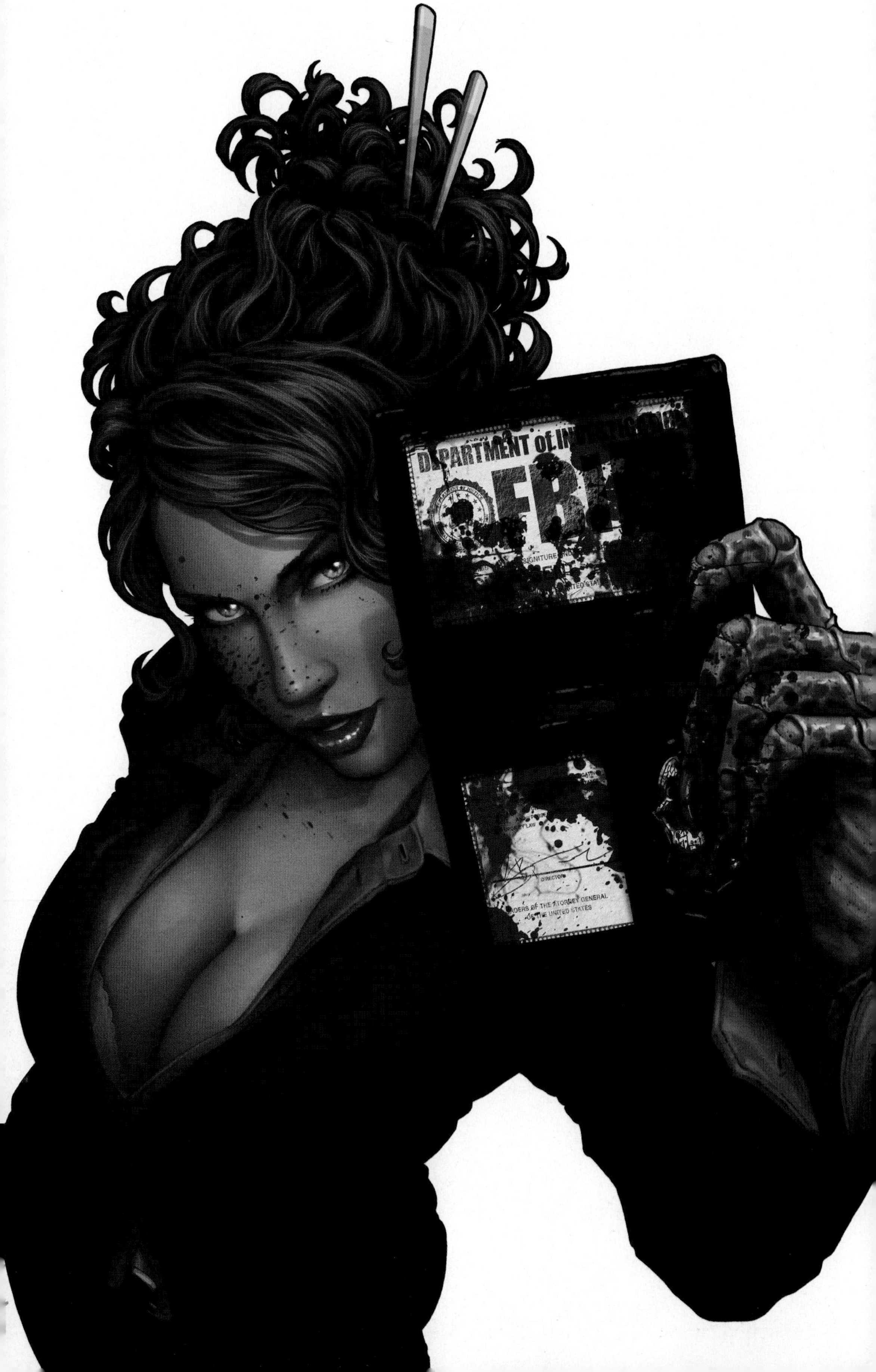
DEPARTMENT of
SIGNITURE
DIRECTOR
ORDERS OF THE ATTORNEY GENERAL
OF THE UNITED STATES

cover art by
JOHN TYLER CHRISTOPHER

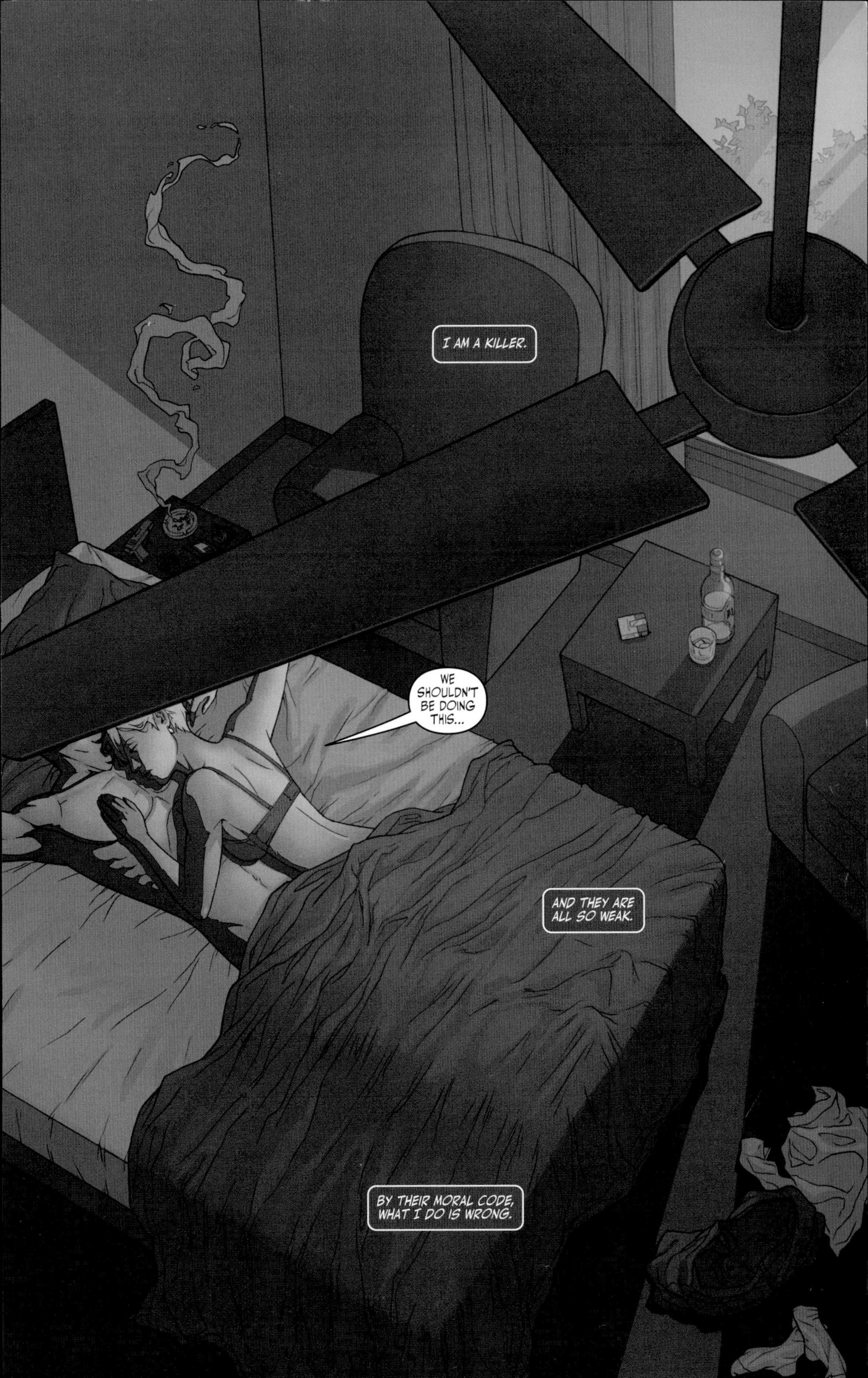
I AM A KILLER.
WE SHOULDN'T BE DOING THIS...
AND THEY ARE ALL SO WEAK.
BY THEIR MORAL CODE, WHAT I DO IS WRONG.

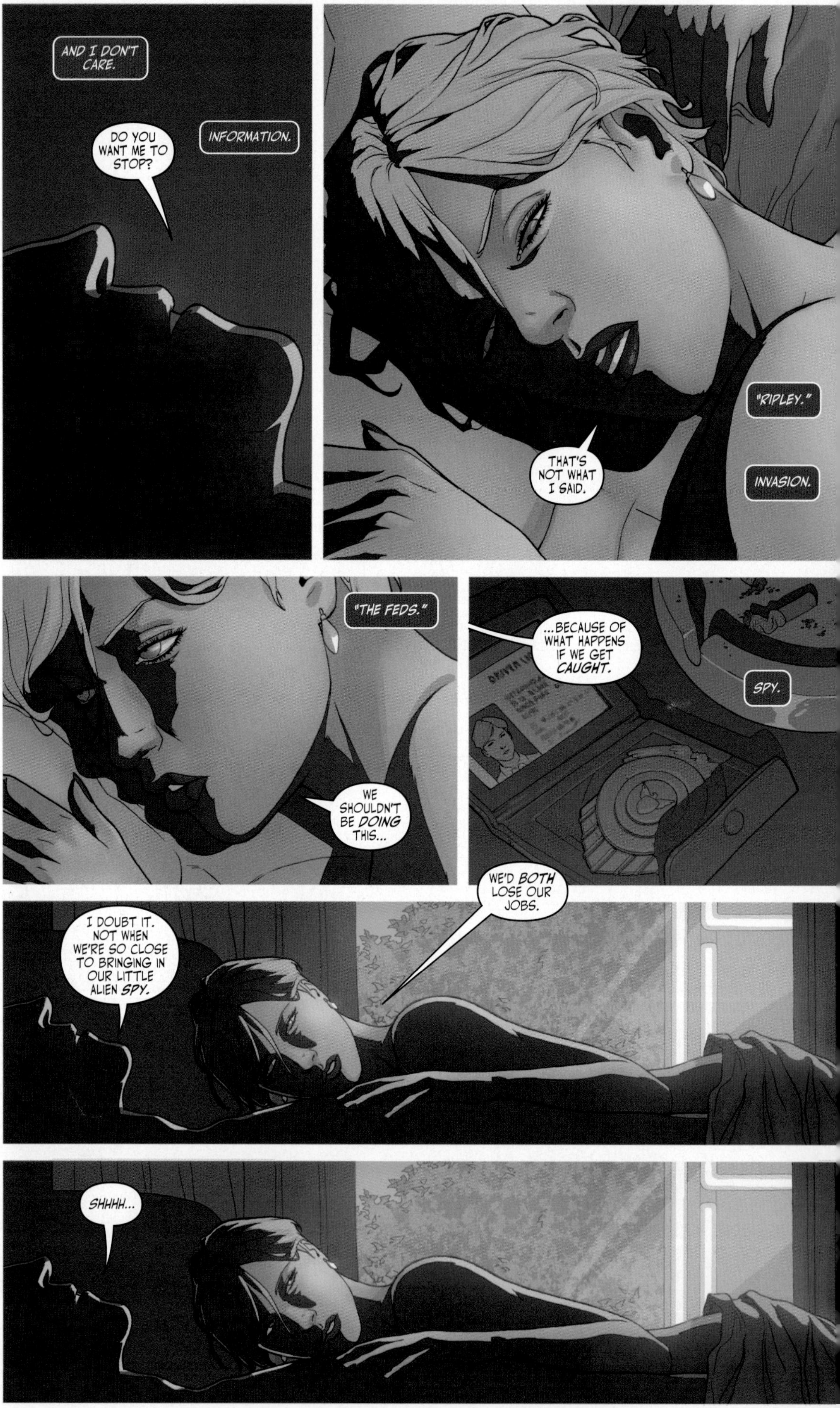
AND I DON'T CARE.
DO YOU WANT ME TO STOP?
INFORMATION.
"RIPLEY."
THAT'S NOT WHAT I SAID.
INVASION.
"THE FEDS."
WE SHOULDN'T BE DOING THIS...
...BECAUSE OF WHAT HAPPENS IF WE GET CAUGHT.
SPY.
WE'D BOTH LOSE OUR JOBS.
I DOUBT IT. NOT WHEN WE'RE SO CLOSE TO BRINGING IN OUR LITTLE ALIEN SPY.
SHHHH...

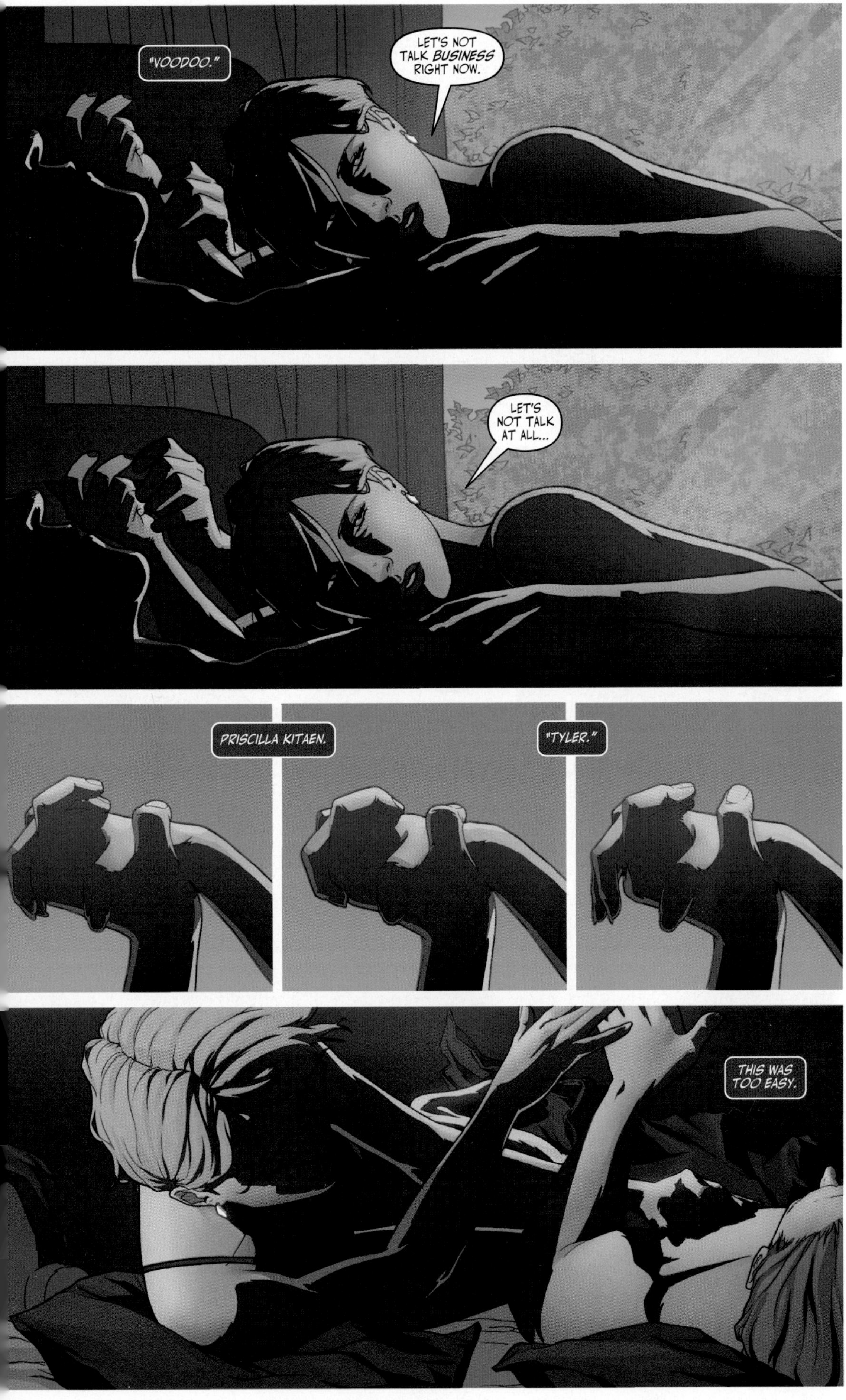
"VOODOO."
LET'S NOT TALK BUSINESS RIGHT NOW.
LET'S NOT TALK AT ALL...
PRISCILLA KITAEN.
"TYLER."
THIS WAS TOO EASY.

AND YET I CAN ALMOST FEEL HOW HE FELT FOR HER.

BECAUSE *I* THOUGHT THAT WAS PRETTY GREAT.

PATHETIC.

I'M TALKING ABOUT *US*. WE SHOULDN'T BE *INVOLVED* AT ALL, EVANS.

WE'RE *PARTNERS*, JESS. DON'T BEAT YOURSELF UP OVER IT. IT HAPPENS.

BUT IT'S NOT *SUPPOSED* TO.

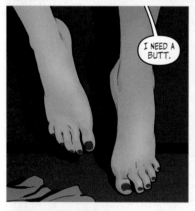

I NEED A BUTT.

NOTHING WRONG WITH *THAT ONE* FROM MY PERSPECTIVE.

KEEP TALKING LIKE THAT, I *MIGHT* FORGIVE YOU FOR ACTING LIKE A HORNY TEENAGER IN THE CLUB TONIGHT.

THAT TRAMP *DOES* HAVE A TIGHT LITTLE BODY...

breeep

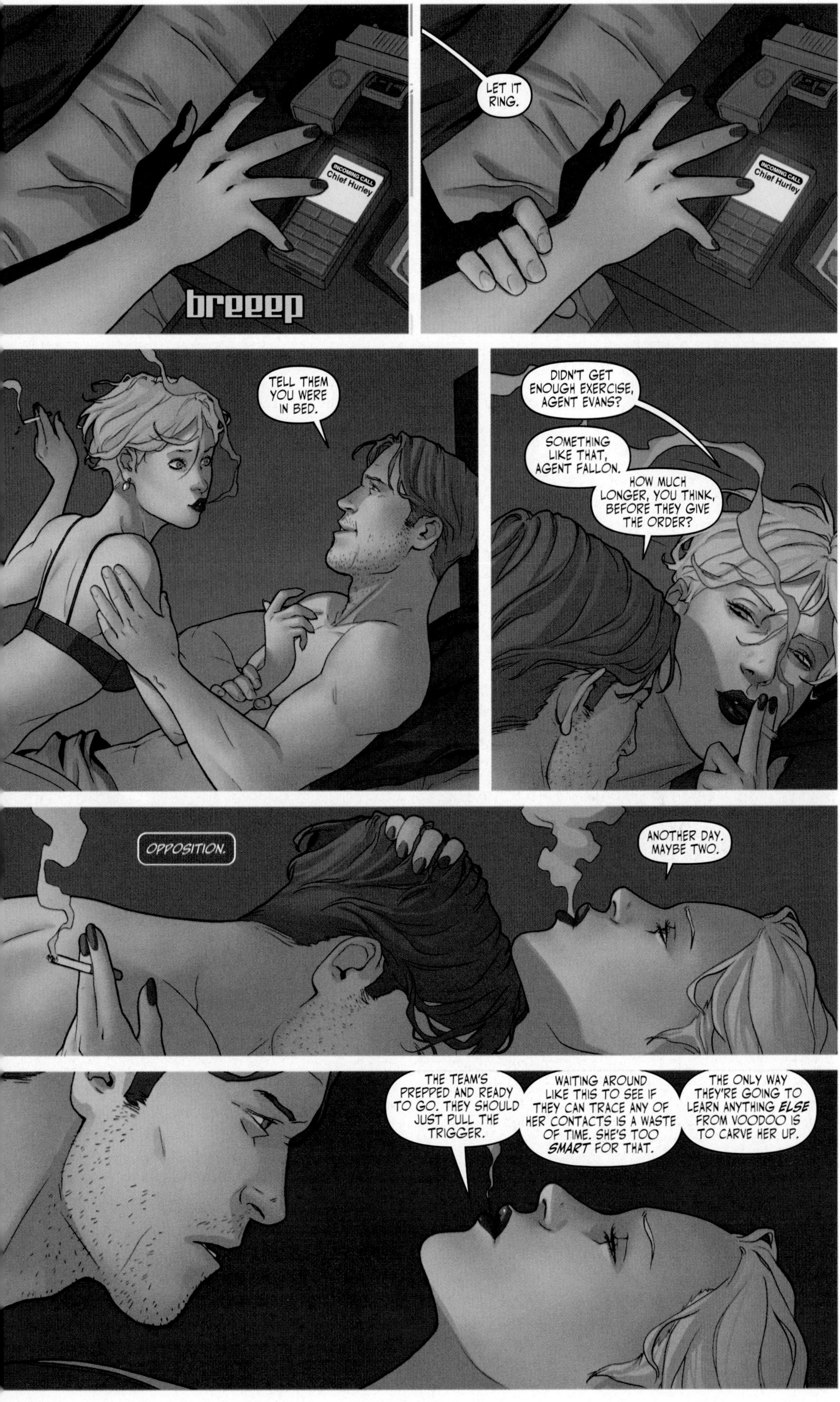
INCOMING CALL
Chief Hurley
breeep
LET IT RING.
INCOMING CALL
Chief Hurley
TELL THEM YOU WERE IN BED.
DIDN'T GET ENOUGH EXERCISE, AGENT EVANS?
SOMETHING LIKE THAT, AGENT FALLON.
HOW MUCH LONGER, YOU THINK, BEFORE THEY GIVE THE ORDER?
OPPOSITION.
ANOTHER DAY. MAYBE TWO.
THE TEAM'S PREPPED AND READY TO GO. THEY SHOULD JUST PULL THE TRIGGER.
WAITING AROUND LIKE THIS TO SEE IF THEY CAN TRACE ANY OF HER CONTACTS IS A WASTE OF TIME. SHE'S TOO SMART FOR THAT.
THE ONLY WAY THEY'RE GOING TO LEARN ANYTHING ELSE FROM VOODOO IS TO CARVE HER UP.

THAT'S A LITTLE *HARSH,* ISN'T IT?

WHAT, YOU FEEL *SORRY* FOR HER NOW THAT SHE'S BEEN SHAKING HER ASS IN YOUR FACE?

FORGET WHAT I SAID ABOUT BEING FORGIVEN.

YOU'RE RIGHT, I'M *SORRY.* WHAT CAN I DO TO MAKE IT UP TO YOU?

I CAN THINK OF A FEW DIFFERENT WAYS.

I'M ALL FOR DIFFERENT WAYS.

JUST LET ME RUN TO THE BATHROOM. BE RIGHT BACK.

DON'T KEEP ME WAITING.

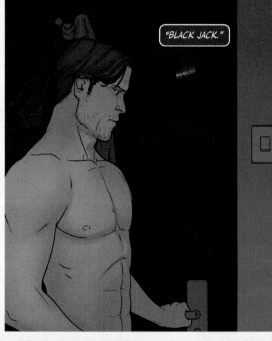

"BLACK JACK."

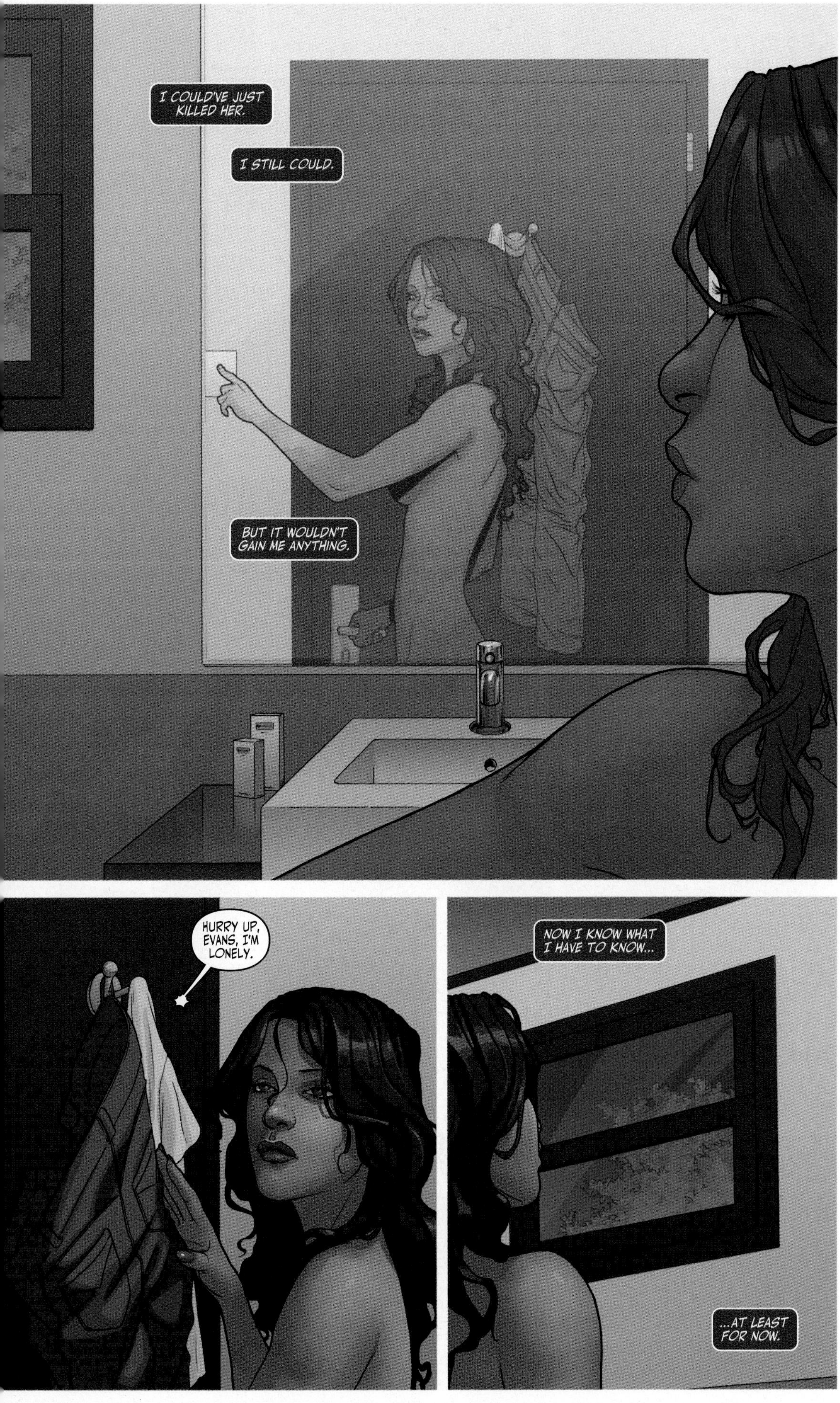
I COULD'VE JUST KILLED HER.
I STILL COULD.
BUT IT WOULDN'T GAIN ME ANYTHING.
HURRY UP, EVANS, I'M LONELY.
NOW I KNOW WHAT I HAVE TO KNOW...
...AT LEAST FOR NOW.

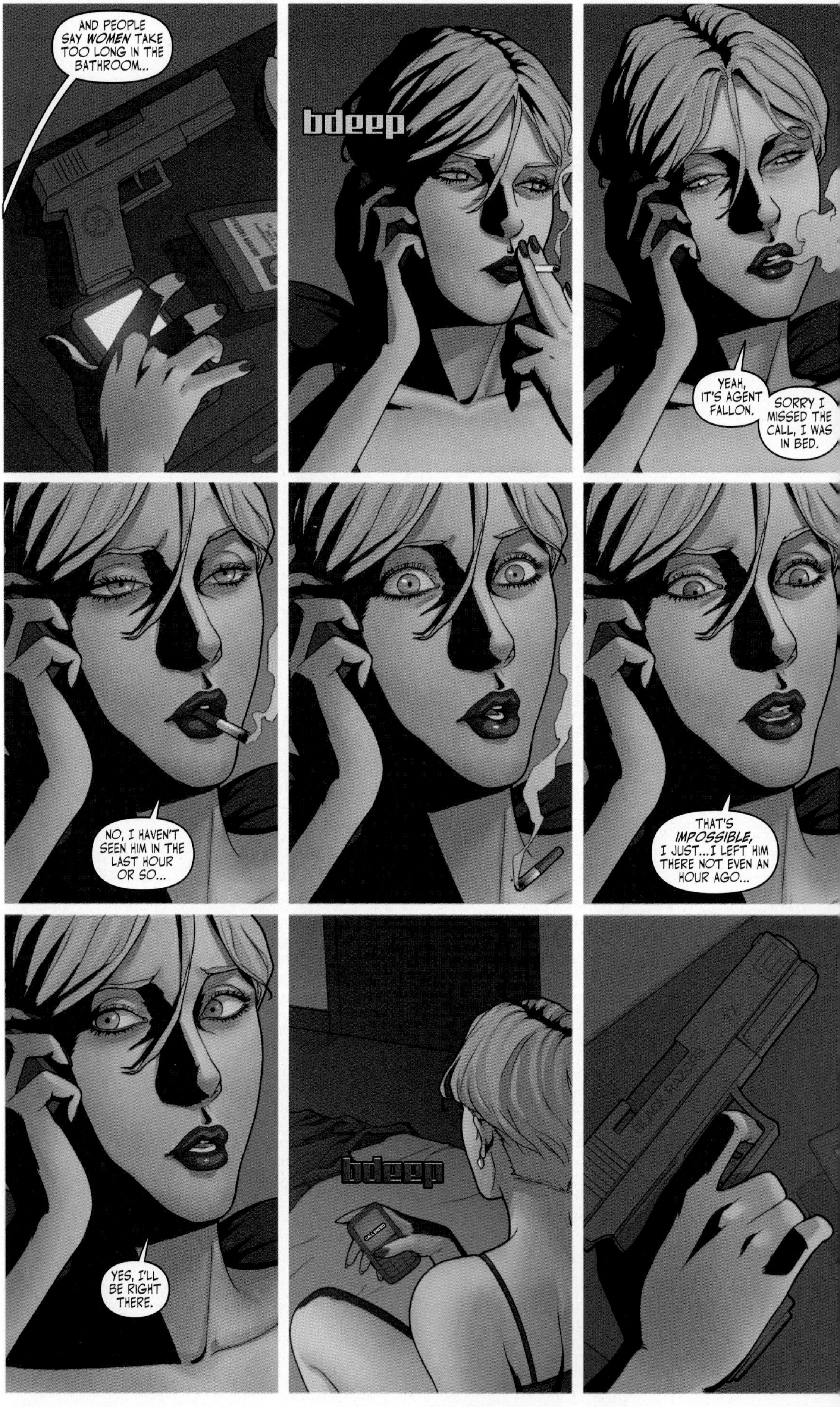
AND PEOPLE SAY WOMEN TAKE TOO LONG IN THE BATHROOM...
BDEEP
YEAH, IT'S AGENT FALLON.
SORRY I MISSED THE CALL, I WAS IN BED.
NO, I HAVEN'T SEEN HIM IN THE LAST HOUR OR SO...
THAT'S IMPOSSIBLE, I JUST...I LEFT HIM THERE NOT EVEN AN HOUR AGO...
YES, I'LL BE RIGHT THERE.
BDEEP
CALL ENDED
BLACK RAZORS
17

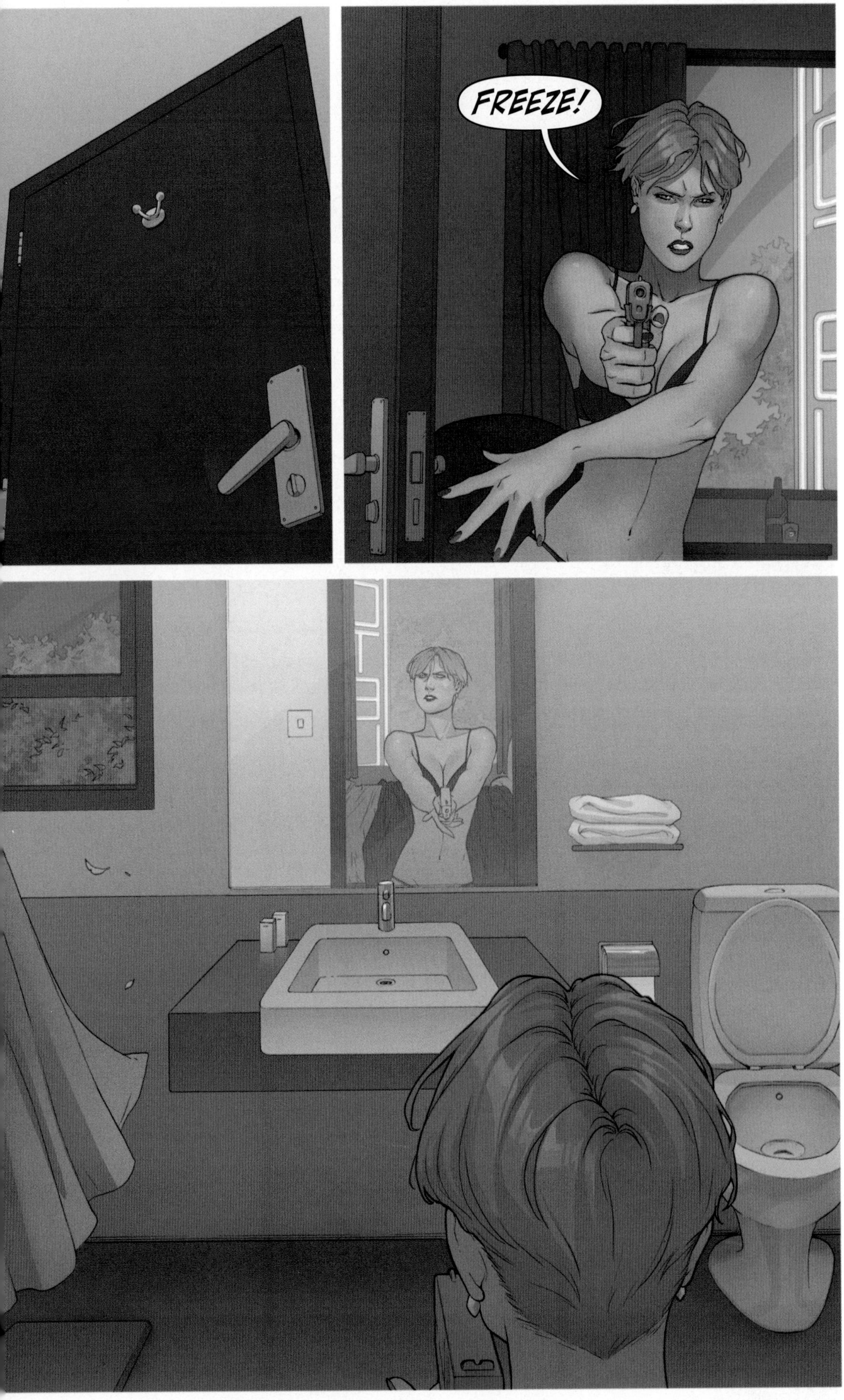
FREEZE!

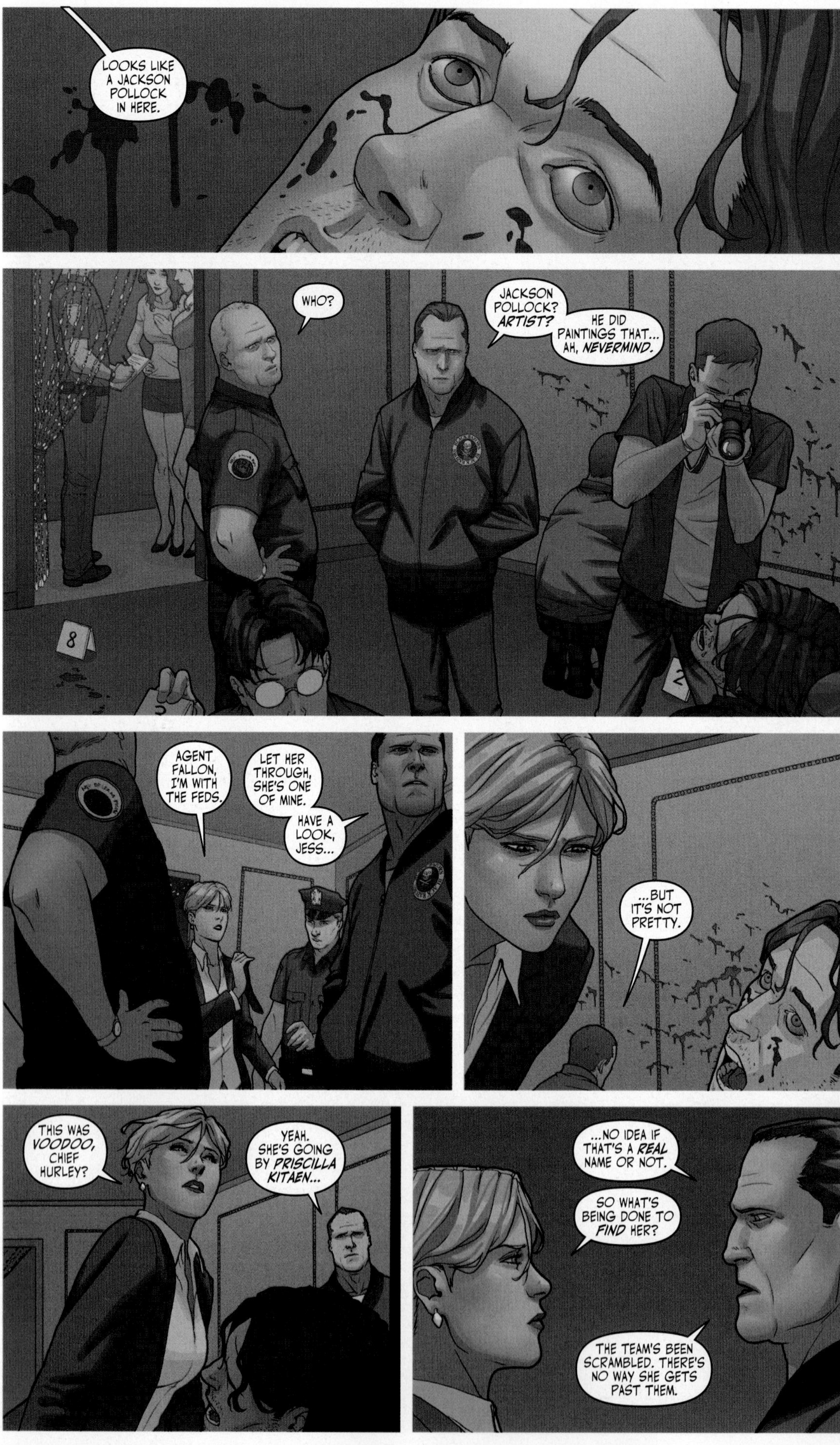

LOOKS LIKE A JACKSON POLLOCK IN HERE.
WHO?
JACKSON POLLOCK? *ARTIST?*
HE DID PAINTINGS THAT... AH, *NEVERMIND.*
8
AGENT FALLON, I'M WITH THE FEDS.
LET HER THROUGH, SHE'S ONE OF MINE.
HAVE A LOOK, JESS...
...BUT IT'S NOT PRETTY.
THIS WAS *VOODOO,* CHIEF HURLEY?
YEAH. SHE'S GOING BY *PRISCILLA KITAEN...*
...NO IDEA IF THAT'S A *REAL* NAME OR NOT.
SO WHAT'S BEING DONE TO *FIND* HER?
THE TEAM'S BEEN SCRAMBLED. THERE'S NO WAY SHE GETS PAST THEM.

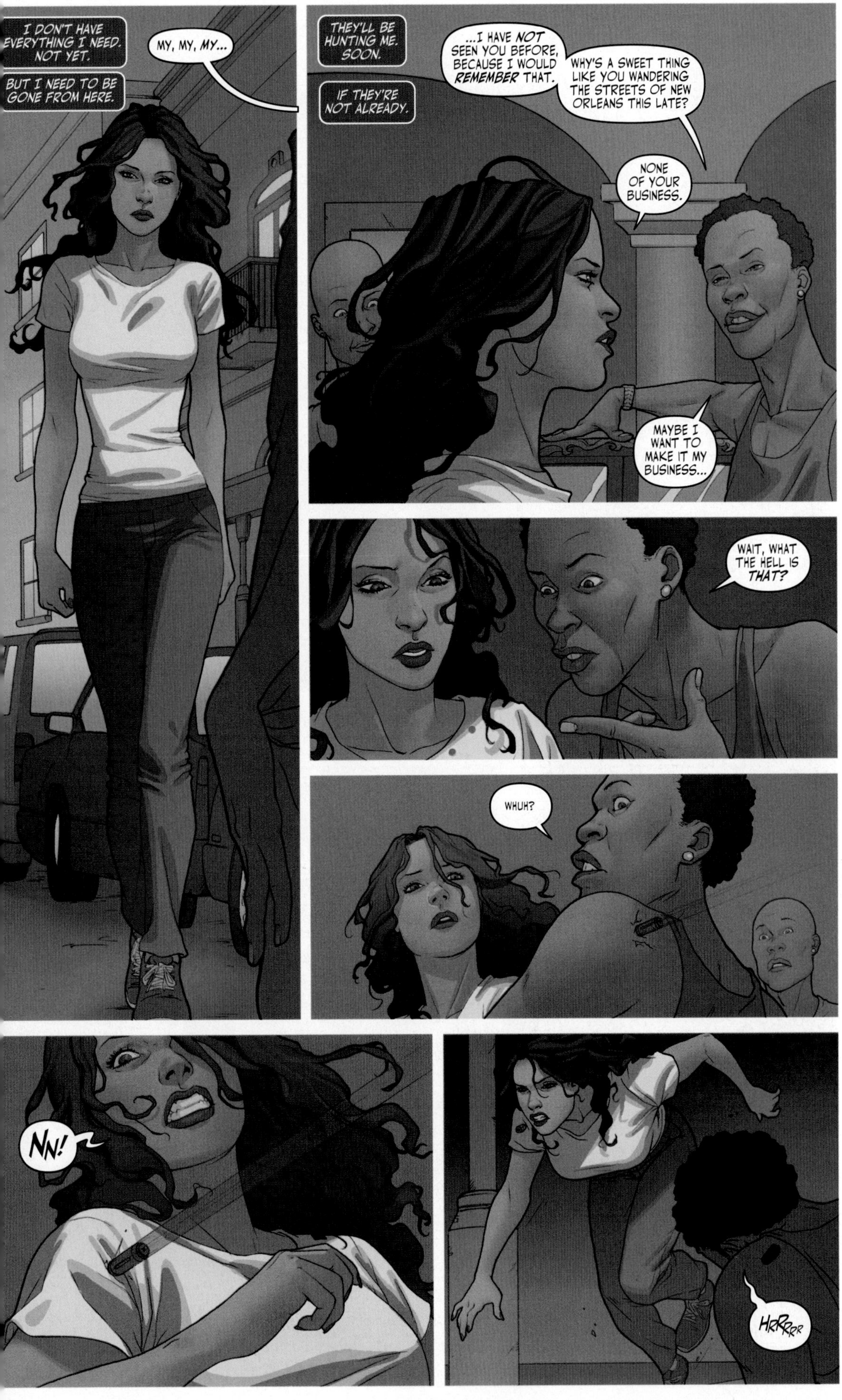

I DON'T HAVE EVERYTHING I NEED. NOT YET.
BUT I NEED TO BE GONE FROM HERE.
MY, MY, MY...
THEY'LL BE HUNTING ME. SOON.
IF THEY'RE NOT ALREADY.
...I HAVE NOT SEEN YOU BEFORE, BECAUSE I WOULD REMEMBER THAT.
WHY'S A SWEET THING LIKE YOU WANDERING THE STREETS OF NEW ORLEANS THIS LATE?
NONE OF YOUR BUSINESS.
MAYBE I WANT TO MAKE IT MY BUSINESS...
WAIT, WHAT THE HELL IS THAT?
WHUH?
NN!
HRRRRR

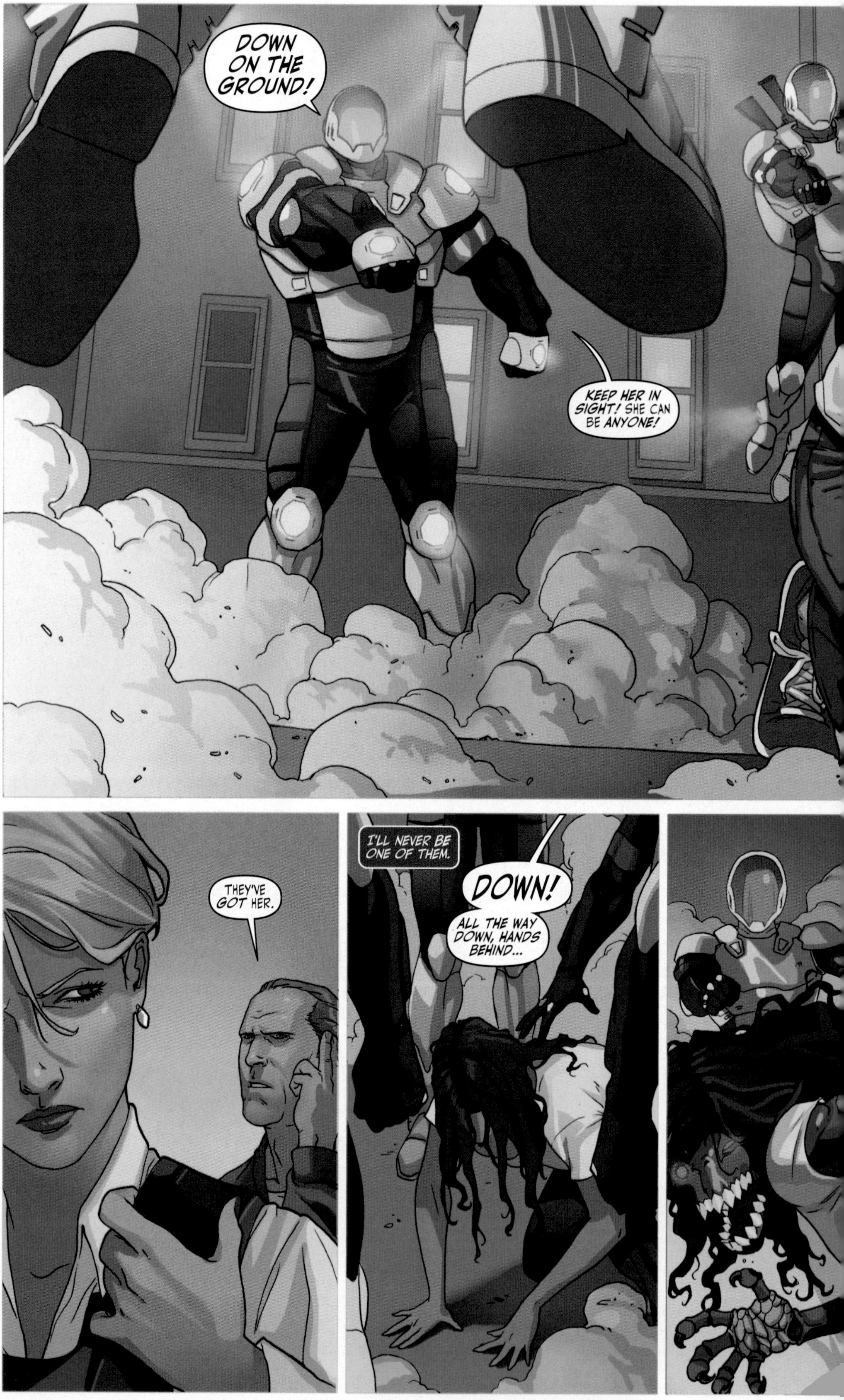
DOWN ON THE GROUND!
KEEP HER IN SIGHT! SHE CAN BE ANYONE!
THEY'VE GOT HER.
I'LL NEVER BE ONE OF THEM.
DOWN!
ALL THE WAY DOWN, HANDS BEHIND...

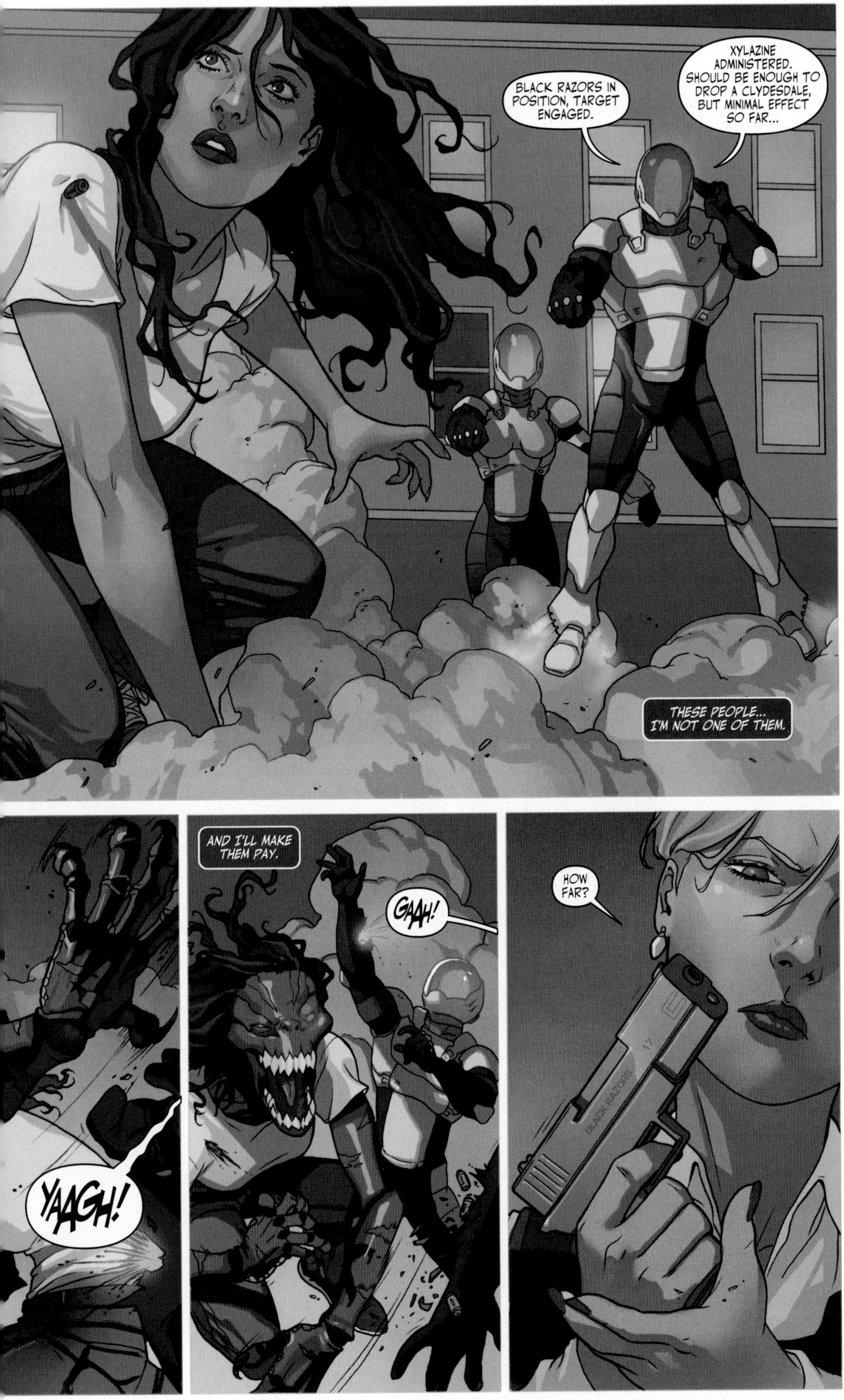
BLACK RAZORS IN POSITION, TARGET ENGAGED.
XYLAZINE ADMINISTERED. SHOULD BE ENOUGH TO DROP A CLYDESDALE, BUT MINIMAL EFFECT SO FAR...
THESE PEOPLE... I'M NOT ONE OF THEM.
YAAGH!
AND I'LL MAKE THEM PAY.
GAAH!
HOW FAR?
BLACK RAZORS
17

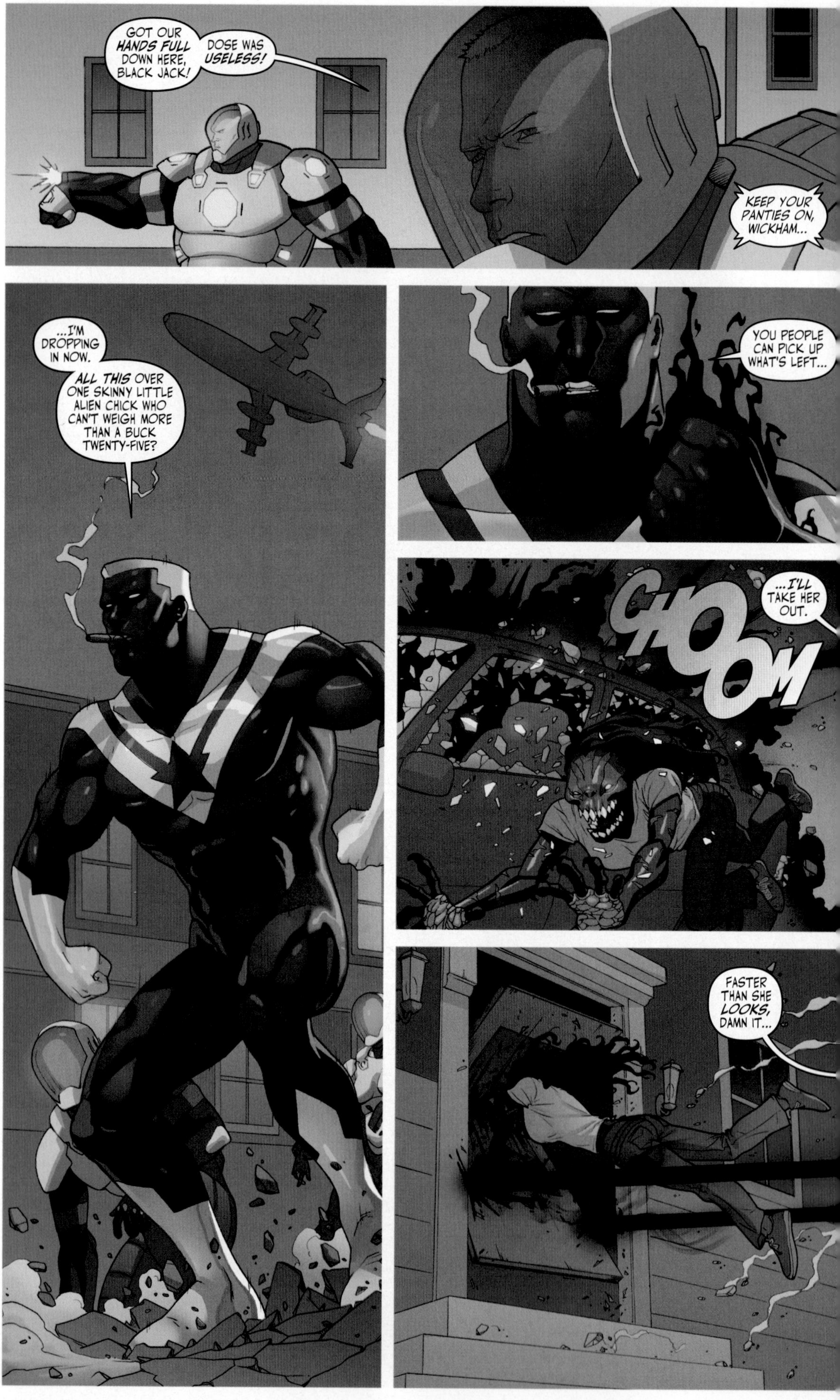
GOT OUR HANDS FULL DOWN HERE, BLACK JACK!
DOSE WAS USELESS!
KEEP YOUR PANTIES ON, WICKHAM...
...I'M DROPPING IN NOW.
ALL THIS OVER ONE SKINNY LITTLE ALIEN CHICK WHO CAN'T WEIGH MORE THAN A BUCK TWENTY-FIVE?
YOU PEOPLE CAN PICK UP WHAT'S LEFT...
CHOOOM
...I'LL TAKE HER OUT.
FASTER THAN SHE LOOKS, DAMN IT...

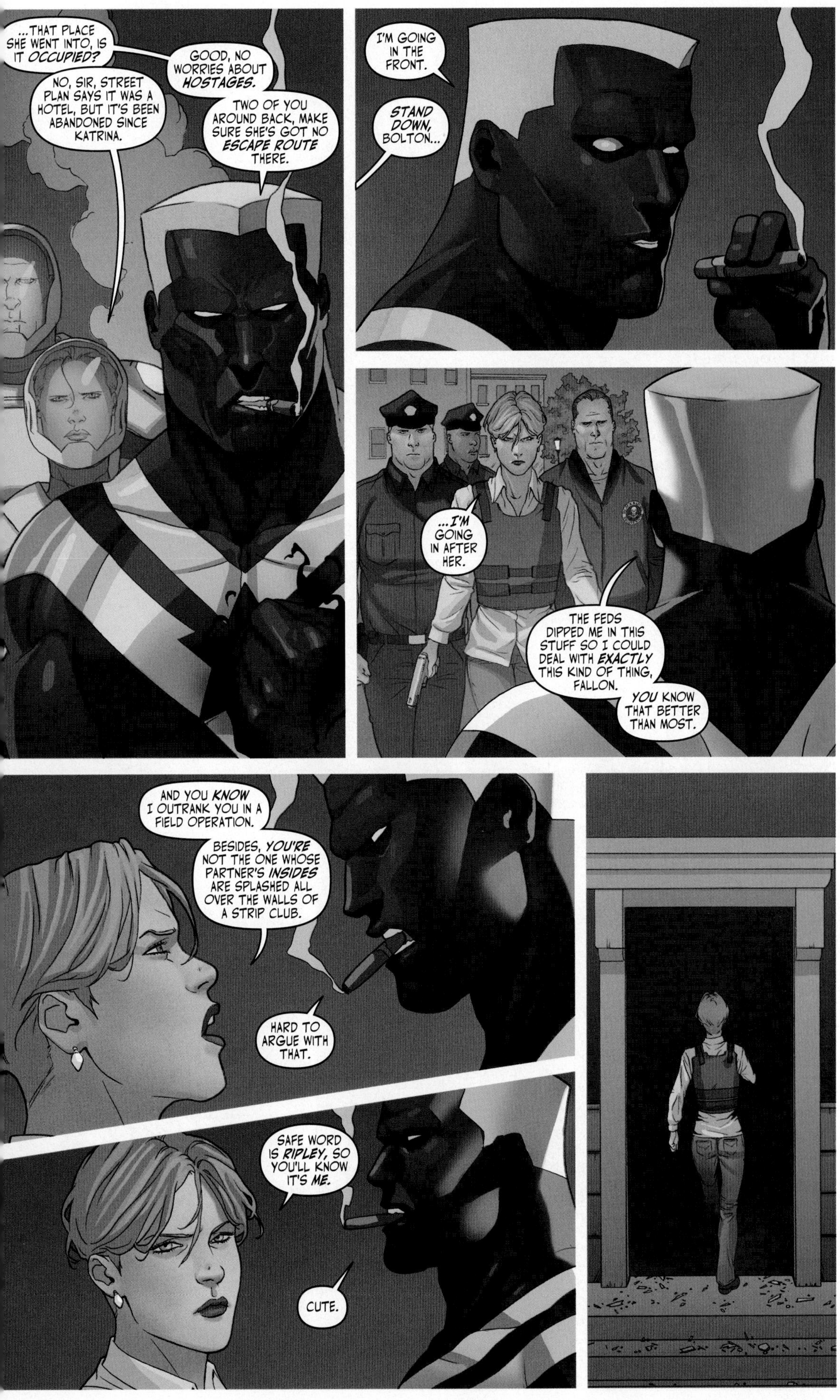
...THAT PLACE SHE WENT INTO, IS IT OCCUPIED?
NO, SIR, STREET PLAN SAYS IT WAS A HOTEL, BUT IT'S BEEN ABANDONED SINCE KATRINA.
GOOD, NO WORRIES ABOUT HOSTAGES.
TWO OF YOU AROUND BACK, MAKE SURE SHE'S GOT NO ESCAPE ROUTE THERE.
I'M GOING IN THE FRONT.
STAND DOWN, BOLTON...
...I'M GOING IN AFTER HER.
THE FEDS DIPPED ME IN THIS STUFF SO I COULD DEAL WITH EXACTLY THIS KIND OF THING, FALLON.
YOU KNOW THAT BETTER THAN MOST.
AND YOU KNOW I OUTRANK YOU IN A FIELD OPERATION.
BESIDES, YOU'RE NOT THE ONE WHOSE PARTNER'S INSIDES ARE SPLASHED ALL OVER THE WALLS OF A STRIP CLUB.
HARD TO ARGUE WITH THAT.
SAFE WORD IS RIPLEY, SO YOU'LL KNOW IT'S ME.
CUTE.

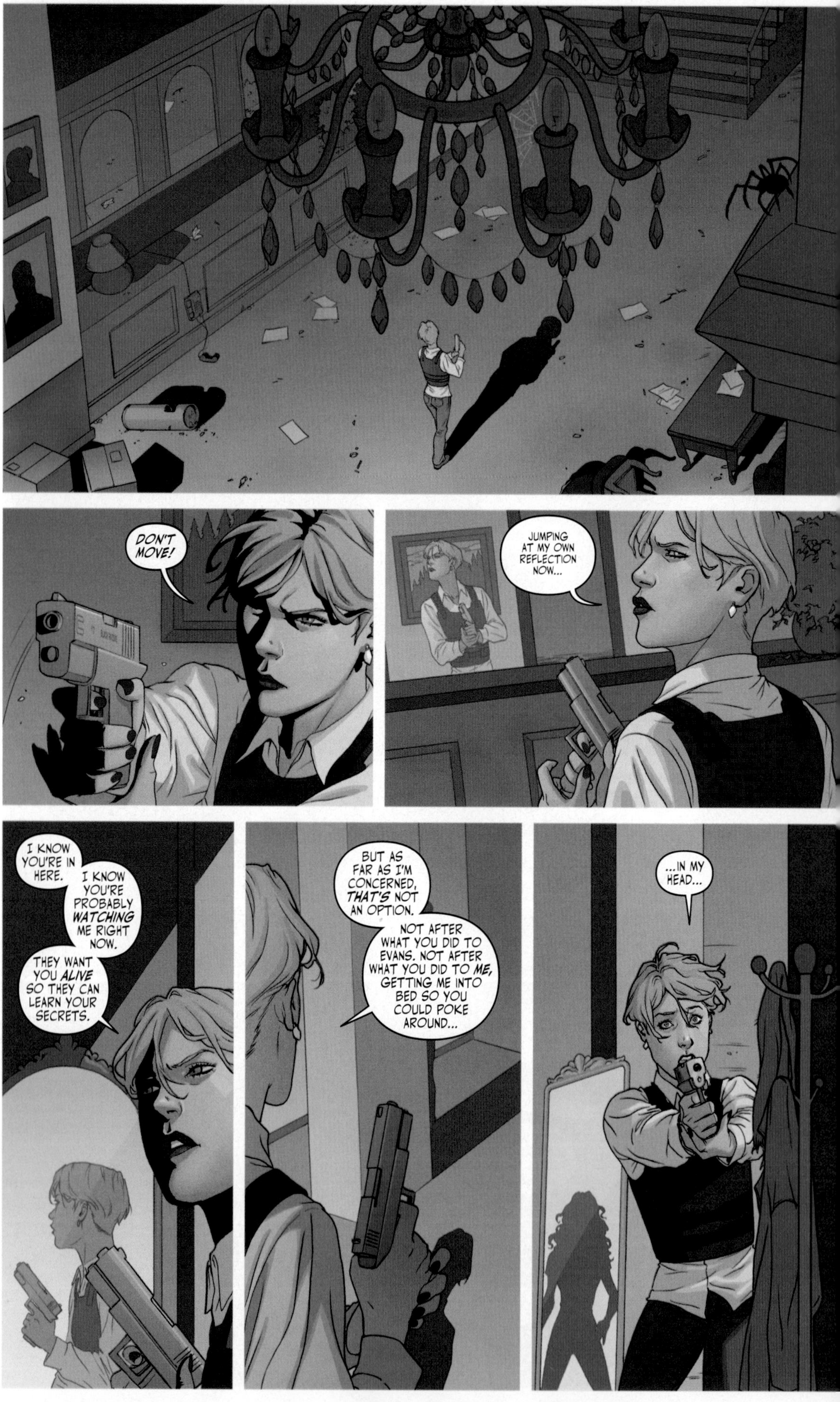
DON'T MOVE!
JUMPING AT MY OWN REFLECTION NOW...
I KNOW YOU'RE IN HERE.
I KNOW YOU'RE PROBABLY WATCHING ME RIGHT NOW.
THEY WANT YOU ALIVE SO THEY CAN LEARN YOUR SECRETS.
BUT AS FAR AS I'M CONCERNED, THAT'S NOT AN OPTION.
NOT AFTER WHAT YOU DID TO EVANS. NOT AFTER WHAT YOU DID TO ME, GETTING ME INTO BED SO YOU COULD POKE AROUND...
...IN MY HEAD...

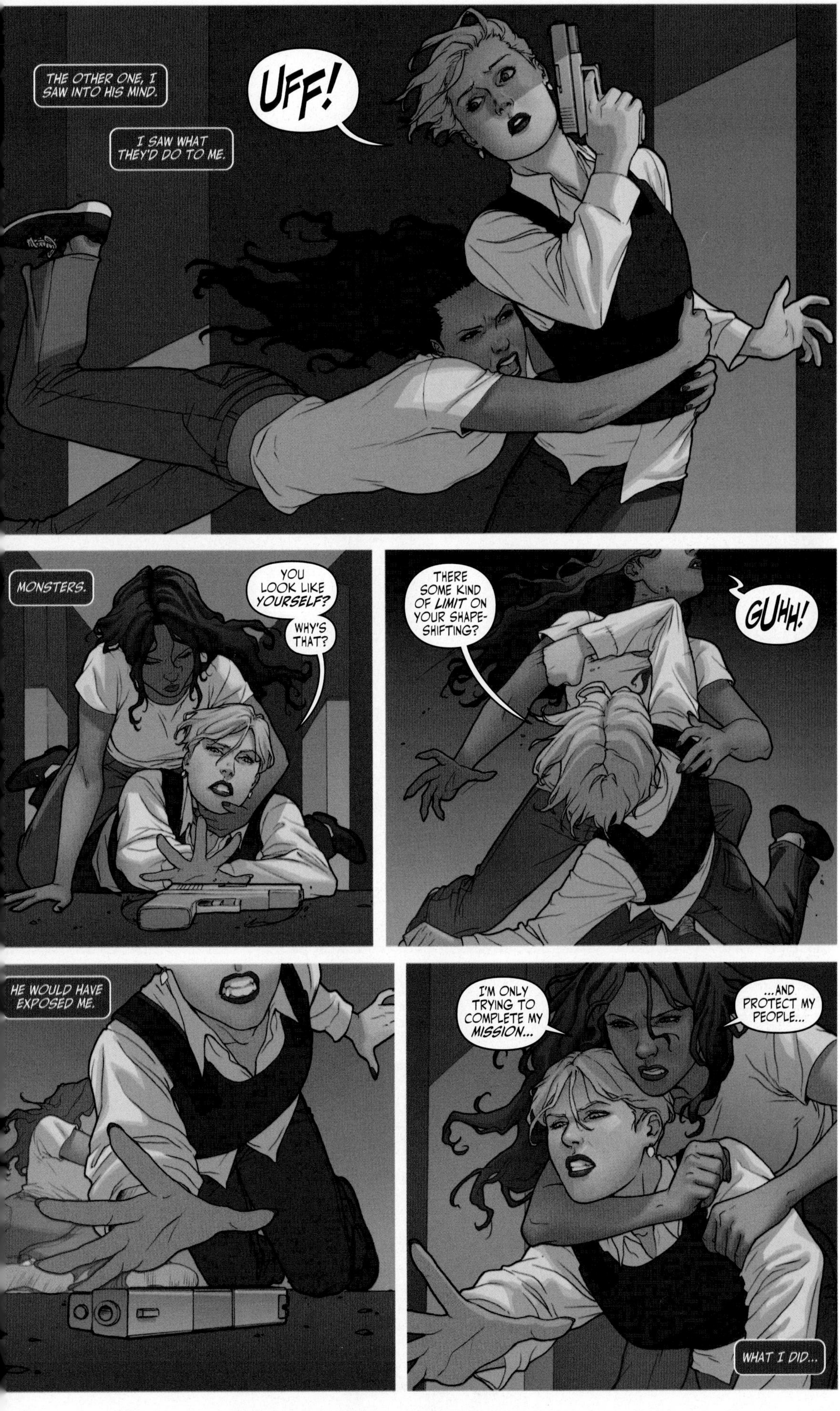
THE OTHER ONE, I SAW INTO HIS MIND.
I SAW WHAT THEY'D DO TO ME.
UFF!
MONSTERS.
YOU LOOK LIKE YOURSELF?
WHY'S THAT?
THERE SOME KIND OF LIMIT ON YOUR SHAPE-SHIFTING?
GUHH!
HE WOULD HAVE EXPOSED ME.
I'M ONLY TRYING TO COMPLETE MY MISSION...
...AND PROTECT MY PEOPLE...
WHAT I DID...

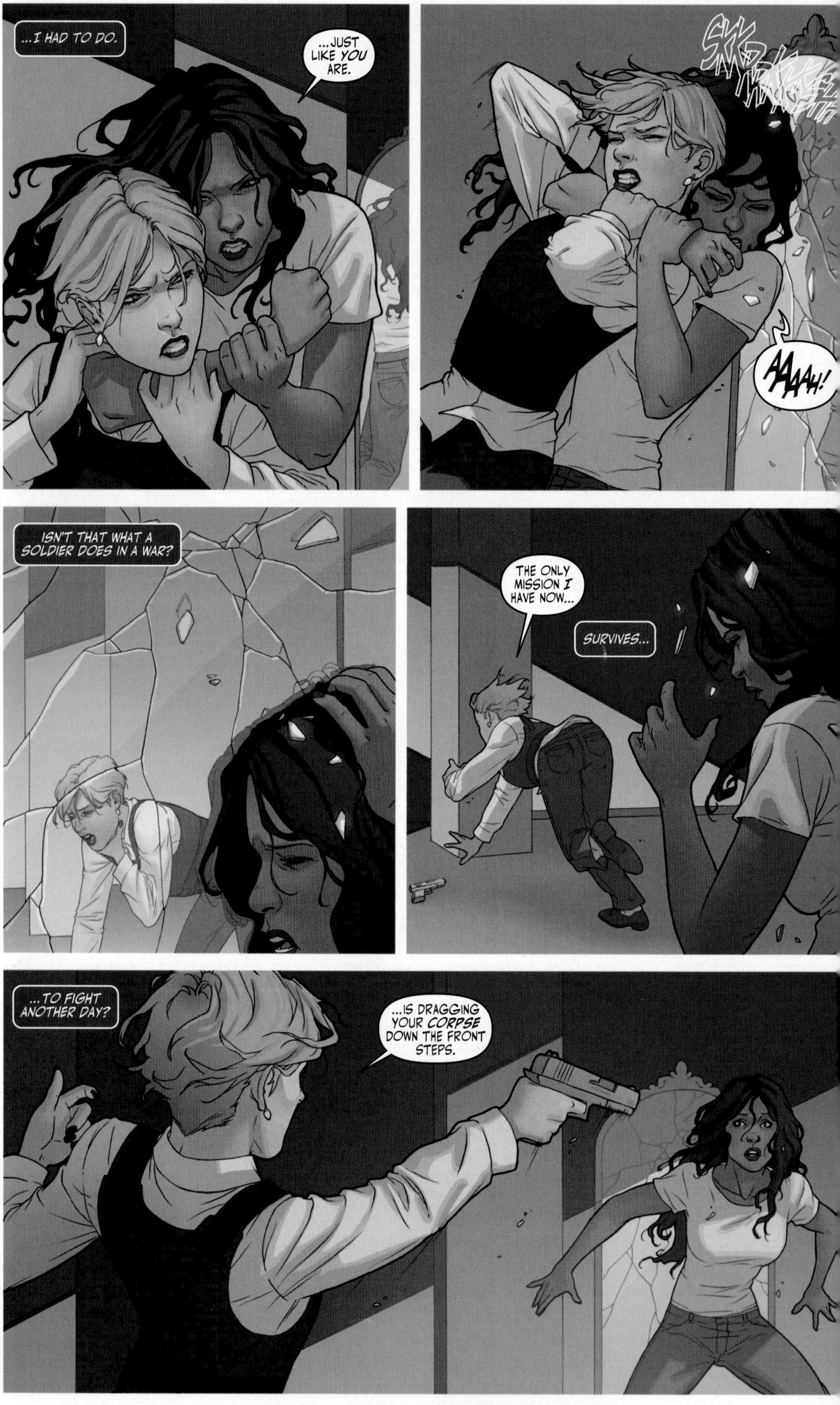

...I HAD TO DO.
...JUST LIKE YOU ARE.
AAAAH!
ISN'T THAT WHAT A SOLDIER DOES IN A WAR?
THE ONLY MISSION I HAVE NOW...
SURVIVES...
...TO FIGHT ANOTHER DAY?
...IS DRAGGING YOUR CORPSE DOWN THE FRONT STEPS.

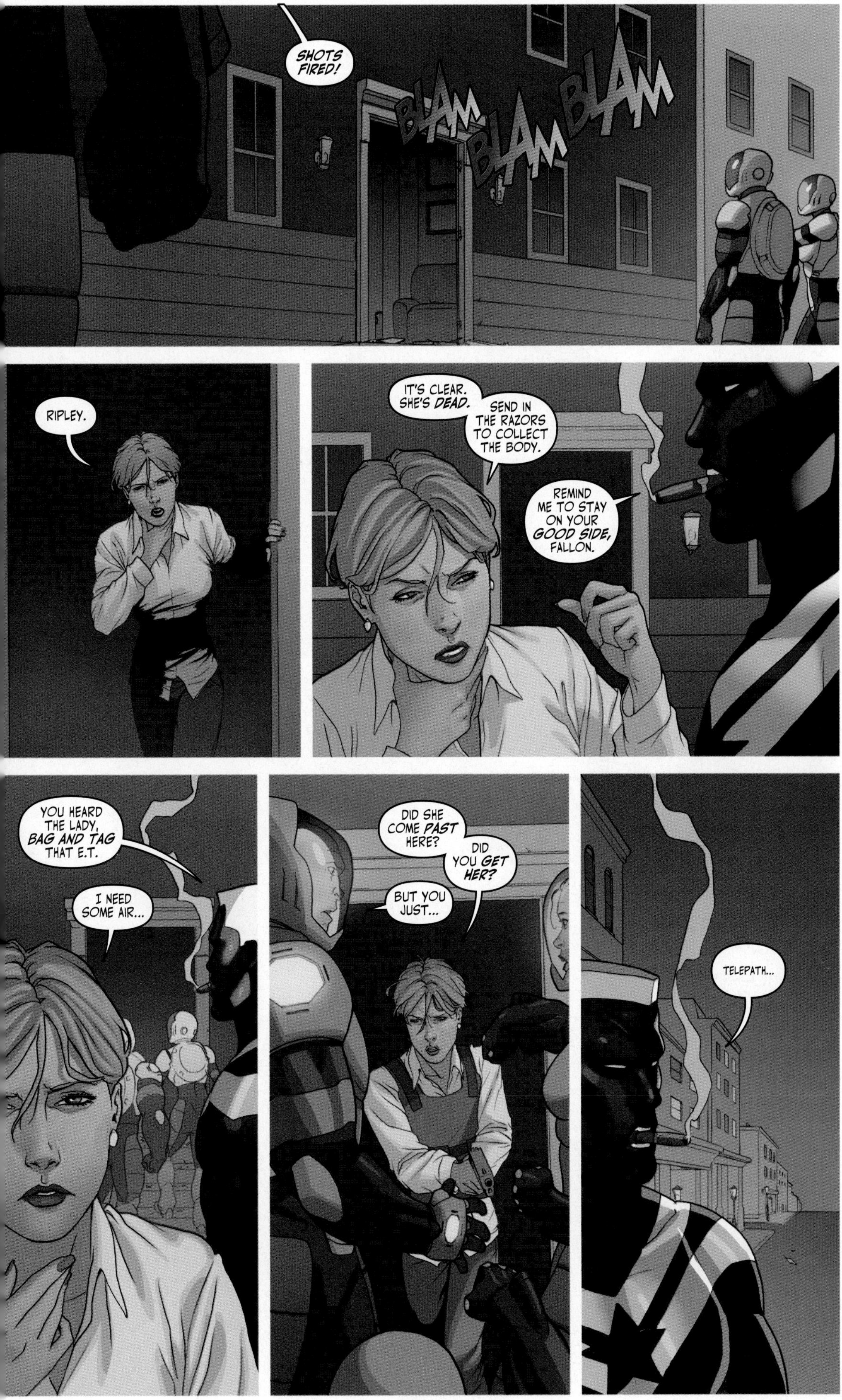
SHOTS FIRED!
BLAM BLAM BLAM
RIPLEY.
IT'S CLEAR. SHE'S *DEAD.*
SEND IN THE RAZORS TO COLLECT THE BODY.
REMIND ME TO STAY ON YOUR *GOOD SIDE,* FALLON.
YOU HEARD THE LADY, *BAG AND TAG* THAT E.T.
I NEED SOME AIR...
DID SHE COME *PAST* HERE?
DID YOU *GET HER?*
BUT YOU JUST...
TELEPATH...

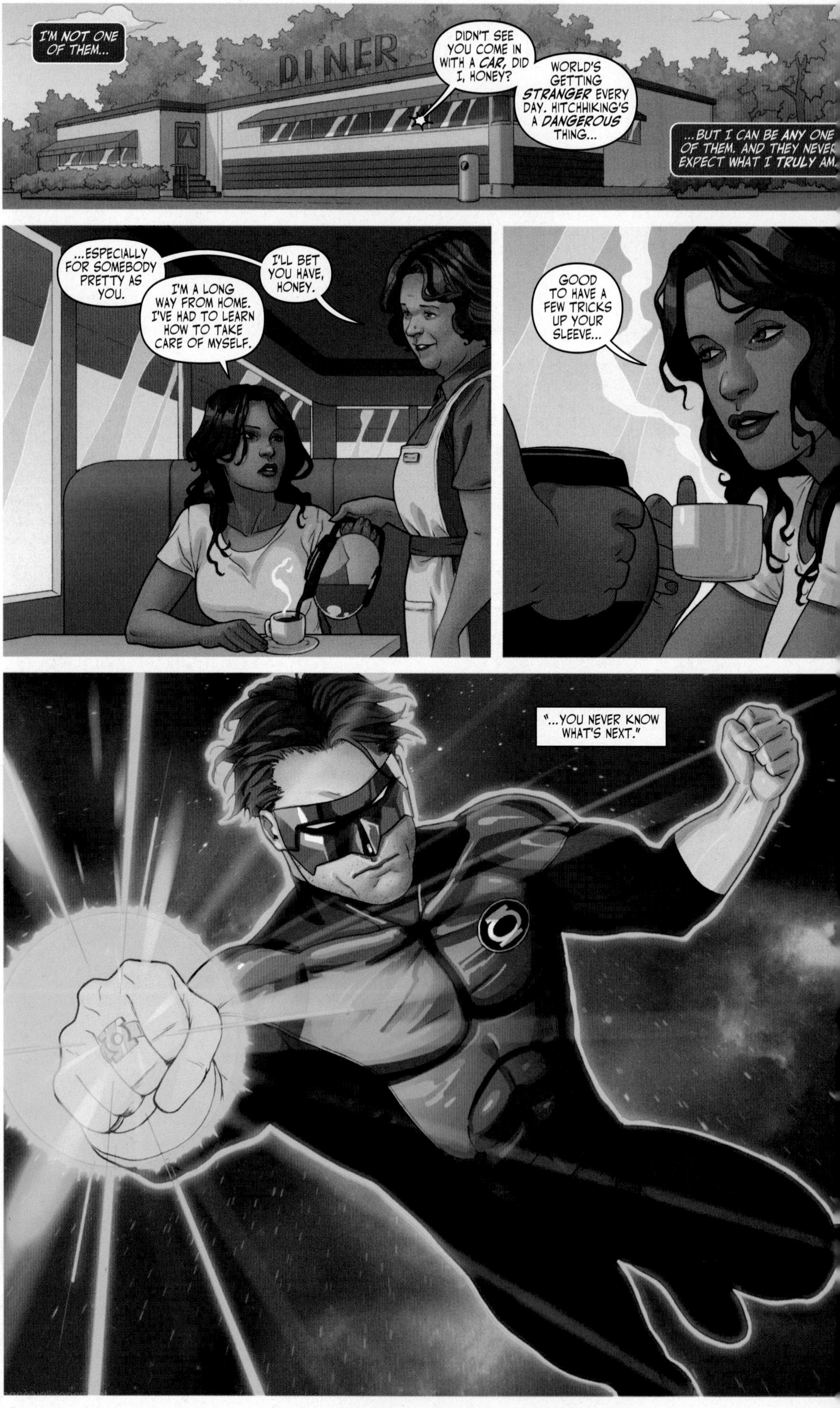
I'M NOT ONE OF THEM...
DIDN'T SEE YOU COME IN WITH A CAR, DID I, HONEY?
WORLD'S GETTING STRANGER EVERY DAY. HITCHHIKING'S A DANGEROUS THING...
...BUT I CAN BE ANY ONE OF THEM. AND THEY NEVER EXPECT WHAT I TRULY AM.
...ESPECIALLY FOR SOMEBODY PRETTY AS YOU.
I'M A LONG WAY FROM HOME. I'VE HAD TO LEARN HOW TO TAKE CARE OF MYSELF.
I'LL BET YOU HAVE, HONEY.
GOOD TO HAVE A FEW TRICKS UP YOUR SLEEVE...
"...YOU NEVER KNOW WHAT'S NEXT."

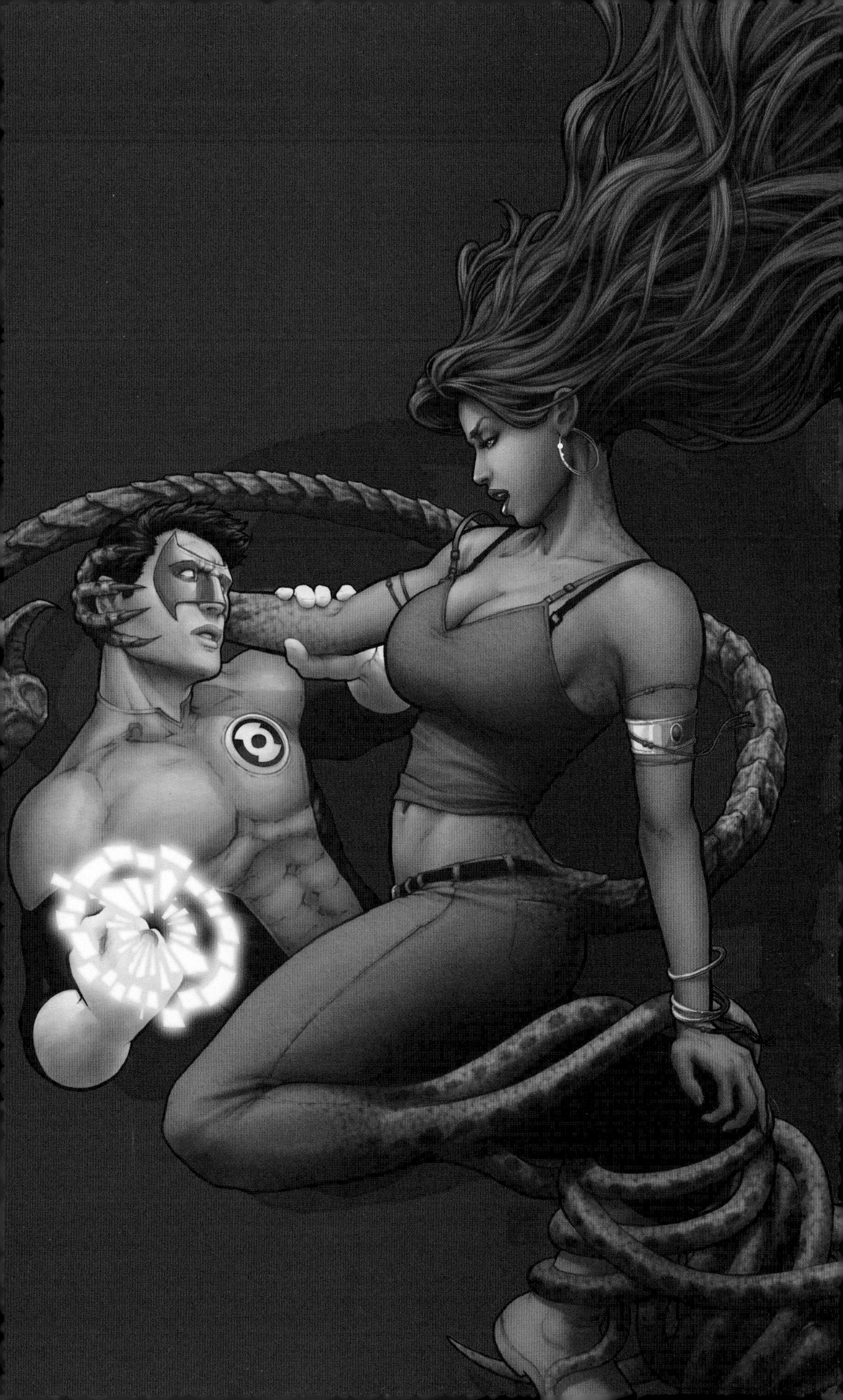

cover art by
JOHN TYLER CHRISTOPHER

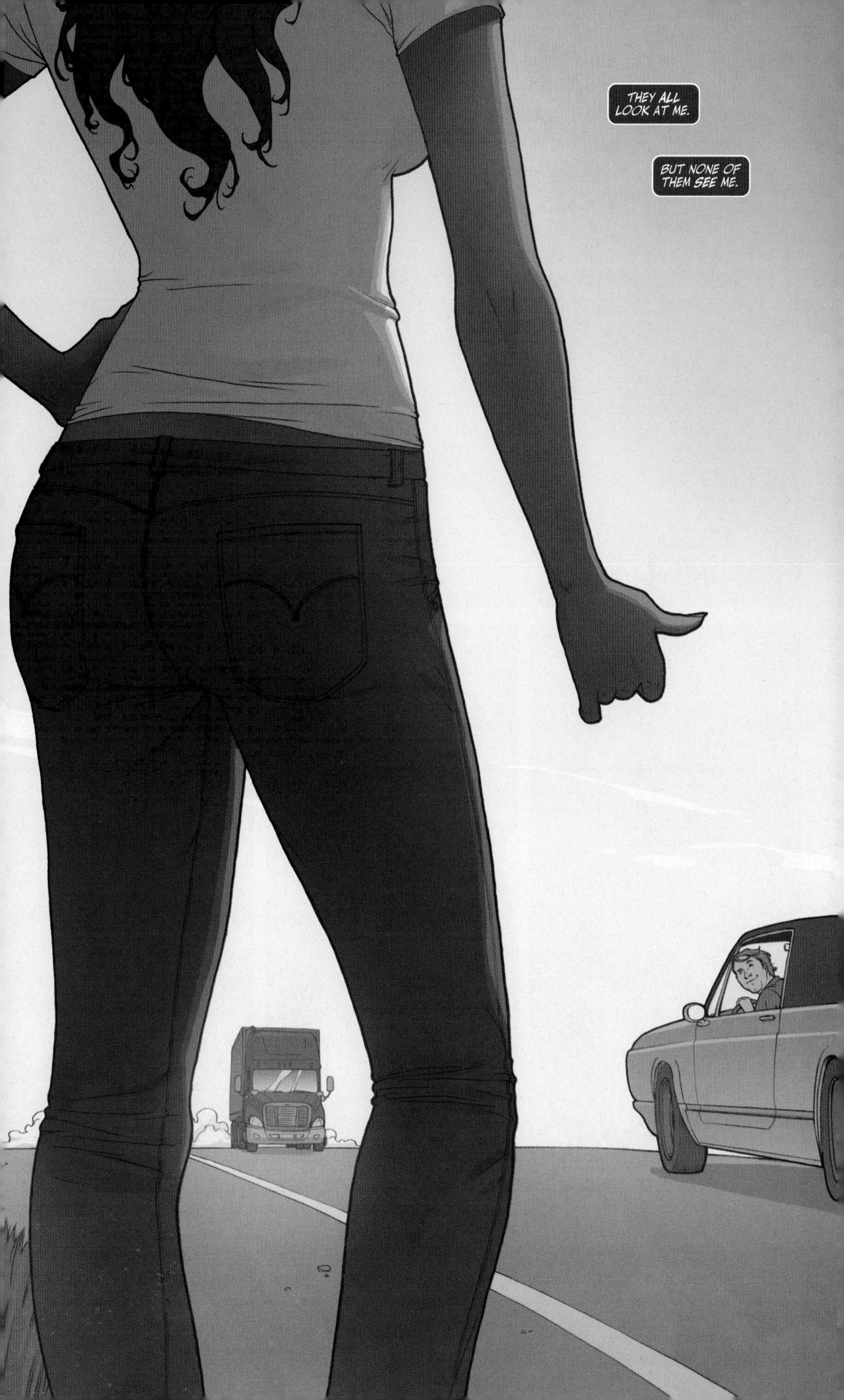
THEY ALL LOOK AT ME.
BUT NONE OF THEM SEE ME.

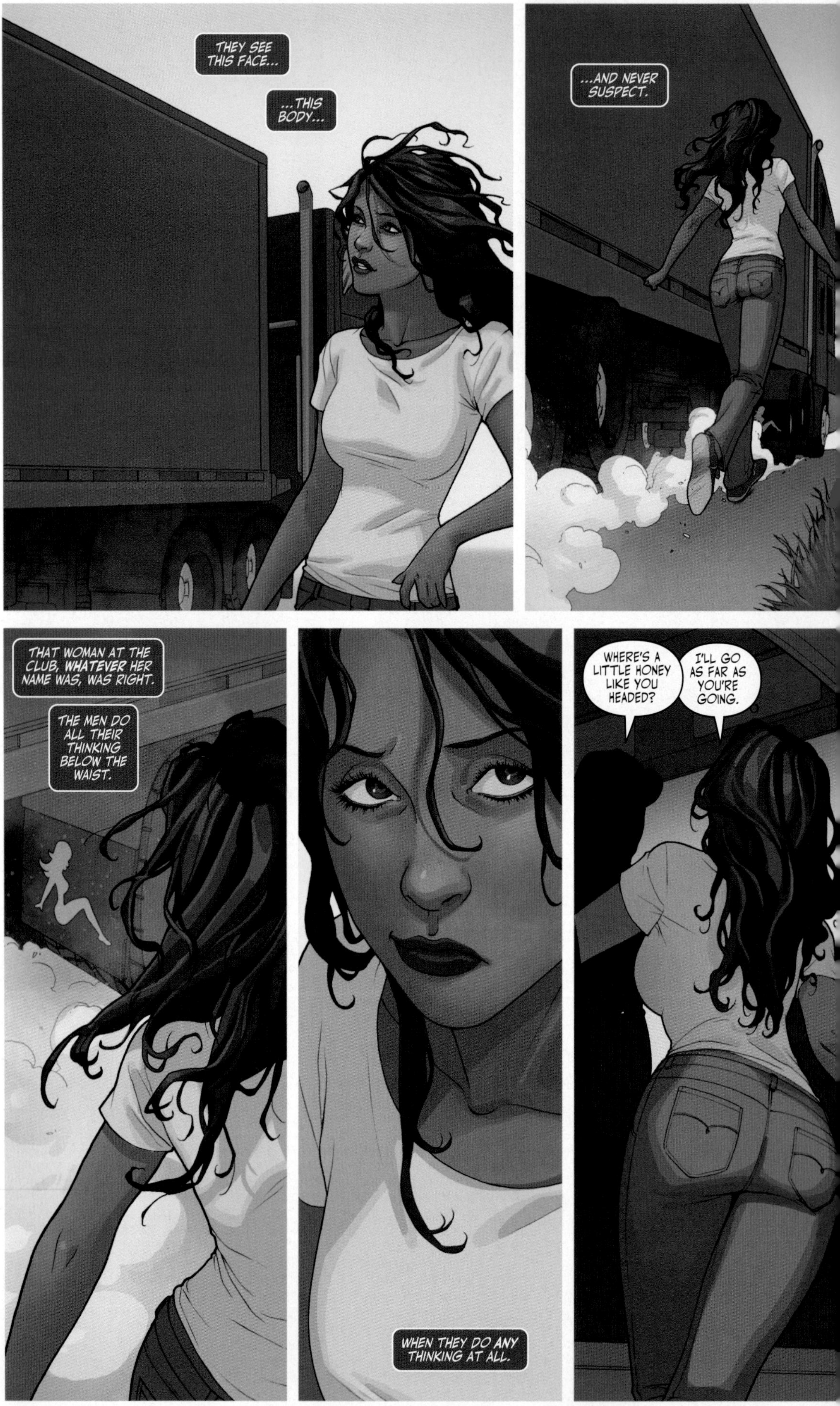
THEY SEE THIS FACE...
...THIS BODY...
...AND NEVER SUSPECT.
THAT WOMAN AT THE CLUB, WHATEVER HER NAME WAS, WAS RIGHT.
THE MEN DO ALL THEIR THINKING BELOW THE WAIST.
WHEN THEY DO ANY THINKING AT ALL.
WHERE'S A LITTLE HONEY LIKE YOU HEADED?
I'LL GO AS FAR AS YOU'RE GOING.

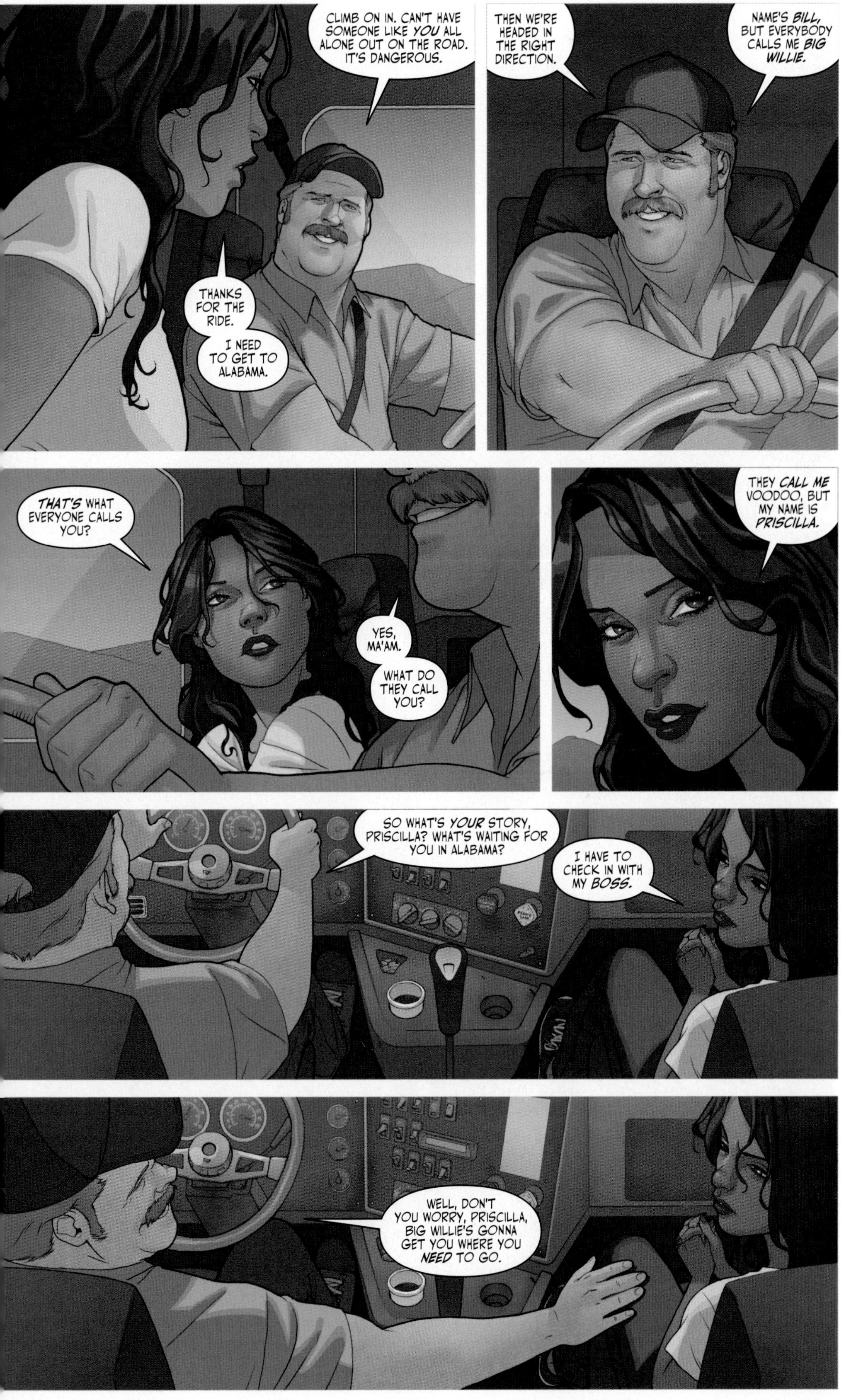
CLIMB ON IN. CAN'T HAVE SOMEONE LIKE YOU ALL ALONE OUT ON THE ROAD. IT'S DANGEROUS.
THANKS FOR THE RIDE.
I NEED TO GET TO ALABAMA.
THEN WE'RE HEADED IN THE RIGHT DIRECTION.
NAME'S BILL, BUT EVERYBODY CALLS ME BIG WILLIE.
THAT'S WHAT EVERYONE CALLS YOU?
YES, MA'AM.
WHAT DO THEY CALL YOU?
THEY CALL ME VOODOO, BUT MY NAME IS PRISCILLA.
SO WHAT'S YOUR STORY, PRISCILLA? WHAT'S WAITING FOR YOU IN ALABAMA?
I HAVE TO CHECK IN WITH MY BOSS.
WELL, DON'T YOU WORRY, PRISCILLA, BIG WILLIE'S GONNA GET YOU WHERE YOU NEED TO GO.

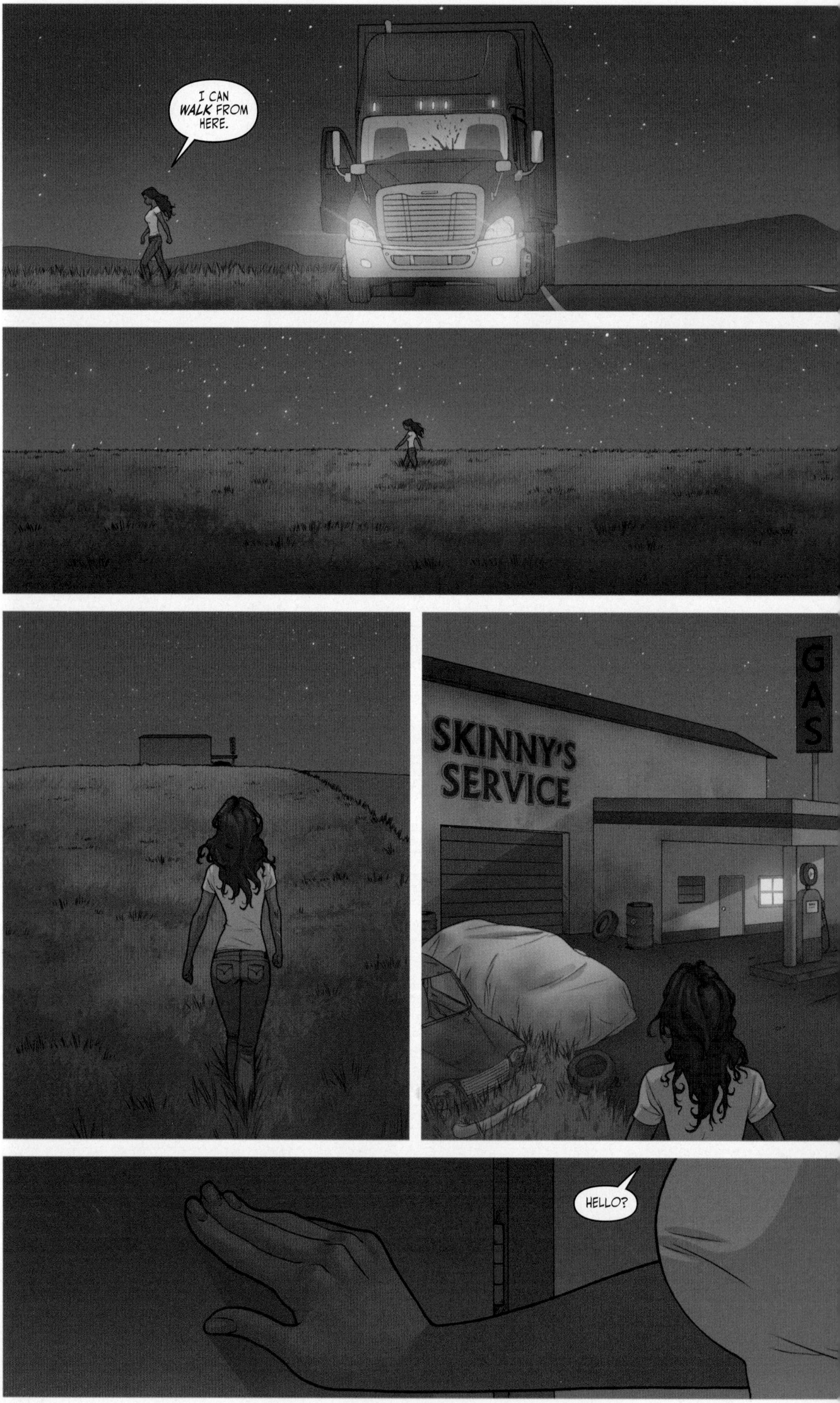
I CAN WALK FROM HERE.
SKINNY'S SERVICE
GAS
HELLO?

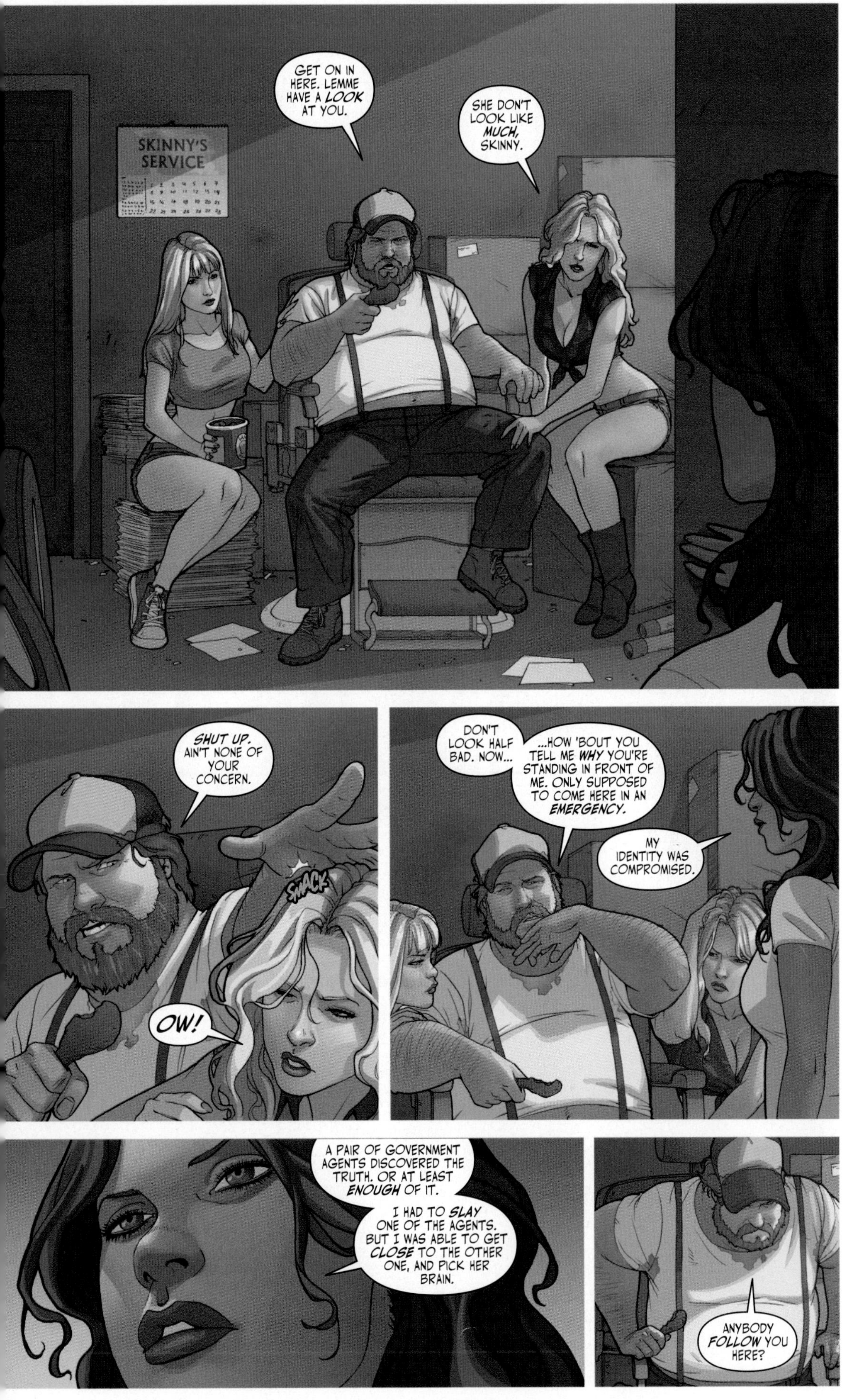
SKINNY'S SERVICE
GET ON IN HERE. LEMME HAVE A LOOK AT YOU.
SHE DON'T LOOK LIKE MUCH, SKINNY.
SHUT UP. AIN'T NONE OF YOUR CONCERN.
SMACK
OW!
DON'T LOOK HALF BAD. NOW...
...HOW 'BOUT YOU TELL ME WHY YOU'RE STANDING IN FRONT OF ME. ONLY SUPPOSED TO COME HERE IN AN EMERGENCY.
MY IDENTITY WAS COMPROMISED.
A PAIR OF GOVERNMENT AGENTS DISCOVERED THE TRUTH. OR AT LEAST ENOUGH OF IT.
I HAD TO SLAY ONE OF THE AGENTS. BUT I WAS ABLE TO GET CLOSE TO THE OTHER ONE, AND PICK HER BRAIN.
ANYBODY FOLLOW YOU HERE?

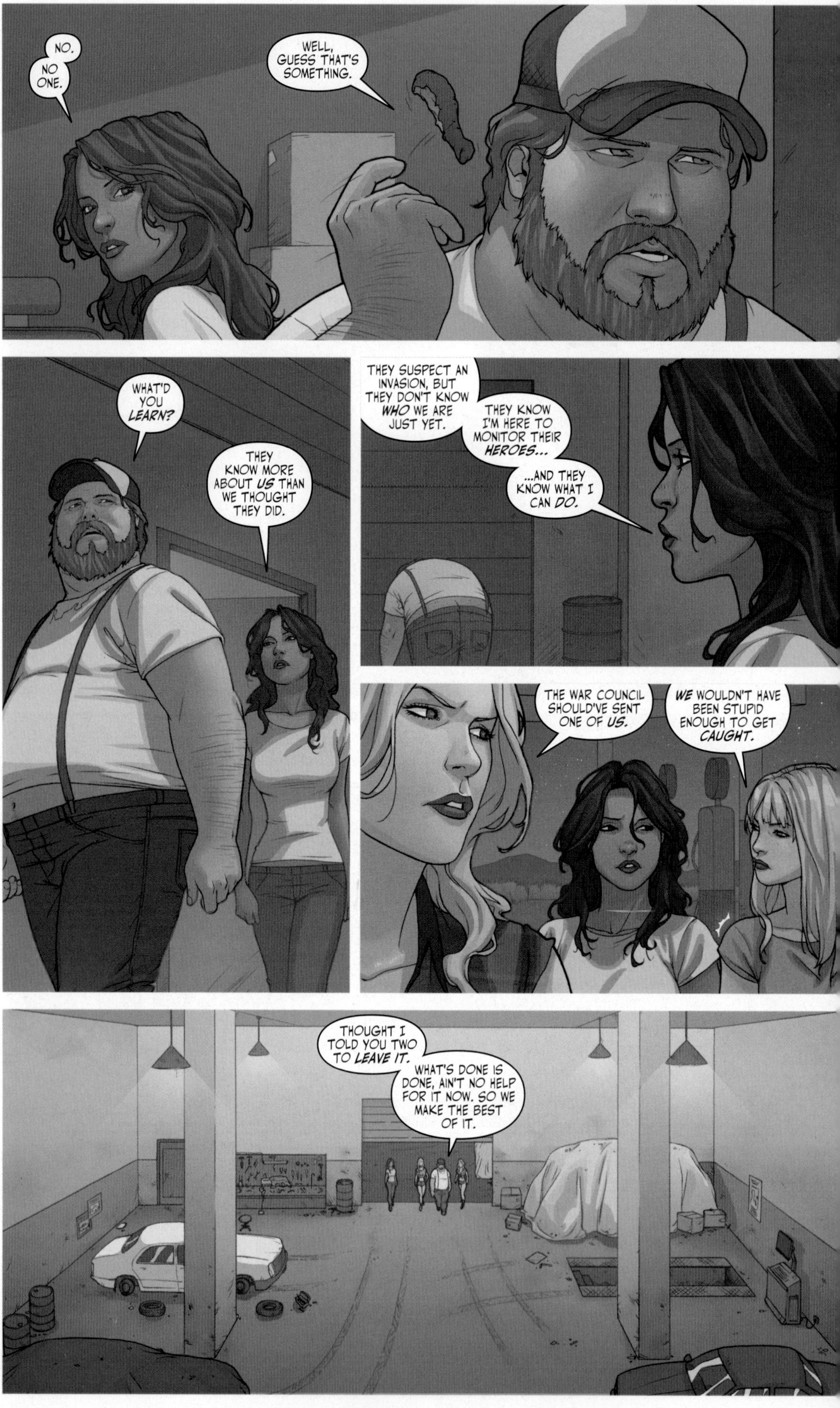
NO.
NO ONE.
WELL, GUESS THAT'S SOMETHING.
WHAT'D YOU LEARN?
THEY KNOW MORE ABOUT US THAN WE THOUGHT THEY DID.
THEY SUSPECT AN INVASION, BUT THEY DON'T KNOW WHO WE ARE JUST YET.
THEY KNOW I'M HERE TO MONITOR THEIR HEROES...
...AND THEY KNOW WHAT I CAN DO.
THE WAR COUNCIL SHOULD'VE SENT ONE OF US.
WE WOULDN'T HAVE BEEN STUPID ENOUGH TO GET CAUGHT.
THOUGHT I TOLD YOU TWO TO LEAVE IT.
WHAT'S DONE IS DONE, AIN'T NO HELP FOR IT NOW. SO WE MAKE THE BEST OF IT.

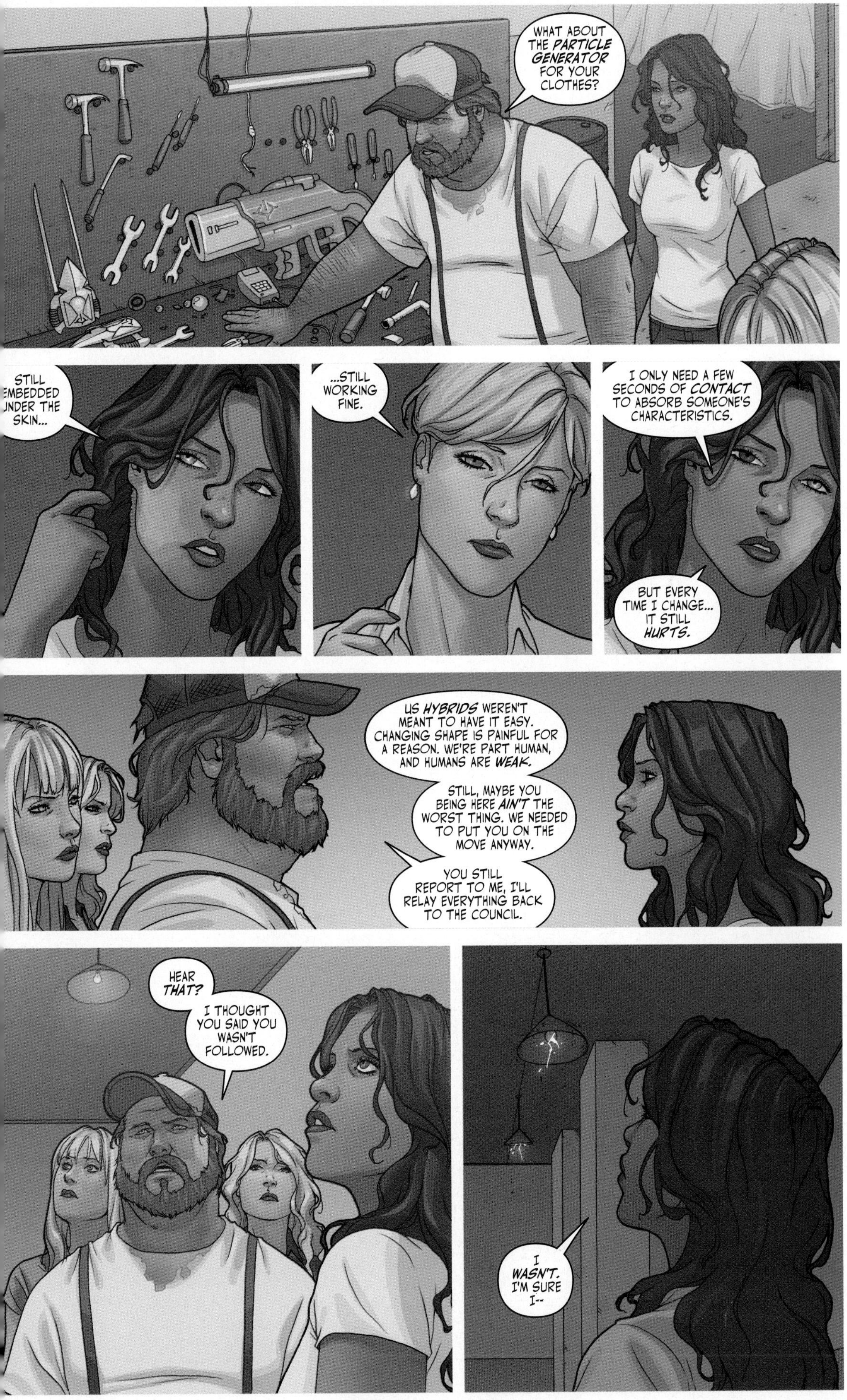
WHAT ABOUT THE PARTICLE GENERATOR FOR YOUR CLOTHES?
STILL EMBEDDED UNDER THE SKIN...
...STILL WORKING FINE.
I ONLY NEED A FEW SECONDS OF CONTACT TO ABSORB SOMEONE'S CHARACTERISTICS.
BUT EVERY TIME I CHANGE... IT STILL HURTS.
US HYBRIDS WEREN'T MEANT TO HAVE IT EASY. CHANGING SHAPE IS PAINFUL FOR A REASON. WE'RE PART HUMAN, AND HUMANS ARE WEAK.
STILL, MAYBE YOU BEING HERE AIN'T THE WORST THING. WE NEEDED TO PUT YOU ON THE MOVE ANYWAY.
YOU STILL REPORT TO ME, I'LL RELAY EVERYTHING BACK TO THE COUNCIL.
HEAR THAT?
I THOUGHT YOU SAID YOU WASN'T FOLLOWED.
I WASN'T. I'M SURE I--

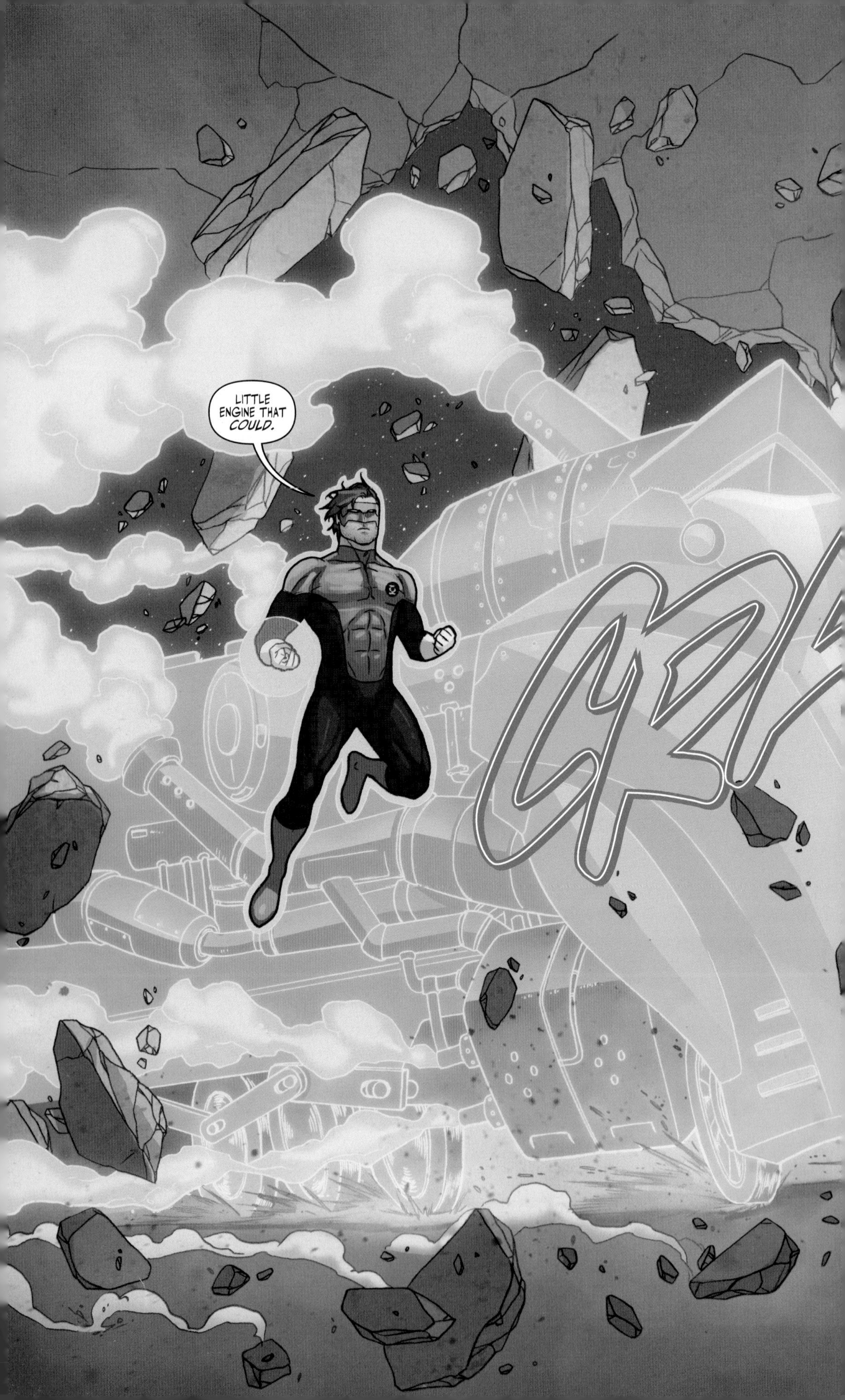
LITTLE ENGINE THAT COULD.

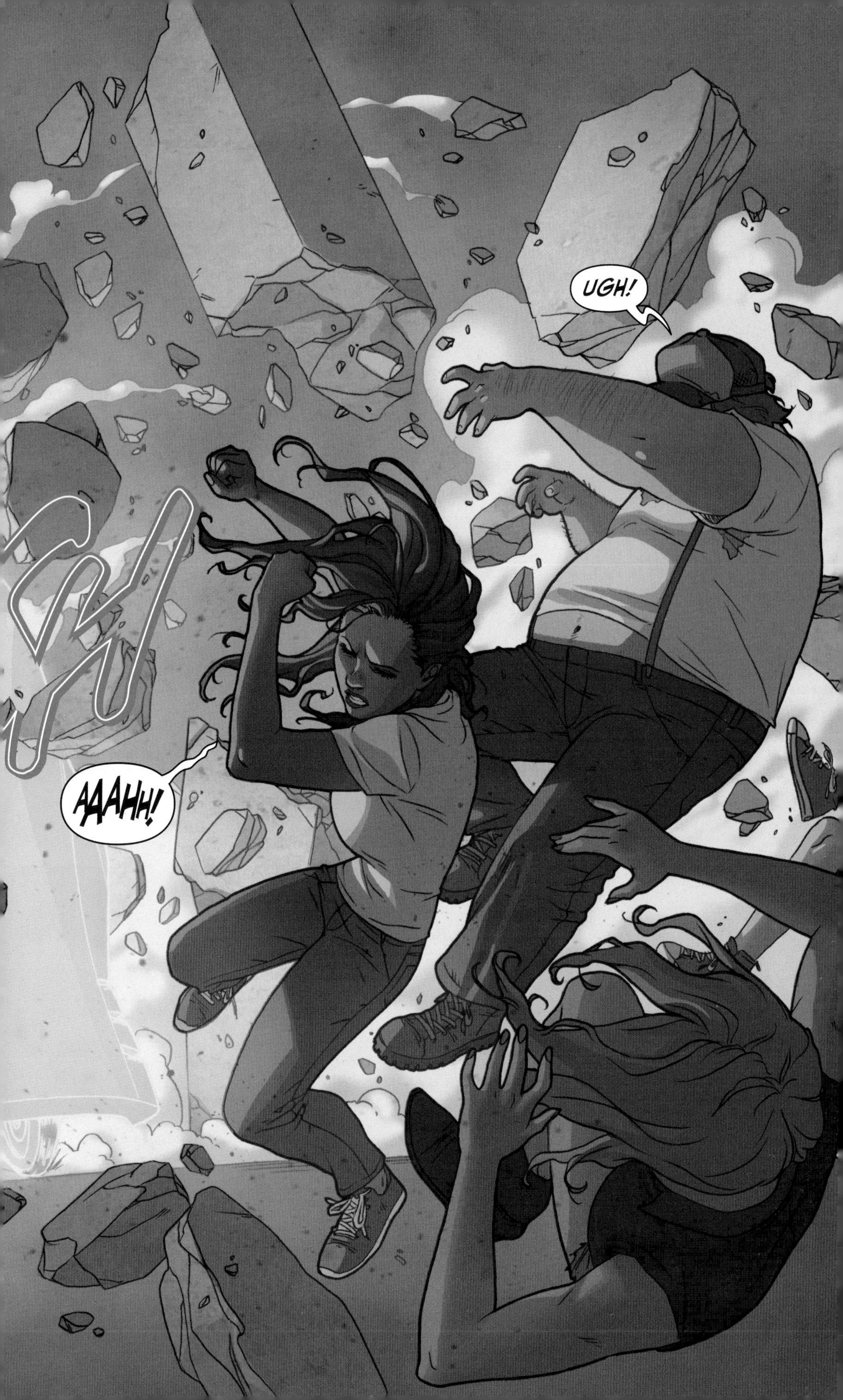
UGH!
AAAHH!

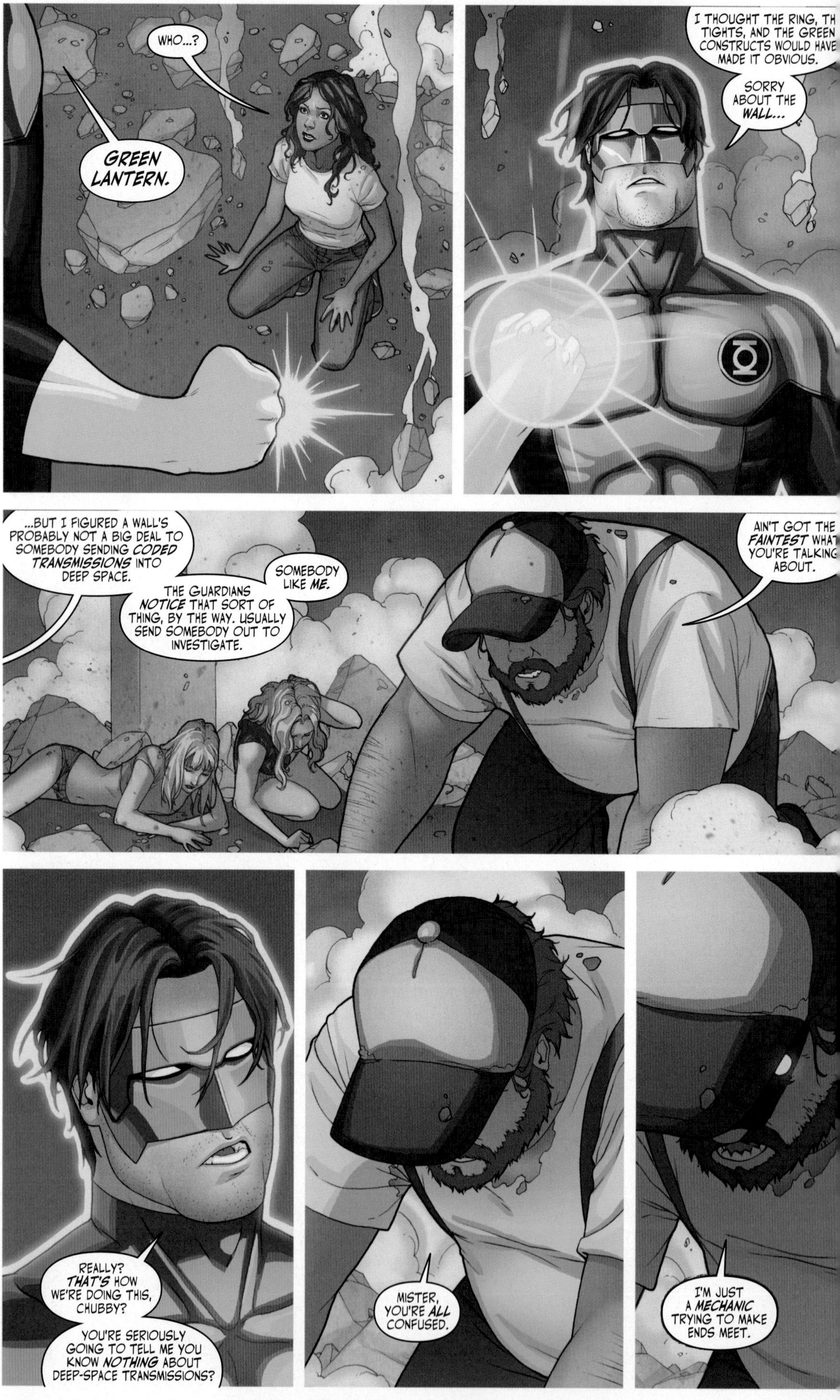
WHO...?
GREEN LANTERN.
I THOUGHT THE RING, TH TIGHTS, AND THE GREEN CONSTRUCTS WOULD HAVE MADE IT OBVIOUS.
SORRY ABOUT THE WALL...
...BUT I FIGURED A WALL'S PROBABLY NOT A BIG DEAL TO SOMEBODY SENDING CODED TRANSMISSIONS INTO DEEP SPACE.
SOMEBODY LIKE ME.
THE GUARDIANS NOTICE THAT SORT OF THING, BY THE WAY. USUALLY SEND SOMEBODY OUT TO INVESTIGATE.
AIN'T GOT THE FAINTEST WHAT YOU'RE TALKING ABOUT.
REALLY? THAT'S HOW WE'RE DOING THIS, CHUBBY?
YOU'RE SERIOUSLY GOING TO TELL ME YOU KNOW NOTHING ABOUT DEEP-SPACE TRANSMISSIONS?
MISTER, YOU'RE ALL CONFUSED.
I'M JUST A MECHANIC TRYING TO MAKE ENDS MEET.

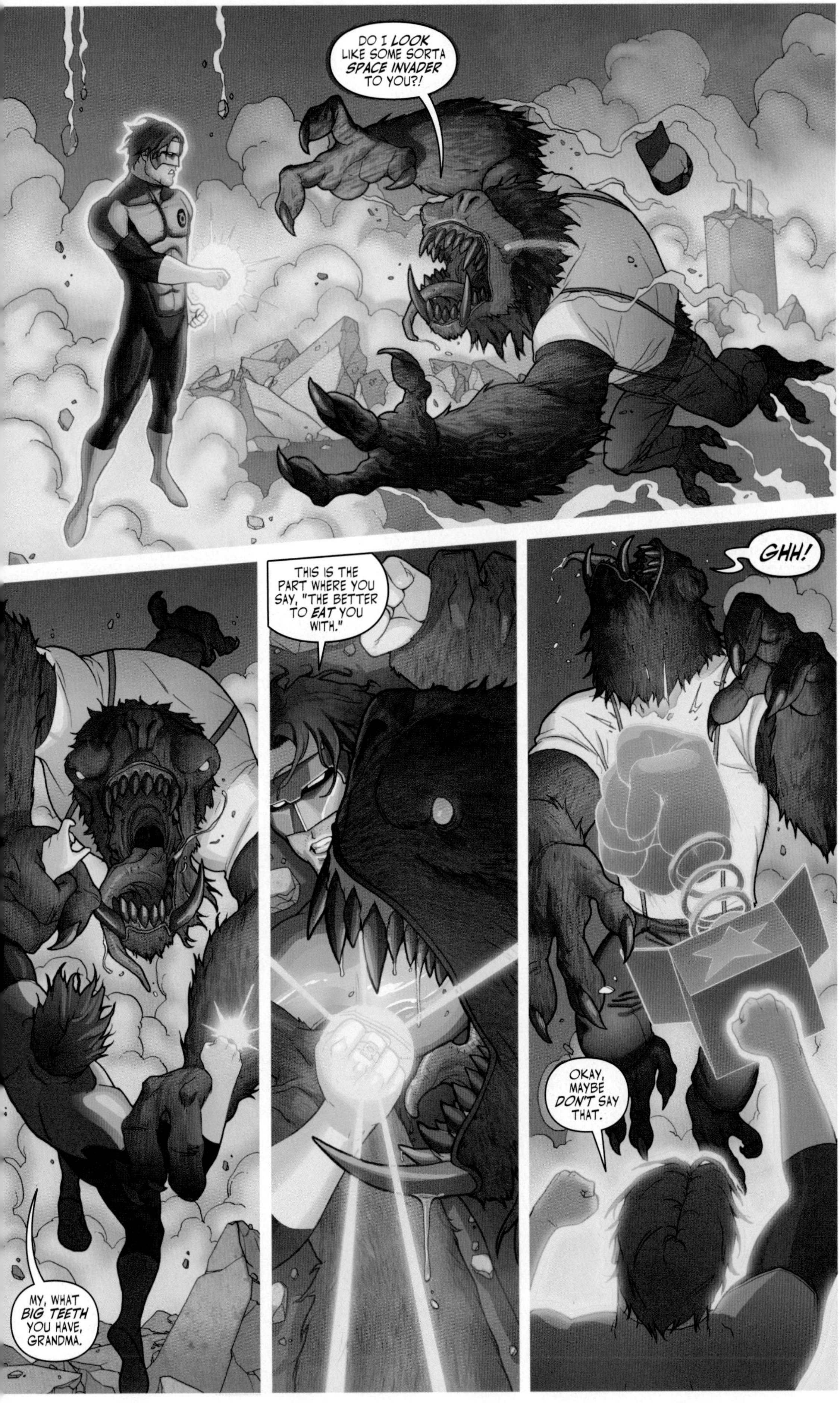
DO I LOOK LIKE SOME SORTA SPACE INVADER TO YOU?!
MY, WHAT BIG TEETH YOU HAVE, GRANDMA.
THIS IS THE PART WHERE YOU SAY, "THE BETTER TO EAT YOU WITH."
GHH!
OKAY, MAYBE DON'T SAY THAT.

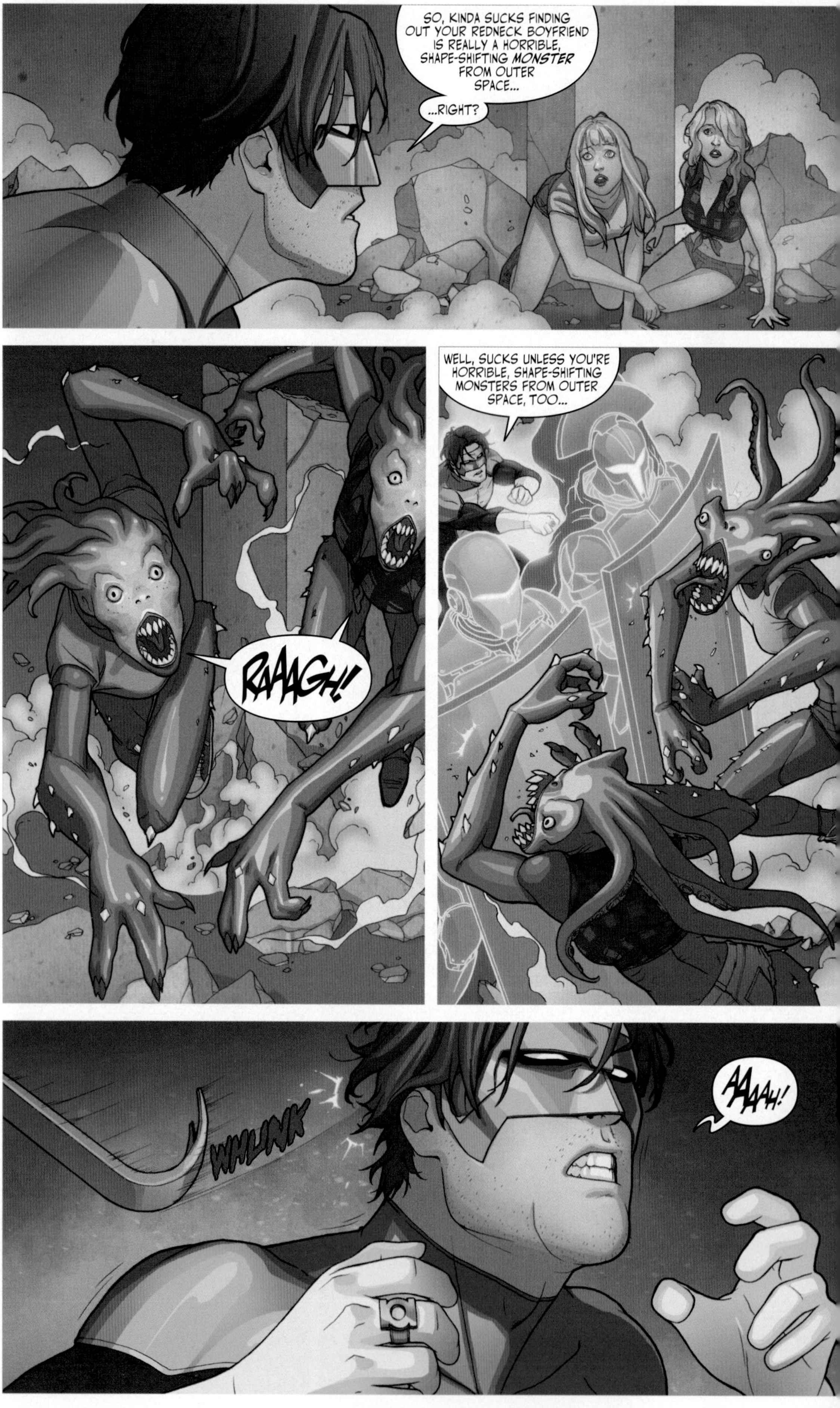
SO, KINDA SUCKS FINDING OUT YOUR REDNECK BOYFRIEND IS REALLY A HORRIBLE, SHAPE-SHIFTING *MONSTER* FROM OUTER SPACE...
...RIGHT?
RAAAGH!
WELL, SUCKS UNLESS YOU'RE HORRIBLE, SHAPE-SHIFTING MONSTERS FROM OUTER SPACE, TOO...
WHLINK
AAAAH!

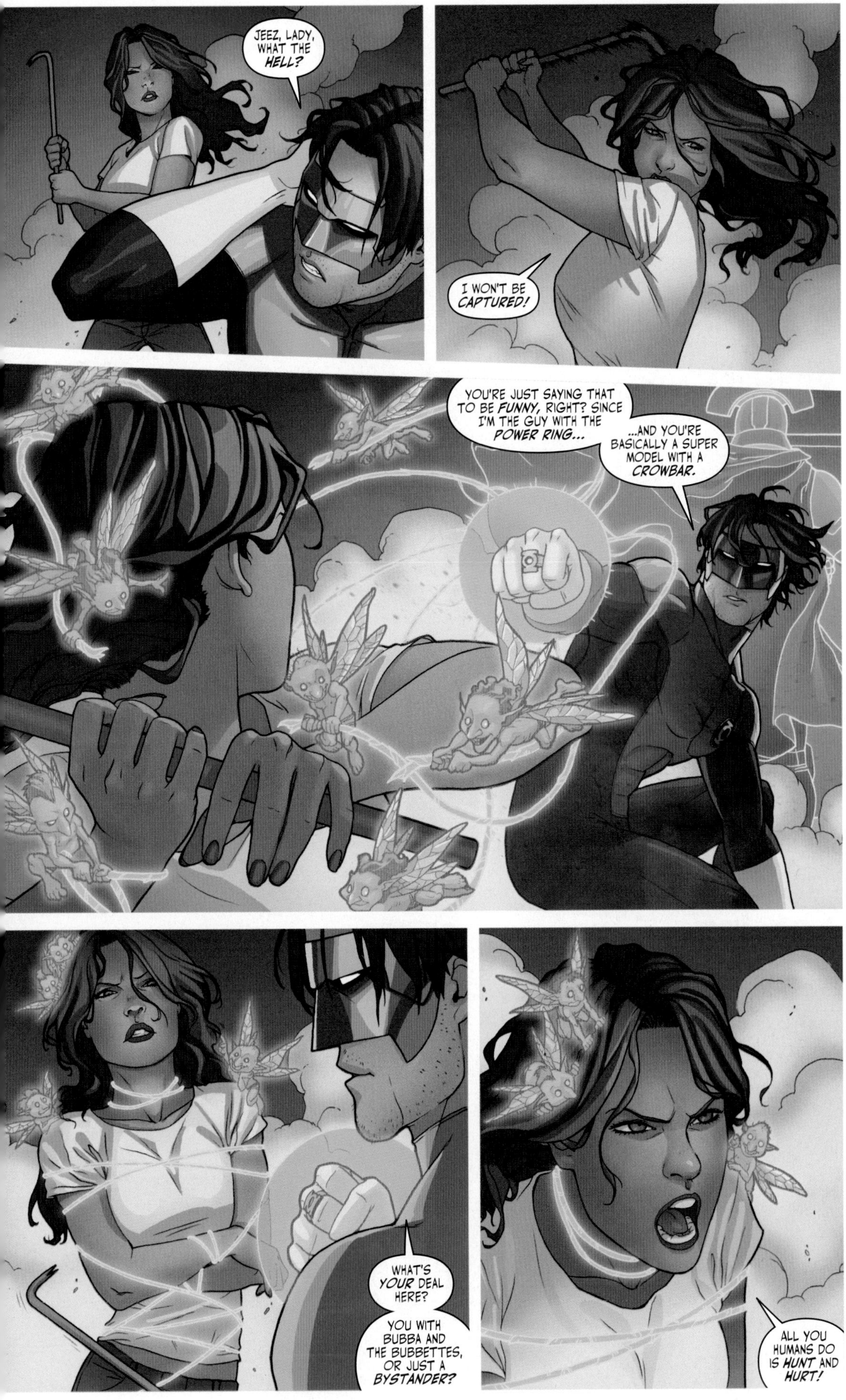
JEEZ, LADY, WHAT THE HELL?
I WON'T BE CAPTURED!
YOU'RE JUST SAYING THAT TO BE FUNNY, RIGHT? SINCE I'M THE GUY WITH THE POWER RING...
...AND YOU'RE BASICALLY A SUPER MODEL WITH A CROWBAR.
WHAT'S YOUR DEAL HERE?
YOU WITH BUBBA AND THE BUBBETTES, OR JUST A BYSTANDER?
ALL YOU HUMANS DO IS HUNT AND HURT!

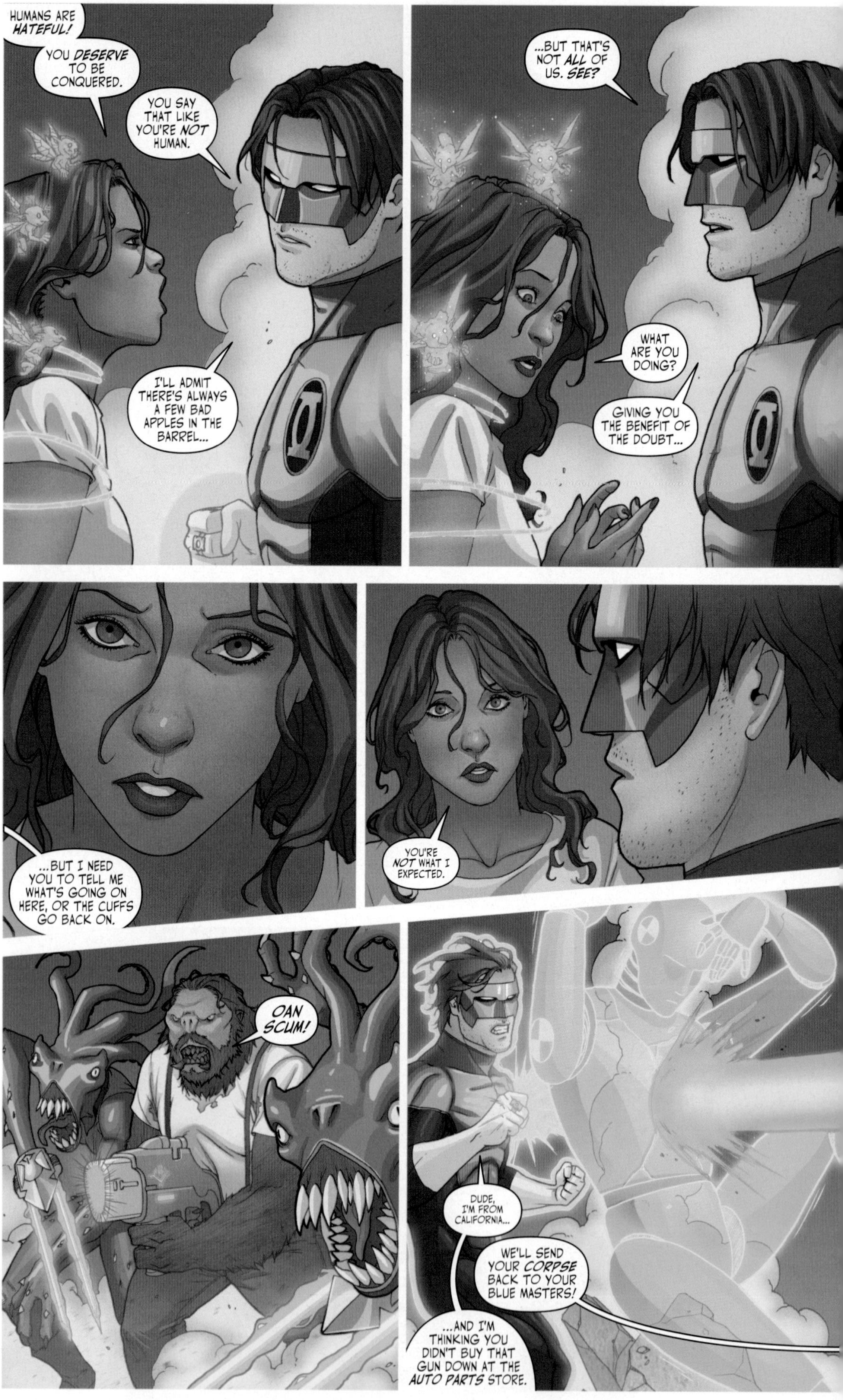

HUMANS ARE HATEFUL!
YOU DESERVE TO BE CONQUERED.
YOU SAY THAT LIKE YOU'RE NOT HUMAN.
I'LL ADMIT THERE'S ALWAYS A FEW BAD APPLES IN THE BARREL...
...BUT THAT'S NOT ALL OF US. SEE?
WHAT ARE YOU DOING?
GIVING YOU THE BENEFIT OF THE DOUBT...
...BUT I NEED YOU TO TELL ME WHAT'S GOING ON HERE, OR THE CUFFS GO BACK ON.
YOU'RE NOT WHAT I EXPECTED.
OAN SCUM!
DUDE, I'M FROM CALIFORNIA...
WE'LL SEND YOUR CORPSE BACK TO YOUR BLUE MASTERS!
...AND I'M THINKING YOU DIDN'T BUY THAT GUN DOWN AT THE AUTO PARTS STORE.

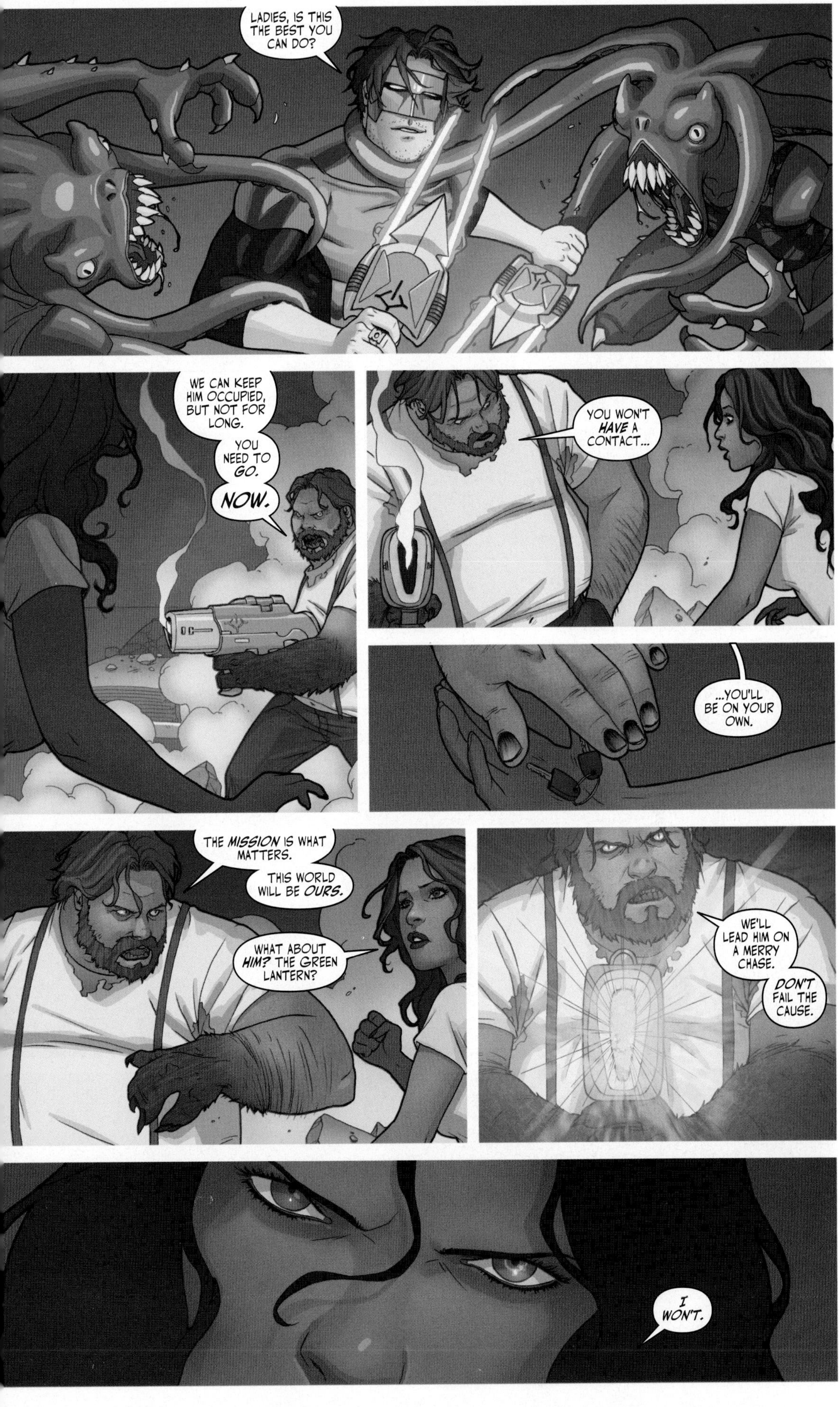

LADIES, IS THIS THE BEST YOU CAN DO?
WE CAN KEEP HIM OCCUPIED, BUT NOT FOR LONG.
YOU NEED TO GO.
NOW.
YOU WON'T HAVE A CONTACT...
...YOU'LL BE ON YOUR OWN.
THE MISSION IS WHAT MATTERS.
THIS WORLD WILL BE OURS.
WHAT ABOUT HIM? THE GREEN LANTERN?
WE'LL LEAD HIM ON A MERRY CHASE.
DON'T FAIL THE CAUSE.
I WON'T.

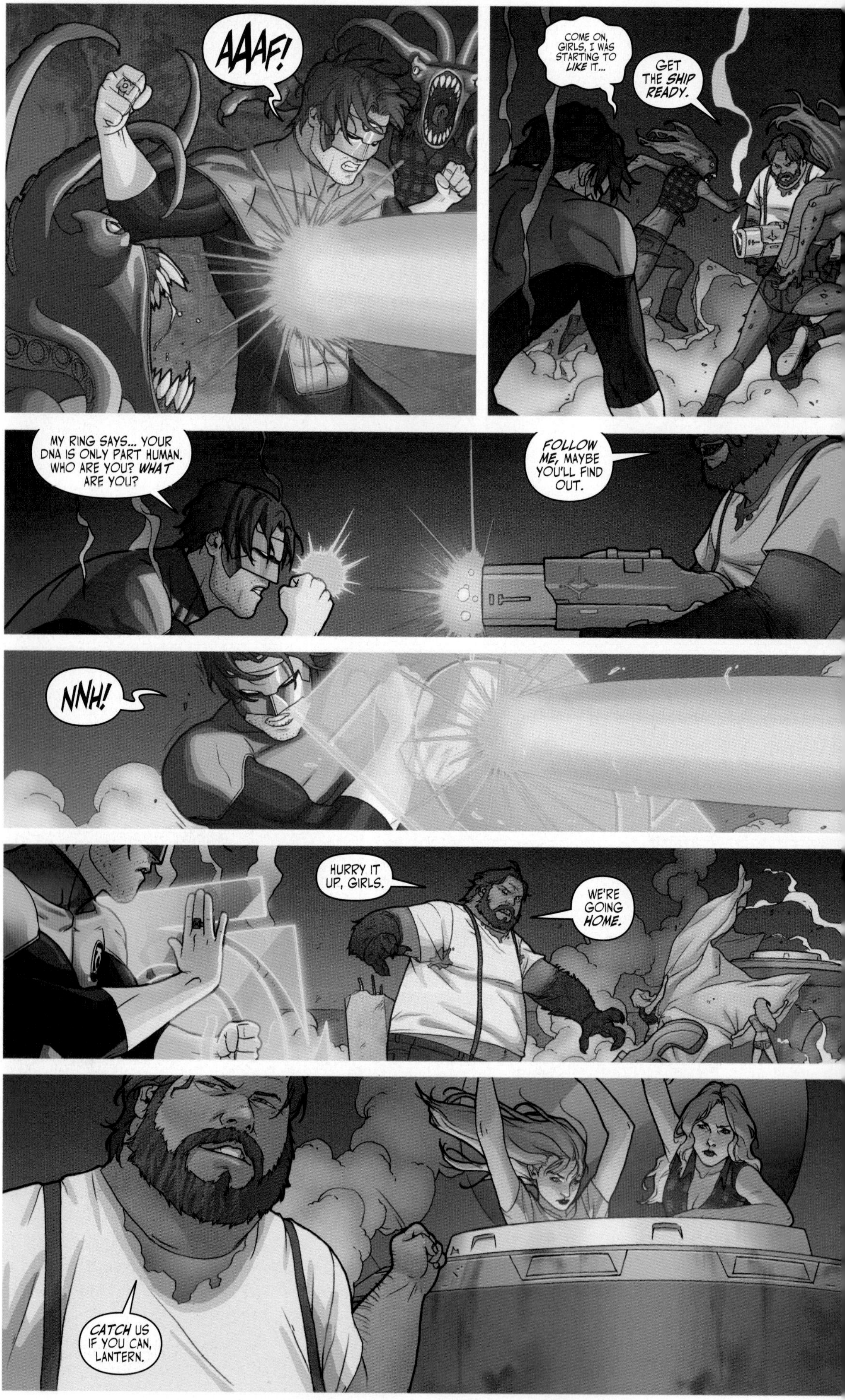
AAAF!
COME ON, GIRLS, I WAS STARTING TO LIKE IT...
GET THE SHIP READY.
MY RING SAYS... YOUR DNA IS ONLY PART HUMAN. WHO ARE YOU? WHAT ARE YOU?
FOLLOW ME, MAYBE YOU'LL FIND OUT.
NNH!
HURRY IT UP, GIRLS.
WE'RE GOING HOME.
CATCH US IF YOU CAN, LANTERN.

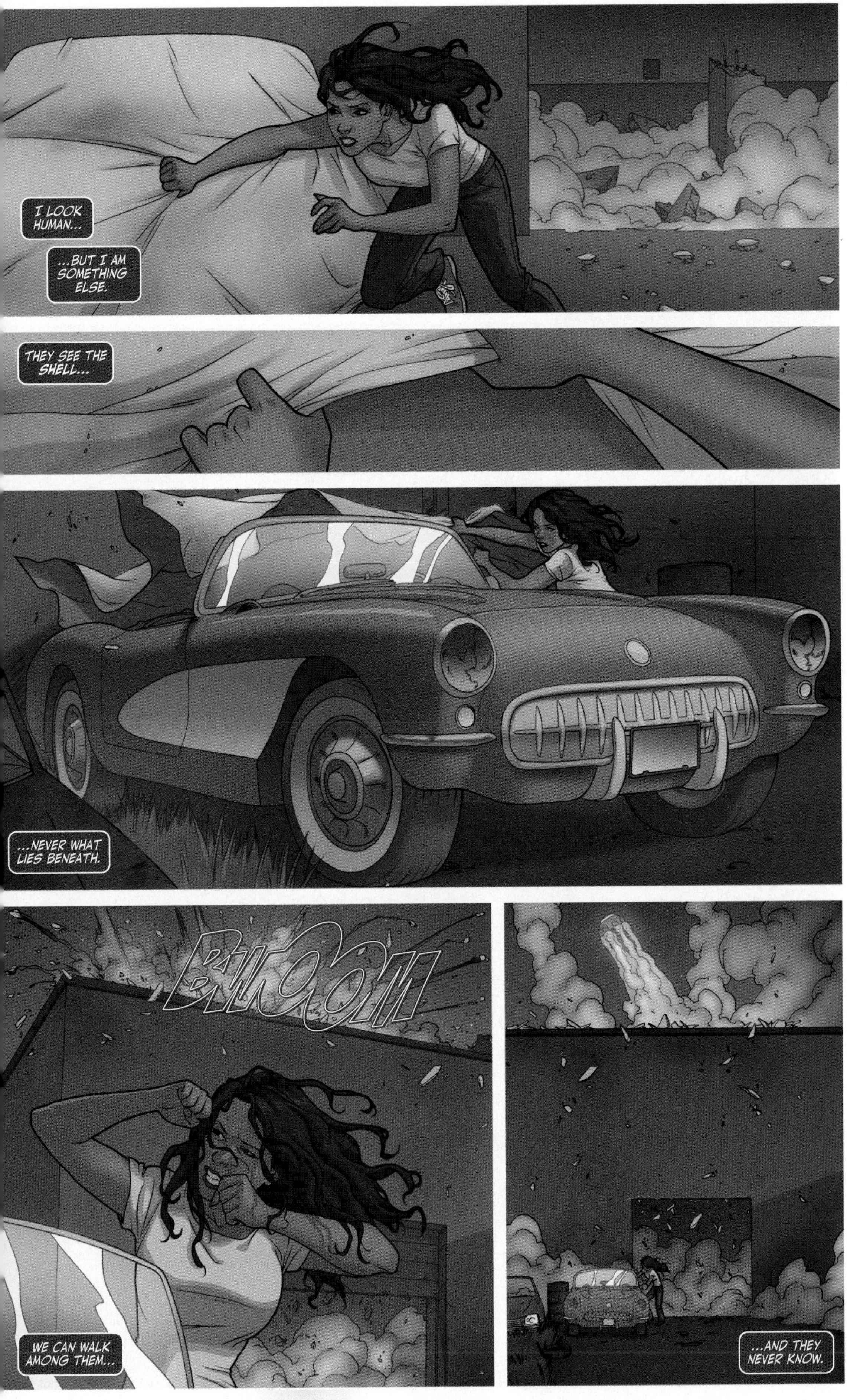
I LOOK HUMAN...
...BUT I AM SOMETHING ELSE.
THEY SEE THE SHELL...
...NEVER WHAT LIES BENEATH.
BWOOM
WE CAN WALK AMONG THEM...
...AND THEY NEVER KNOW.

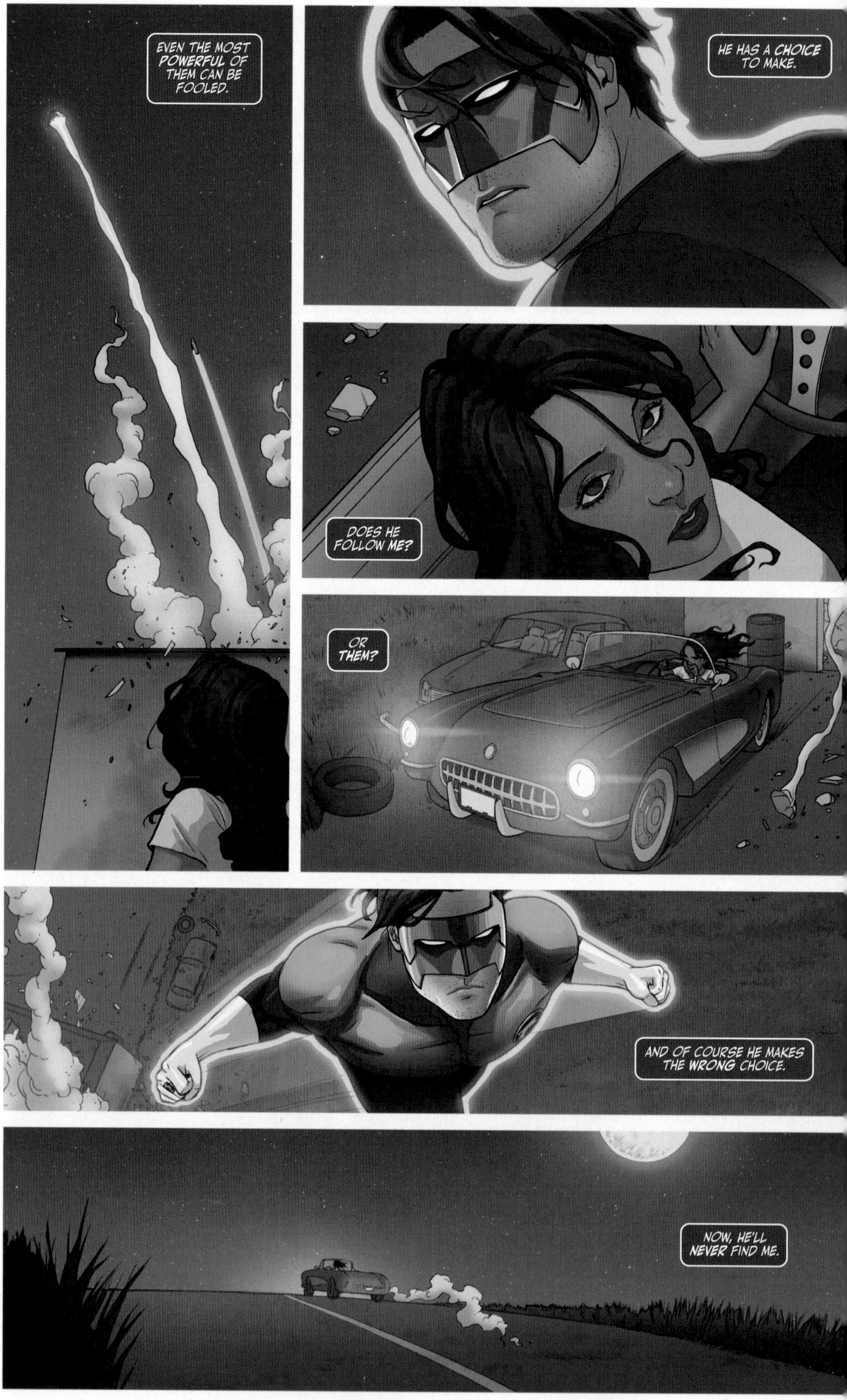
EVEN THE MOST POWERFUL OF THEM CAN BE FOOLED.
HE HAS A CHOICE TO MAKE.
DOES HE FOLLOW ME?
OR THEM?
AND OF COURSE HE MAKES THE WRONG CHOICE.
NOW, HE'LL NEVER FIND ME.

NO, NO, NO...

...YOU ARE *NOT* DISAPPEARING INTO A WARP HOLE.

THAT IS *NOT* HAPPENING.

OKAY, MAYBE IT *IS*...

...JUST A *LITTLE*...

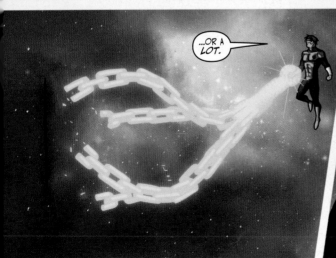

...OR A LOT.

WHO THE HELL *ARE* YOU PEOPLE?

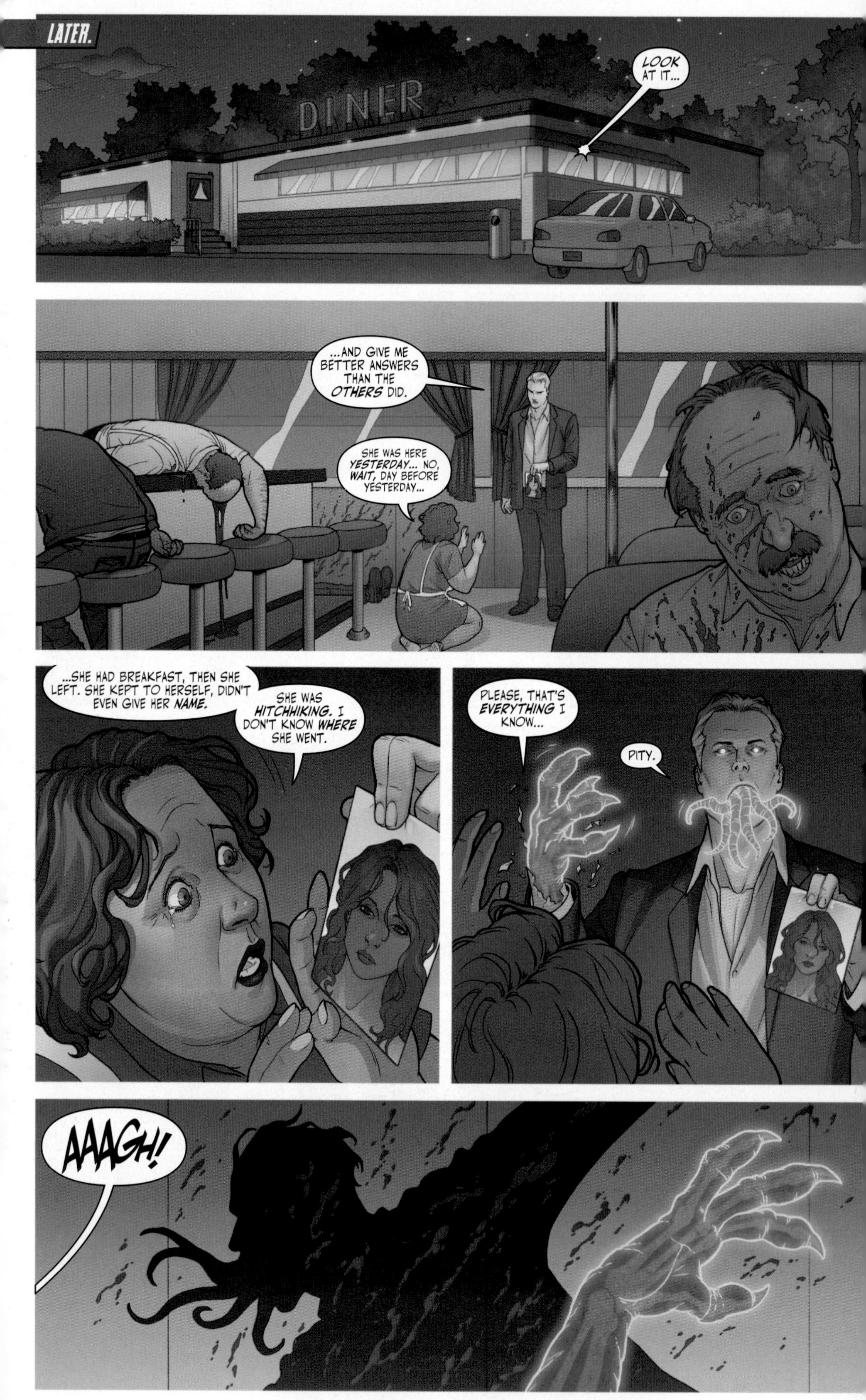
LATER.
DINER
LOOK AT IT...
...AND GIVE ME BETTER ANSWERS THAN THE OTHERS DID.
SHE WAS HERE YESTERDAY... NO, WAIT, DAY BEFORE YESTERDAY...
...SHE HAD BREAKFAST, THEN SHE LEFT. SHE KEPT TO HERSELF, DIDN'T EVEN GIVE HER NAME.
SHE WAS HITCHHIKING. I DON'T KNOW WHERE SHE WENT.
PLEASE, THAT'S EVERYTHING I KNOW...
PITY.
AAAGH!

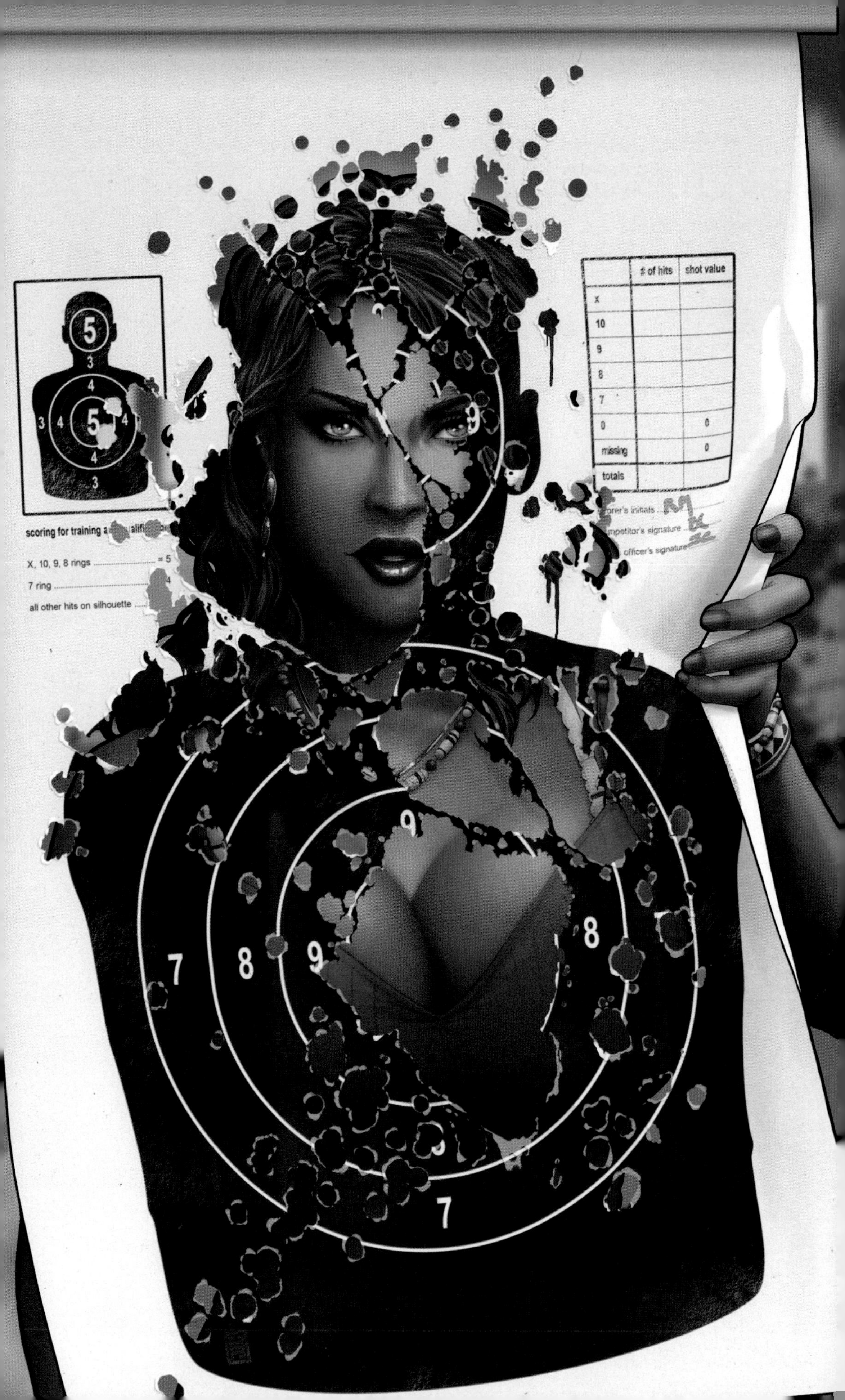

scoring for training a
X, 10, 9, 8 rings = 5
7 ring 4
all other hits on silhouette
# of hits
shot value
x
10
9
8
7
0
0
missing
0
totals

cover art by
JOHN TYLER CHRISTOPHER

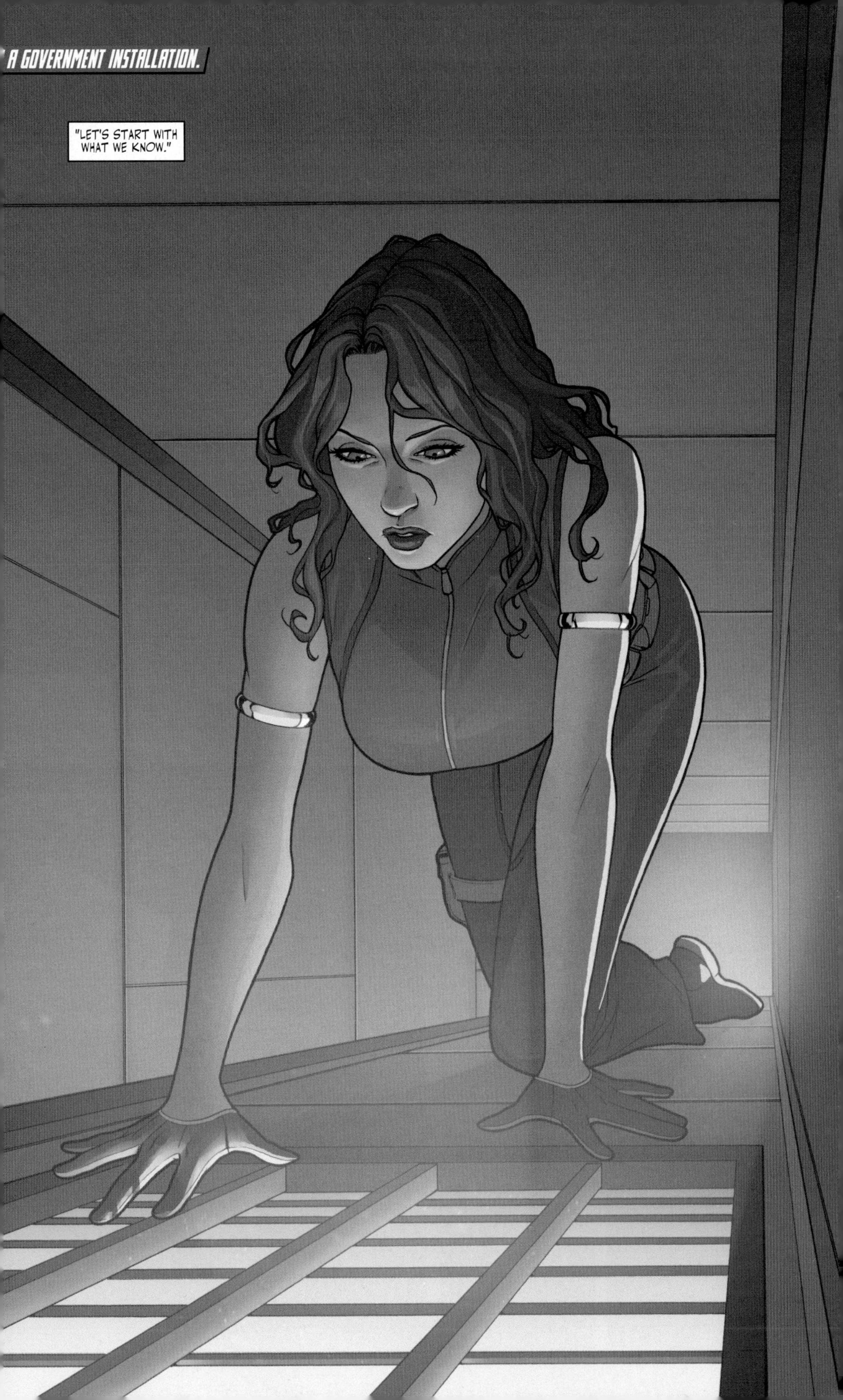
A GOVERNMENT INSTALLATION.
"LET'S START WITH WHAT WE KNOW."

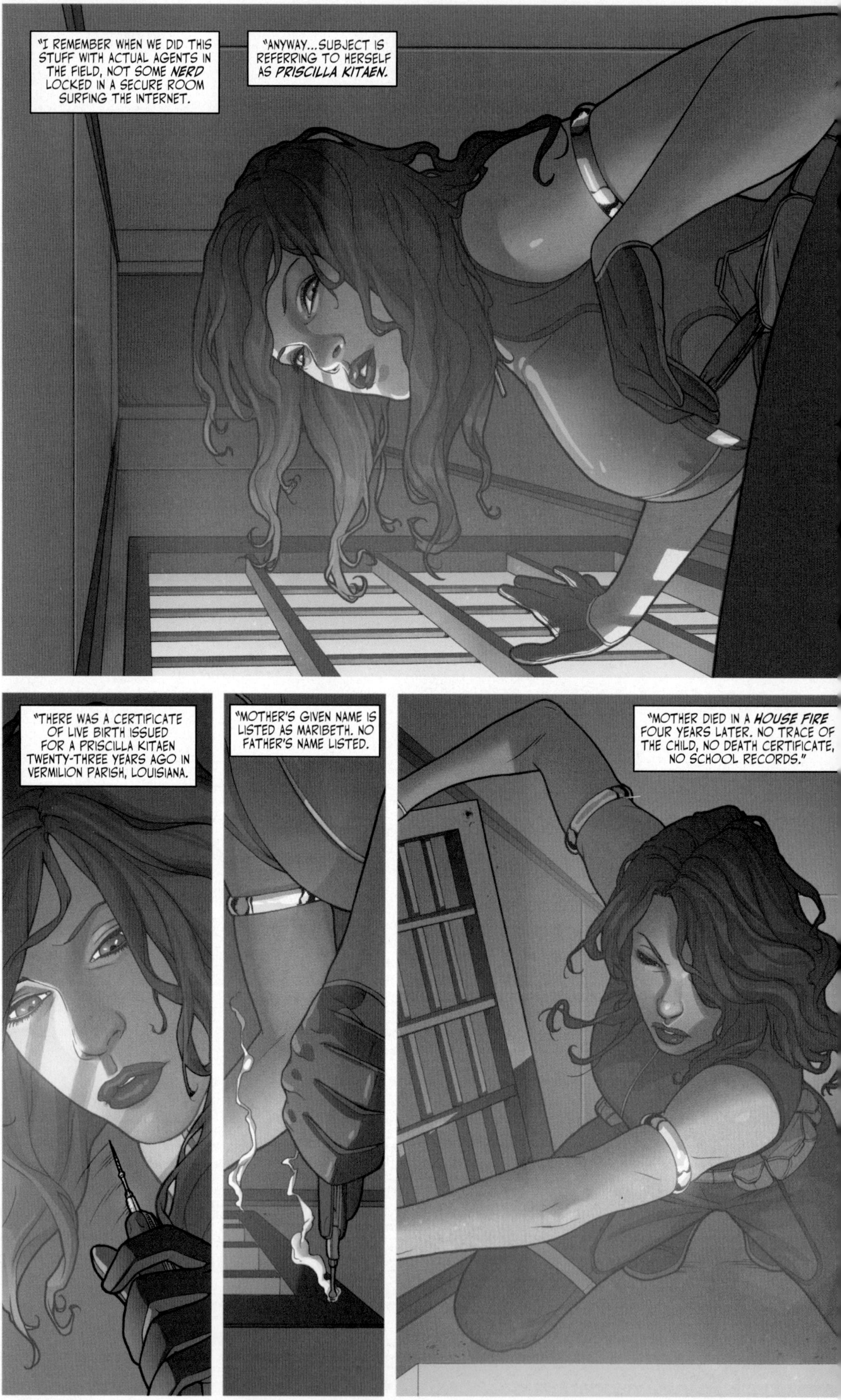
"I REMEMBER WHEN WE DID THIS STUFF WITH ACTUAL AGENTS IN THE FIELD, NOT SOME NERD LOCKED IN A SECURE ROOM SURFING THE INTERNET.
"ANYWAY...SUBJECT IS REFERRING TO HERSELF AS PRISCILLA KITAEN.
"THERE WAS A CERTIFICATE OF LIVE BIRTH ISSUED FOR A PRISCILLA KITAEN TWENTY-THREE YEARS AGO IN VERMILION PARISH, LOUISIANA.
"MOTHER'S GIVEN NAME IS LISTED AS MARIBETH. NO FATHER'S NAME LISTED.
"MOTHER DIED IN A HOUSE FIRE FOUR YEARS LATER. NO TRACE OF THE CHILD, NO DEATH CERTIFICATE, NO SCHOOL RECORDS."

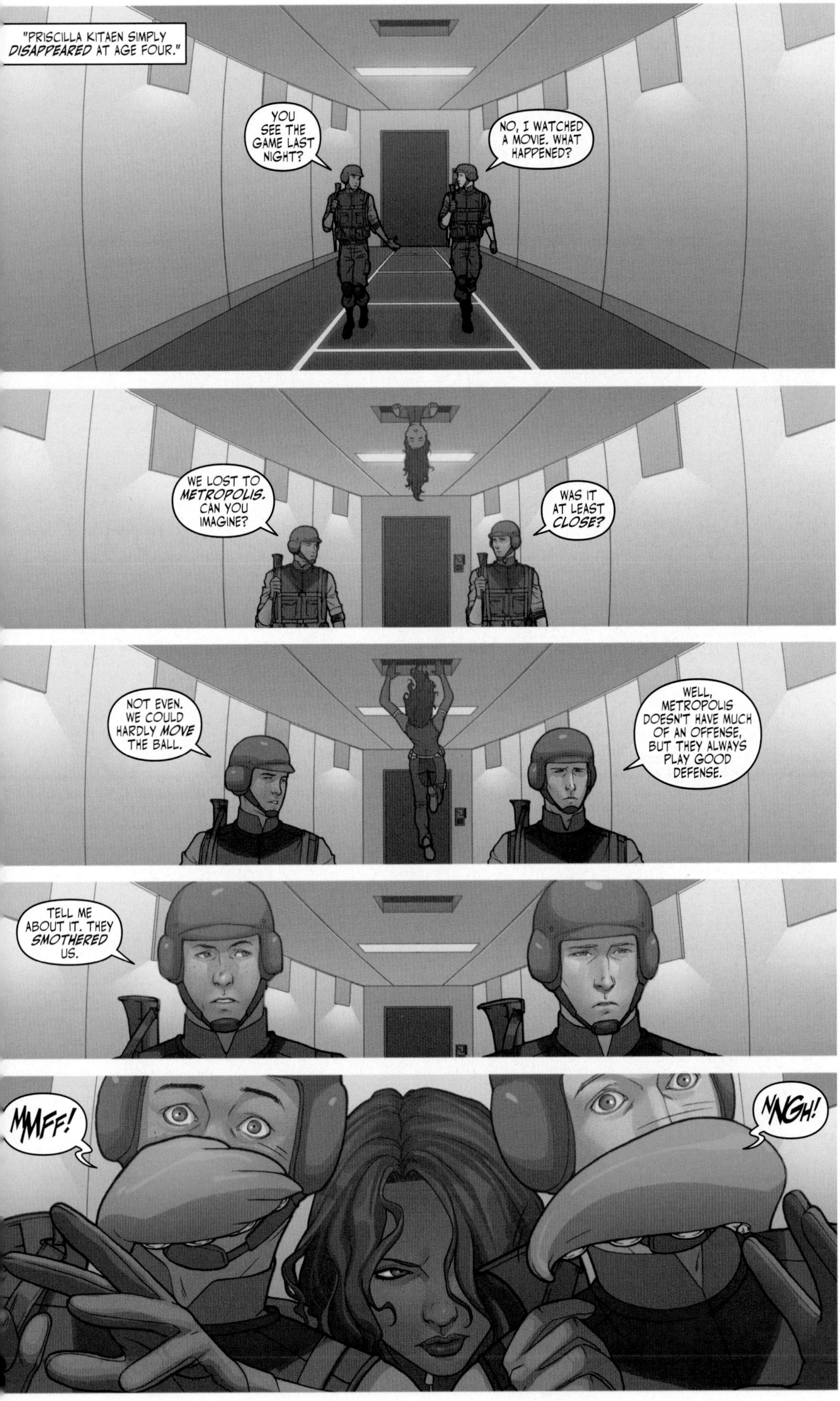
"PRISCILLA KITAEN SIMPLY *DISAPPEARED* AT AGE FOUR."
YOU SEE THE GAME LAST NIGHT?
NO, I WATCHED A MOVIE. WHAT HAPPENED?
WE LOST TO *METROPOLIS.* CAN YOU IMAGINE?
WAS IT AT LEAST *CLOSE?*
NOT EVEN. WE COULD HARDLY *MOVE* THE BALL.
WELL, METROPOLIS DOESN'T HAVE MUCH OF AN OFFENSE, BUT THEY ALWAYS PLAY GOOD DEFENSE.
TELL ME ABOUT IT. THEY *SMOTHERED* US.
MMFF!
NNGH!

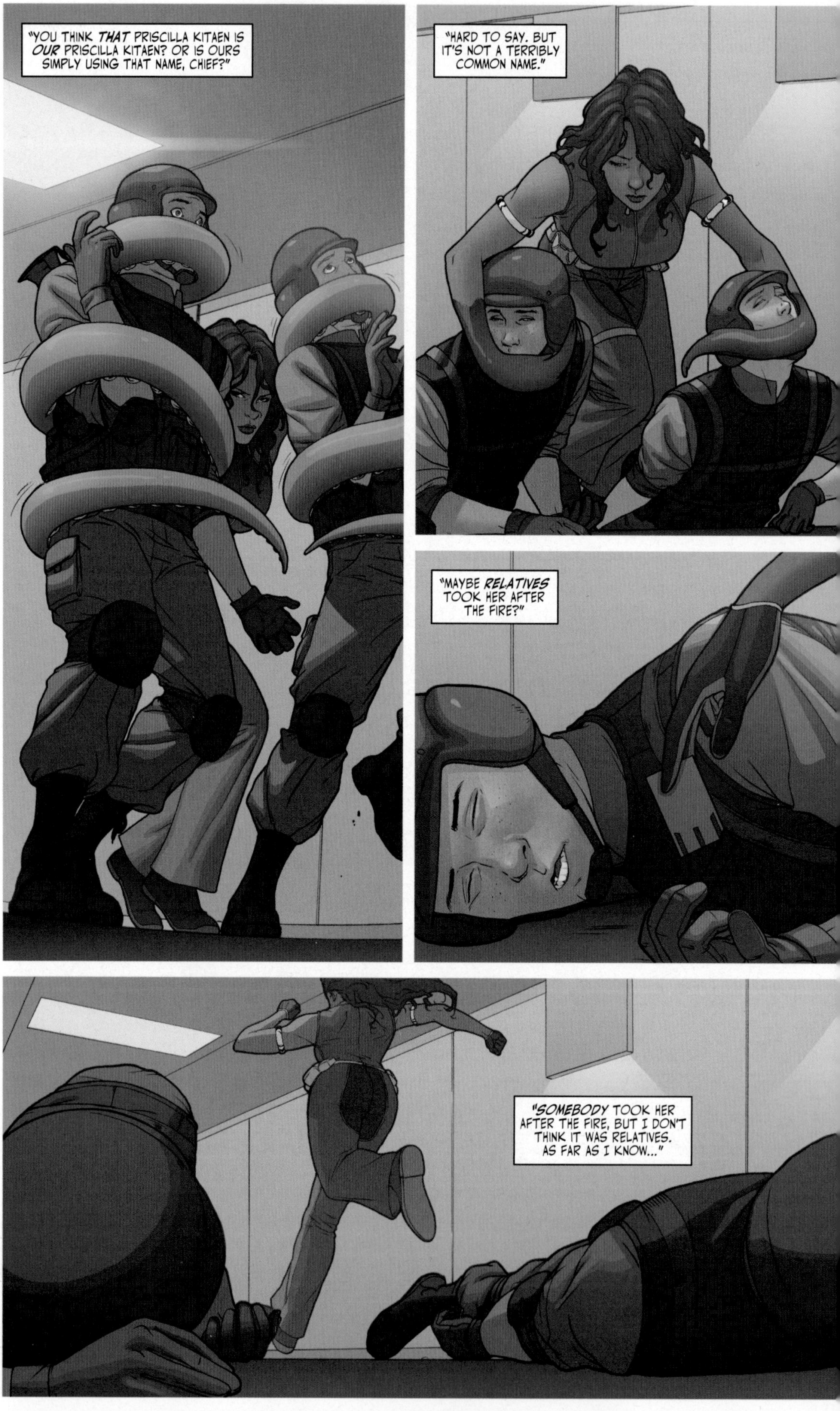
"YOU THINK THAT PRISCILLA KITAEN IS OUR PRISCILLA KITAEN? OR IS OURS SIMPLY USING THAT NAME, CHIEF?"
"HARD TO SAY. BUT IT'S NOT A TERRIBLY COMMON NAME."
"MAYBE RELATIVES TOOK HER AFTER THE FIRE?"
"SOMEBODY TOOK HER AFTER THE FIRE, BUT I DON'T THINK IT WAS RELATIVES. AS FAR AS I KNOW..."

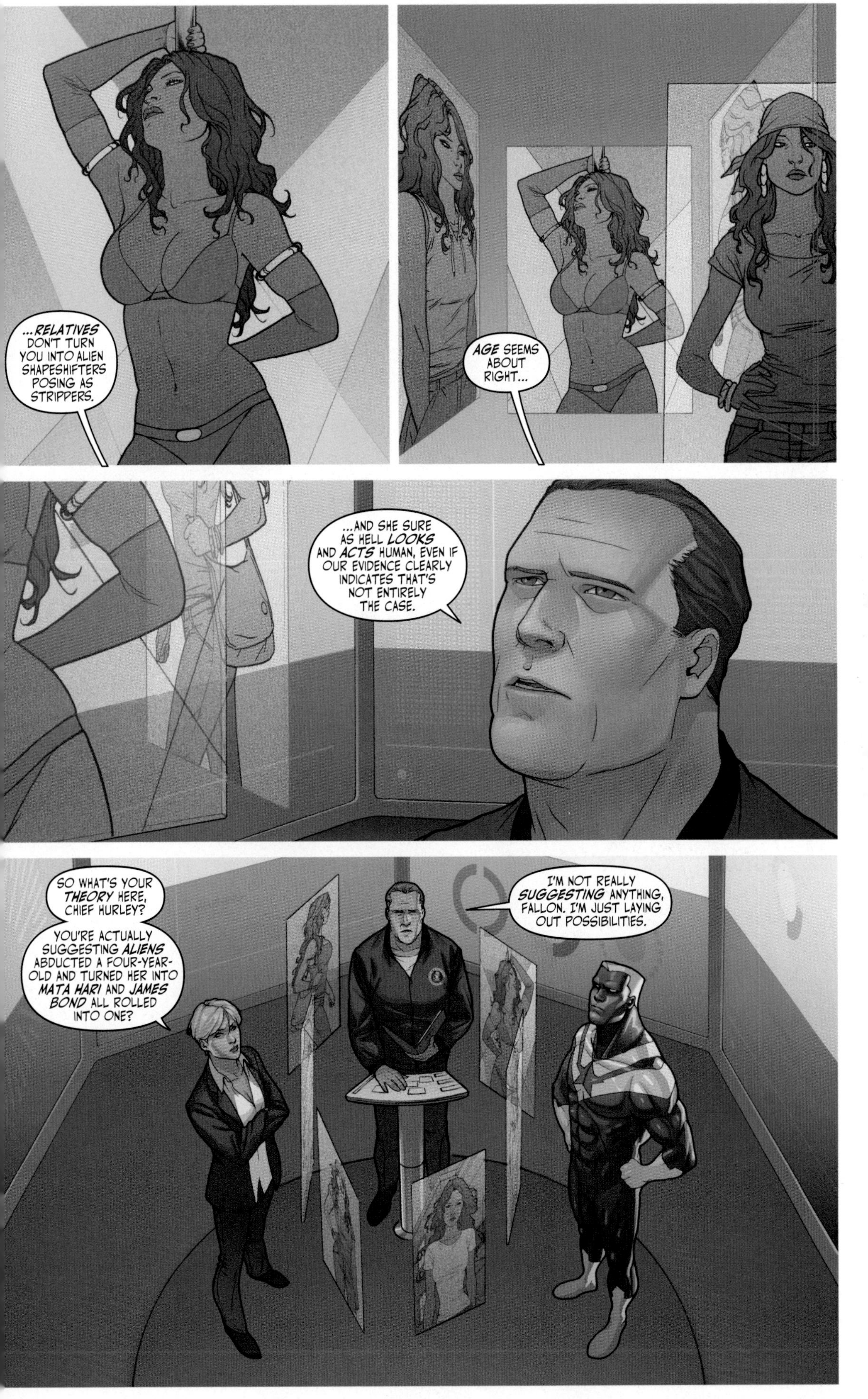
...RELATIVES DON'T TURN YOU INTO ALIEN SHAPESHIFTERS POSING AS STRIPPERS.
AGE SEEMS ABOUT RIGHT...
...AND SHE SURE AS HELL LOOKS AND ACTS HUMAN, EVEN IF OUR EVIDENCE CLEARLY INDICATES THAT'S NOT ENTIRELY THE CASE.
SO WHAT'S YOUR THEORY HERE, CHIEF HURLEY?
YOU'RE ACTUALLY SUGGESTING ALIENS ABDUCTED A FOUR-YEAR-OLD AND TURNED HER INTO MATA HARI AND JAMES BOND ALL ROLLED INTO ONE?
I'M NOT REALLY SUGGESTING ANYTHING, FALLON. I'M JUST LAYING OUT POSSIBILITIES.

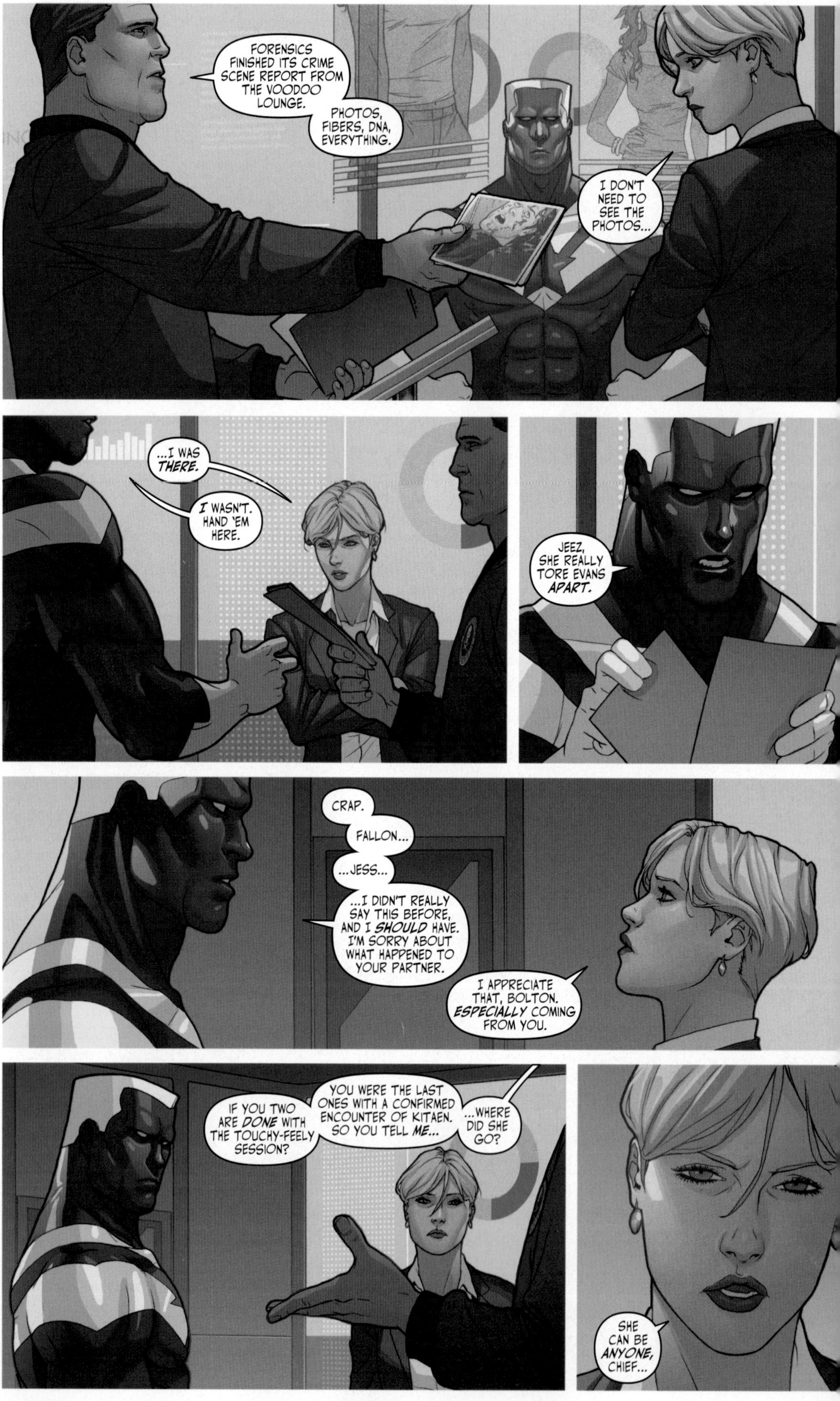
FORENSICS FINISHED ITS CRIME SCENE REPORT FROM THE VOODOO LOUNGE.
PHOTOS, FIBERS, DNA, EVERYTHING.
I DON'T NEED TO SEE THE PHOTOS...
...I WAS *THERE.*
I WASN'T. HAND 'EM HERE.
JEEZ, SHE REALLY TORE EVANS *APART.*
CRAP.
FALLON...
...JESS...
...I DIDN'T REALLY SAY THIS BEFORE, AND I *SHOULD* HAVE. I'M SORRY ABOUT WHAT HAPPENED TO YOUR PARTNER.
I APPRECIATE THAT, BOLTON. *ESPECIALLY* COMING FROM YOU.
IF YOU TWO ARE *DONE* WITH THE TOUCHY-FEELY SESSION?
YOU WERE THE LAST ONES WITH A CONFIRMED ENCOUNTER OF KITAEN. SO YOU TELL *ME*...
...WHERE DID SHE GO?
SHE CAN BE *ANYONE,* CHIEF...

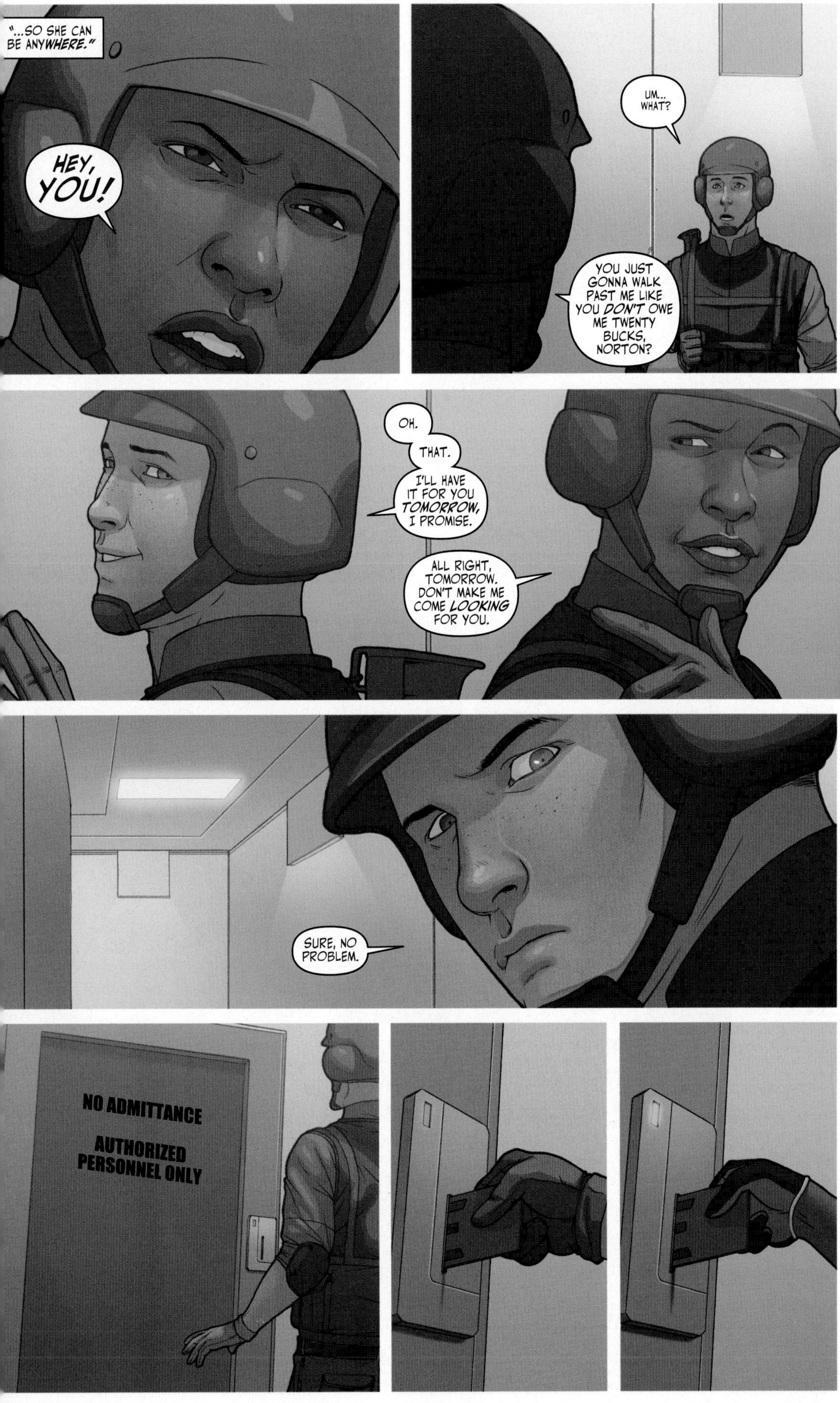

"...SO SHE CAN BE ANYWHERE."
HEY, YOU!
UM... WHAT?
YOU JUST GONNA WALK PAST ME LIKE YOU DON'T OWE ME TWENTY BUCKS, NORTON?
OH.
THAT.
I'LL HAVE IT FOR YOU TOMORROW, I PROMISE.
ALL RIGHT, TOMORROW. DON'T MAKE ME COME LOOKING FOR YOU.
SURE, NO PROBLEM.
NO ADMITTANCE
AUTHORIZED PERSONNEL ONLY

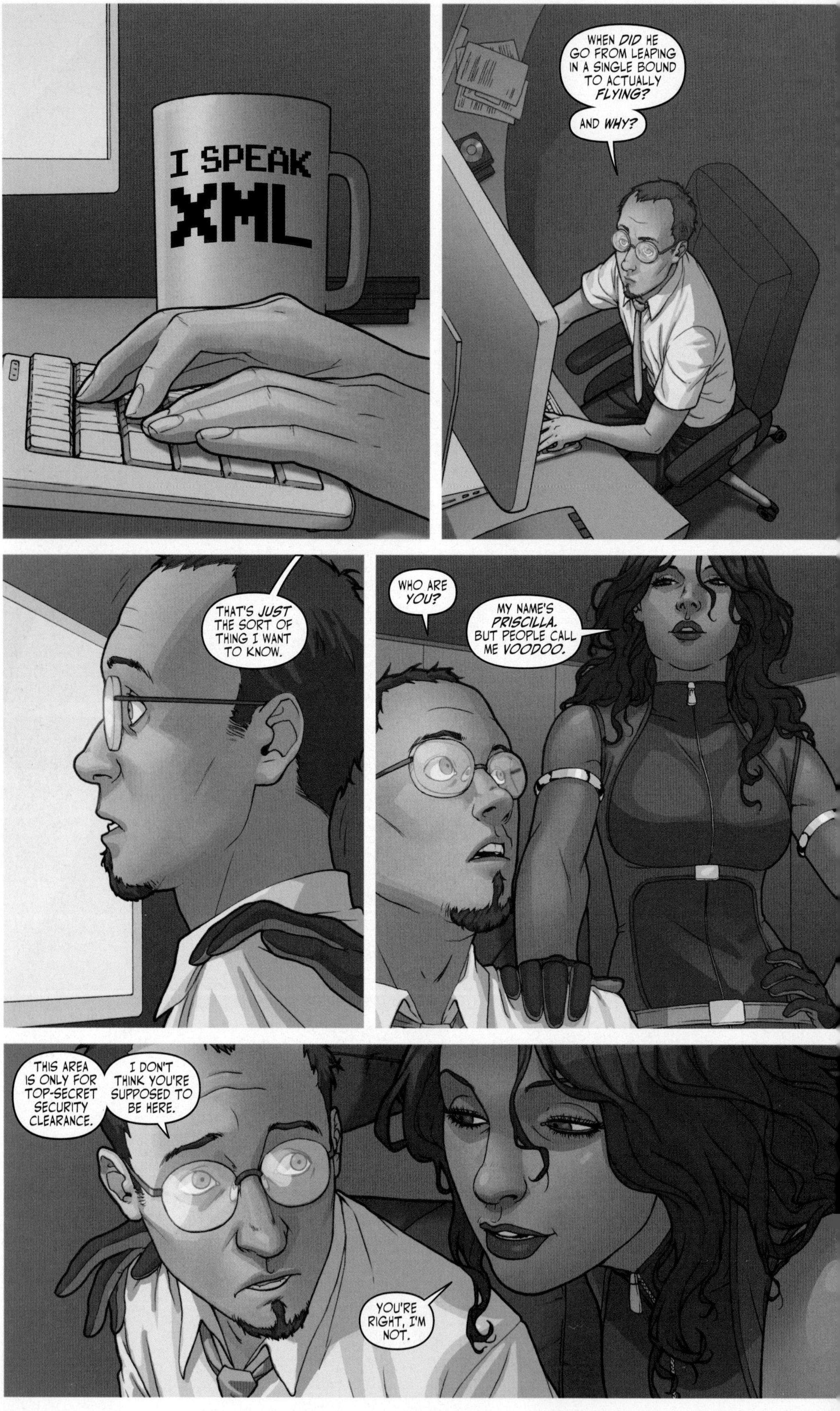
I SPEAK XML
WHEN DID HE GO FROM LEAPING IN A SINGLE BOUND TO ACTUALLY FLYING?
AND WHY?
THAT'S JUST THE SORT OF THING I WANT TO KNOW.
WHO ARE YOU?
MY NAME'S PRISCILLA. BUT PEOPLE CALL ME VOODOO.
THIS AREA IS ONLY FOR TOP-SECRET SECURITY CLEARANCE.
I DON'T THINK YOU'RE SUPPOSED TO BE HERE.
YOU'RE RIGHT, I'M NOT.

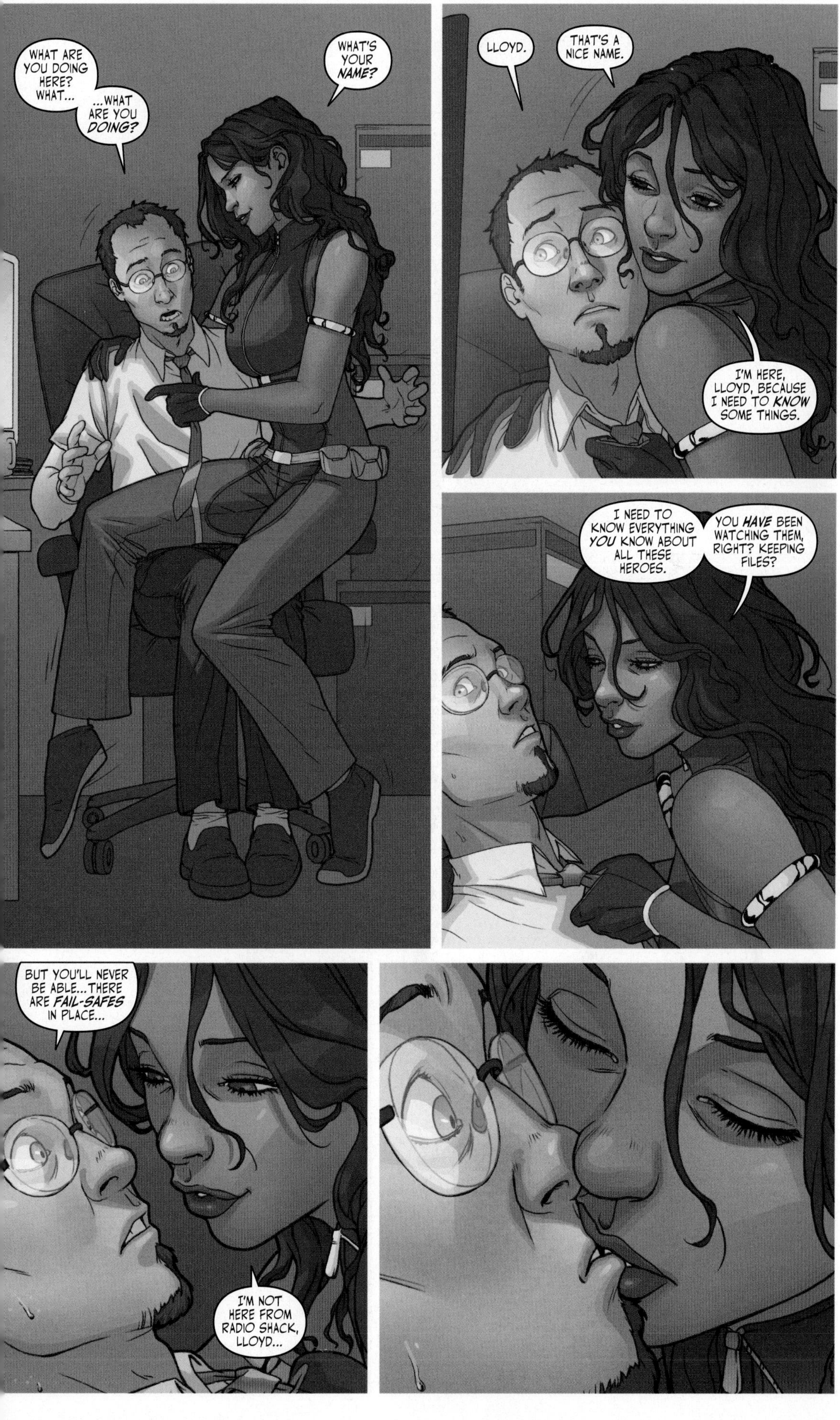
WHAT ARE YOU DOING HERE? WHAT...
...WHAT ARE YOU DOING?
WHAT'S YOUR NAME?
LLOYD.
THAT'S A NICE NAME.
I'M HERE, LLOYD, BECAUSE I NEED TO KNOW SOME THINGS.
I NEED TO KNOW EVERYTHING YOU KNOW ABOUT ALL THESE HEROES.
YOU HAVE BEEN WATCHING THEM, RIGHT? KEEPING FILES?
BUT YOU'LL NEVER BE ABLE...THERE ARE FAIL-SAFES IN PLACE...
I'M NOT HERE FROM RADIO SHACK, LLOYD...

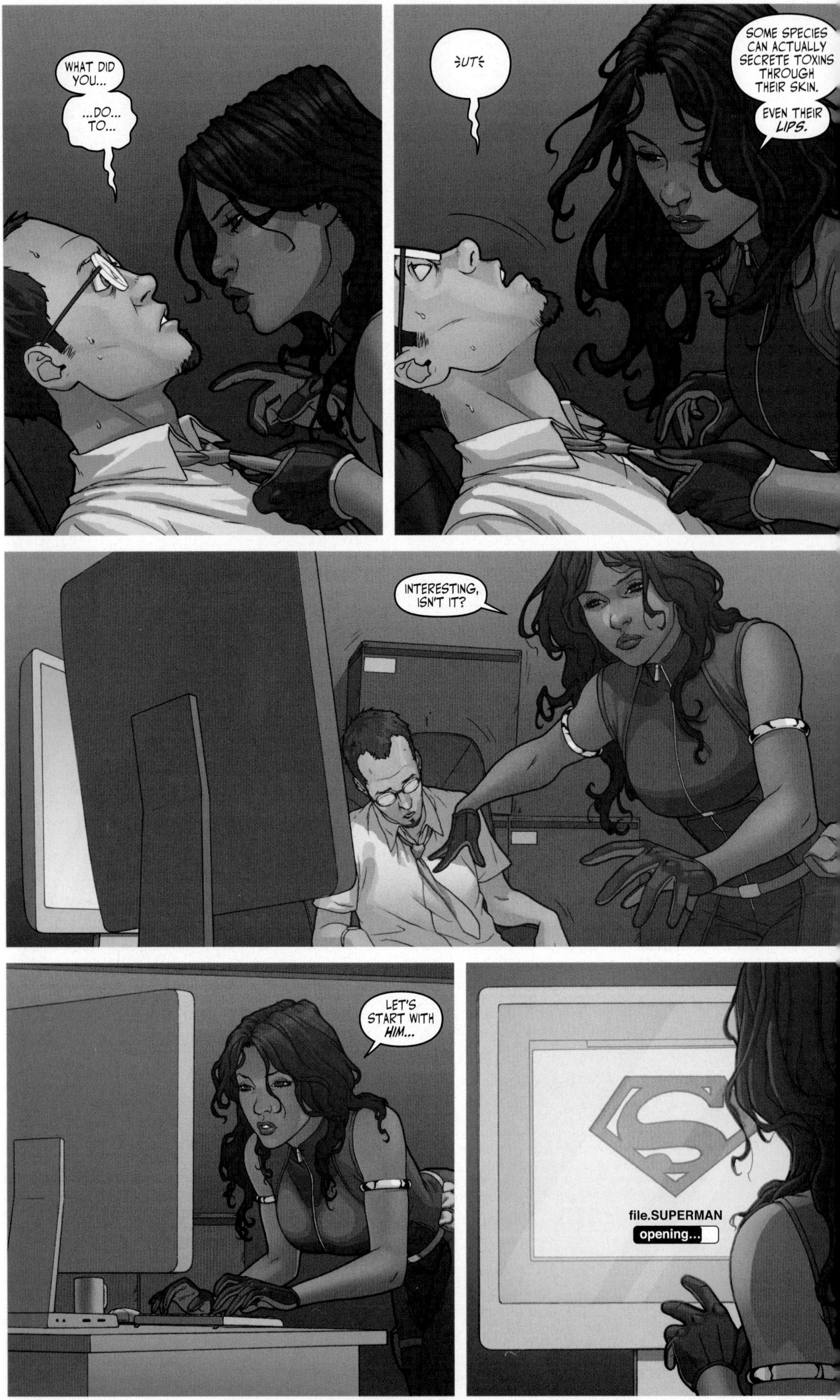
WHAT DID YOU...
...DO... TO...
UT
SOME SPECIES CAN ACTUALLY SECRETE TOXINS THROUGH THEIR SKIN.
EVEN THEIR *LIPS.*
INTERESTING, ISN'T IT?
LET'S START WITH *HIM*...
file.SUPERMAN
opening...

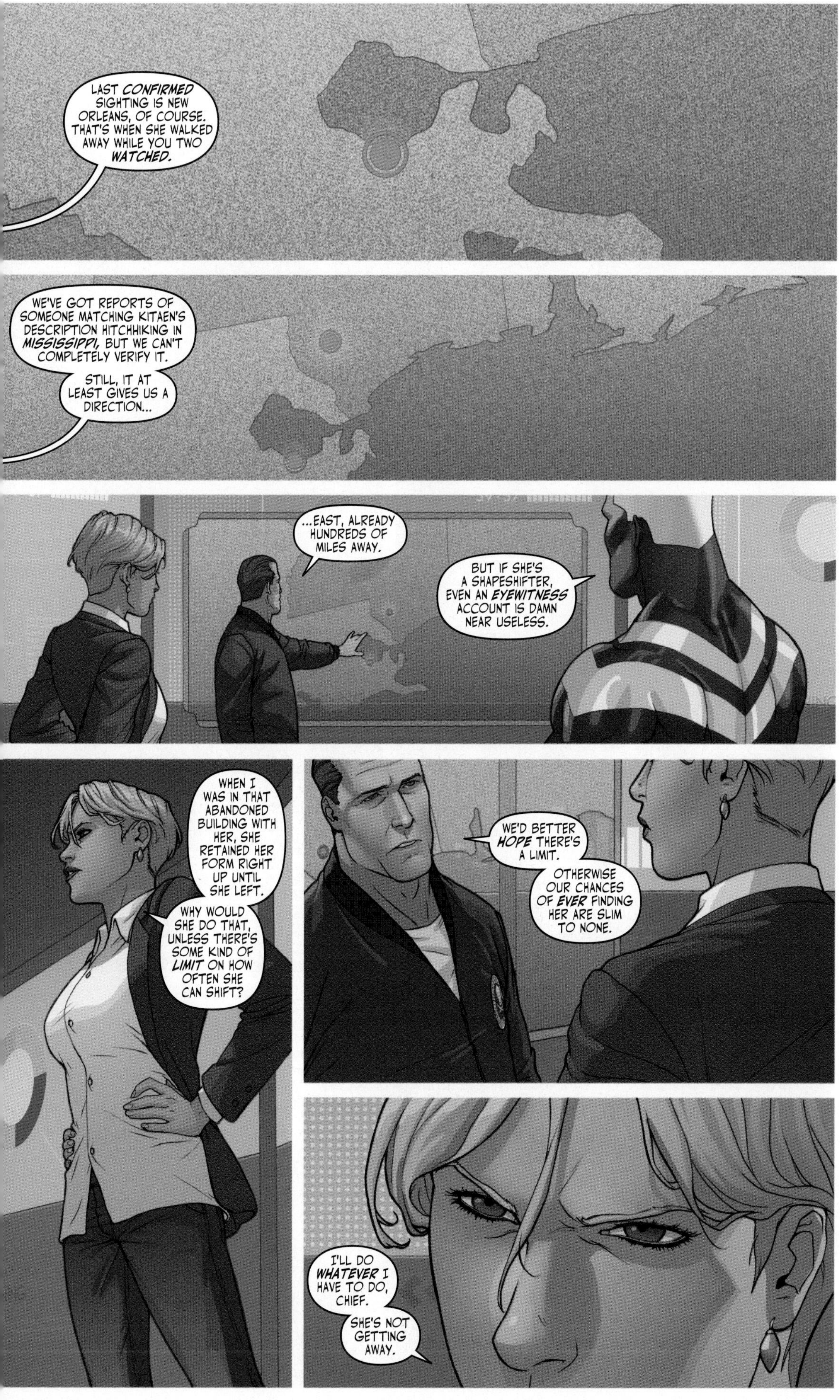
LAST CONFIRMED SIGHTING IS NEW ORLEANS, OF COURSE. THAT'S WHEN SHE WALKED AWAY WHILE YOU TWO WATCHED.
WE'VE GOT REPORTS OF SOMEONE MATCHING KITAEN'S DESCRIPTION HITCHHIKING IN MISSISSIPPI, BUT WE CAN'T COMPLETELY VERIFY IT.
STILL, IT AT LEAST GIVES US A DIRECTION...
...EAST, ALREADY HUNDREDS OF MILES AWAY.
BUT IF SHE'S A SHAPESHIFTER, EVEN AN EYEWITNESS ACCOUNT IS DAMN NEAR USELESS.
WHEN I WAS IN THAT ABANDONED BUILDING WITH HER, SHE RETAINED HER FORM RIGHT UP UNTIL SHE LEFT.
WHY WOULD SHE DO THAT, UNLESS THERE'S SOME KIND OF LIMIT ON HOW OFTEN SHE CAN SHIFT?
WE'D BETTER HOPE THERE'S A LIMIT.
OTHERWISE OUR CHANCES OF EVER FINDING HER ARE SLIM TO NONE.
I'LL DO WHATEVER I HAVE TO DO, CHIEF.
SHE'S NOT GETTING AWAY.

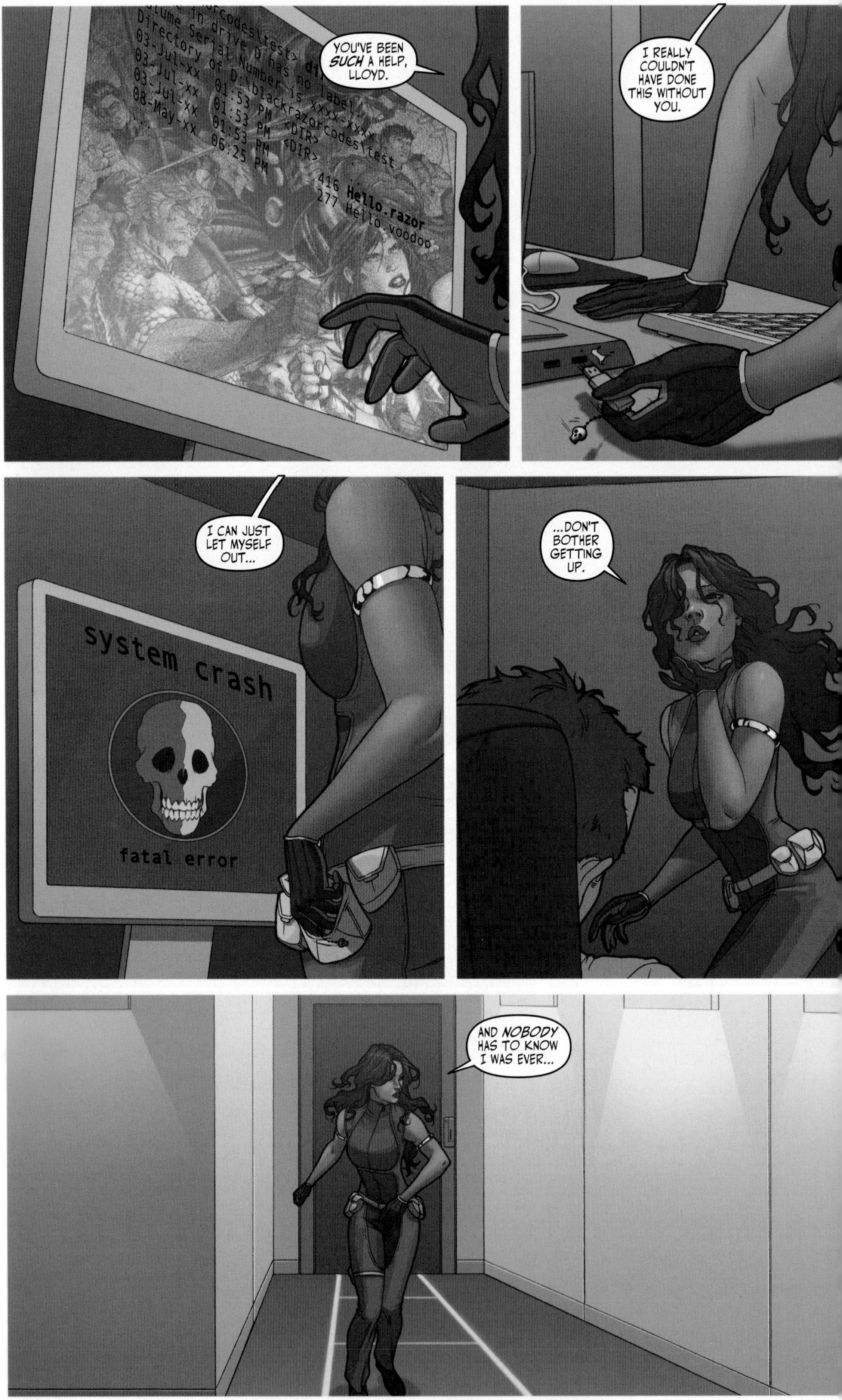
YOU'VE BEEN SUCH A HELP, LLOYD.
I REALLY COULDN'T HAVE DONE THIS WITHOUT YOU.
I CAN JUST LET MYSELF OUT...
system crash
fatal error
...DON'T BOTHER GETTING UP.
AND NOBODY HAS TO KNOW I WAS EVER...

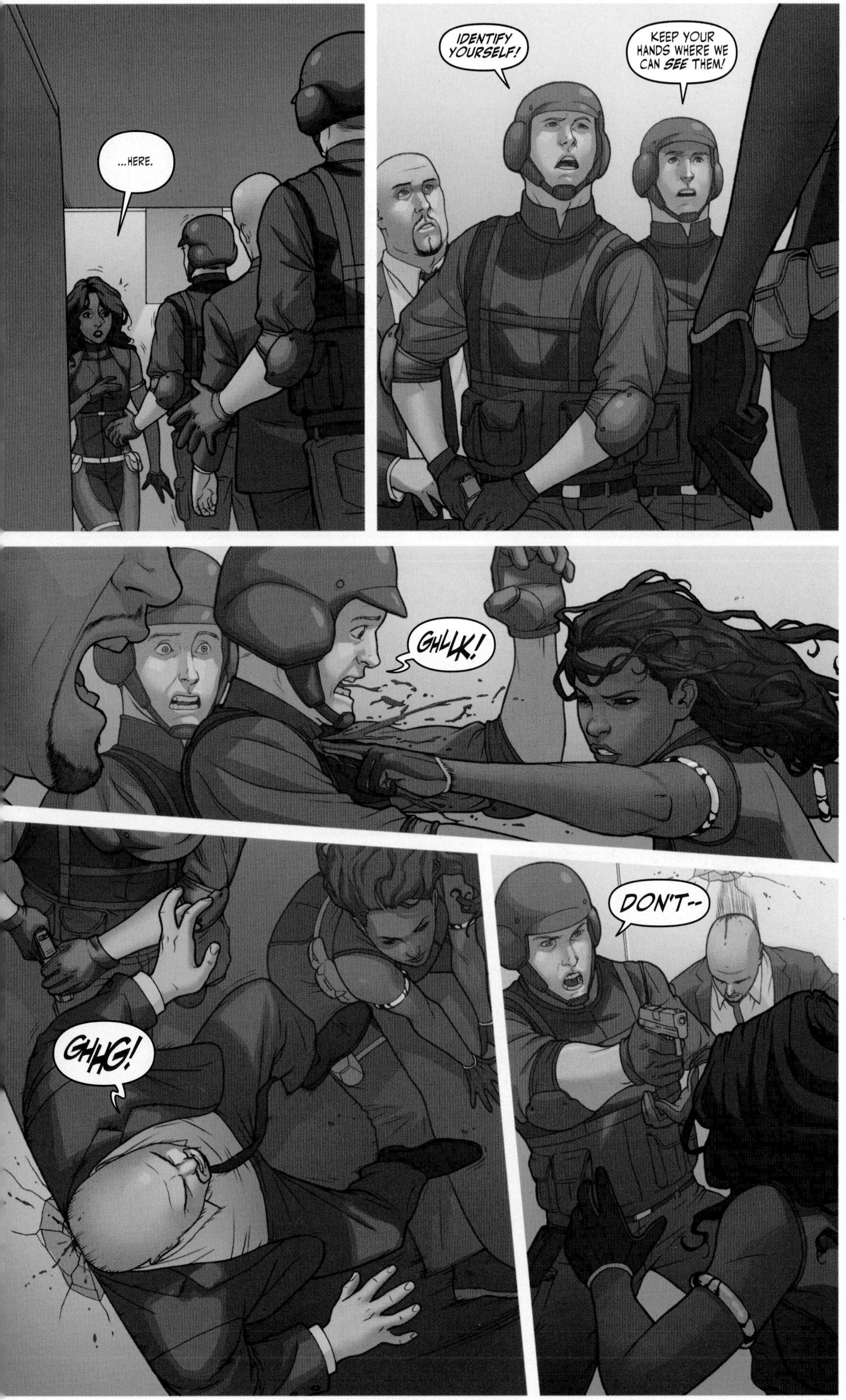
...HERE.
IDENTIFY YOURSELF!
KEEP YOUR HANDS WHERE WE CAN SEE THEM!
GHLLK!
GHHG!
DON'T--

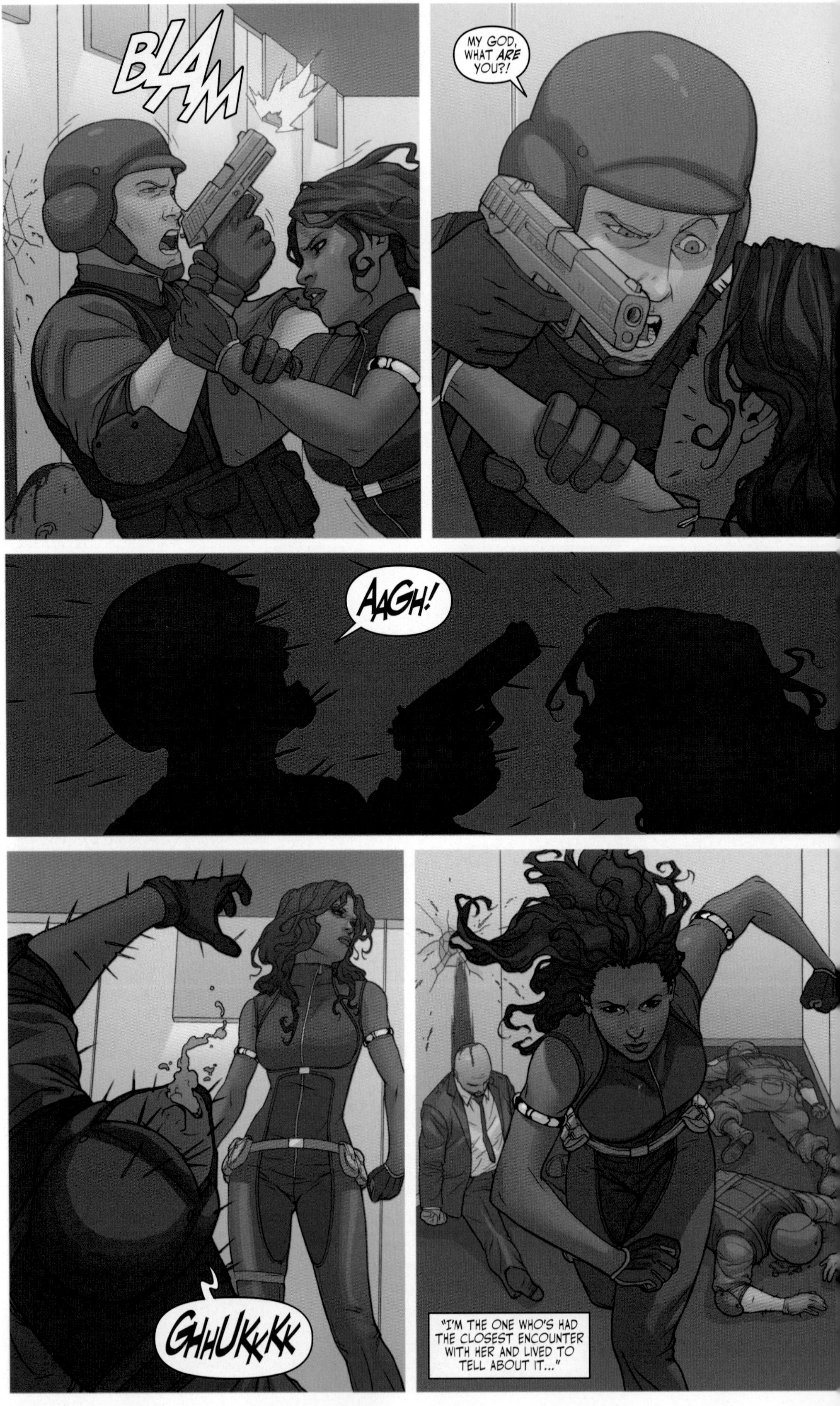
BLAM
MY GOD, WHAT ARE YOU?!
AAGH!
GHHUKKKK
"I'M THE ONE WHO'S HAD THE CLOSEST ENCOUNTER WITH HER AND LIVED TO TELL ABOUT IT..."

...SO HERE'S WHAT I'M THINKING-- LET *ME* GO AFTER HER. *ALONE.*

BRINGING IN THE RAZORS LAST TIME WAS A *MISTAKE.*

NO OFFENSE, BUT IT'LL MEAN TOO MANY BODIES, TOO MUCH CONFUSION. IT PLAYS TO WHAT SHE DOES *BEST.*

AGENT FALLON?

YOU WANT TO USE THEM AS BACKUP, *FINE.* BUT IF YOU LET ME TRACK HER *SOLO...*

AGENT FALLON...

...THIS IS A *GOVERNMENT* FACILITY. THERE'S NO SMOKING IN HERE.

WHAT'RE YOU *DOING,* JESS?

SORRY, SORRY, I'M JUST...

...GUESS I'M STILL PREOCCUPIED WITH EVERYTHING THAT'S HAPPENED.

WEEOOO WEEOOO WEEOOO WEEOOO

WEEOOO WEEOOO WEEOOO WEE

WHAT THE HELL'S *THIS* NOW?

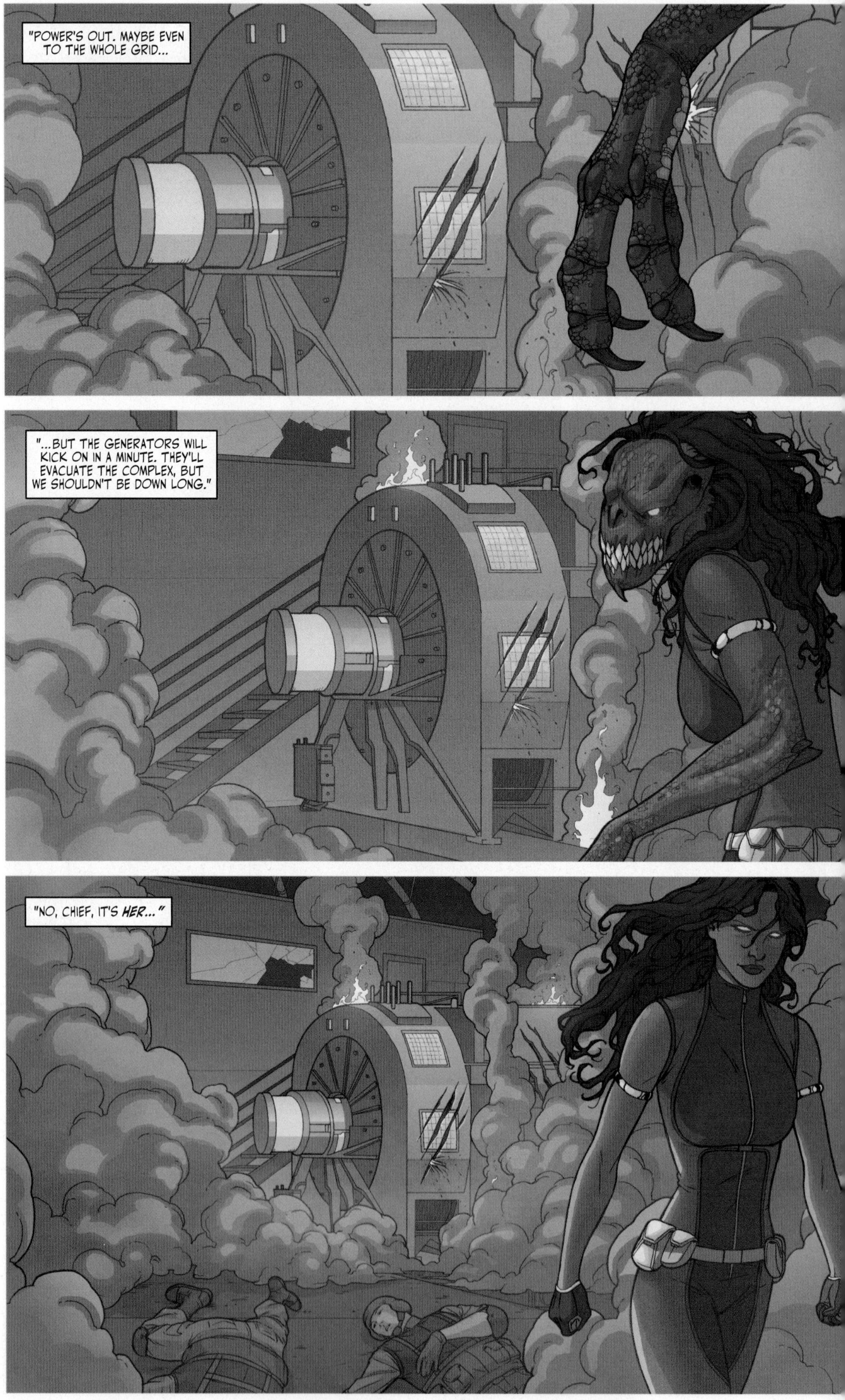
"POWER'S OUT. MAYBE EVEN TO THE WHOLE GRID...
"...BUT THE GENERATORS WILL KICK ON IN A MINUTE. THEY'LL EVACUATE THE COMPLEX, BUT WE SHOULDN'T BE DOWN LONG."
"NO, CHIEF, IT'S *HER*..."

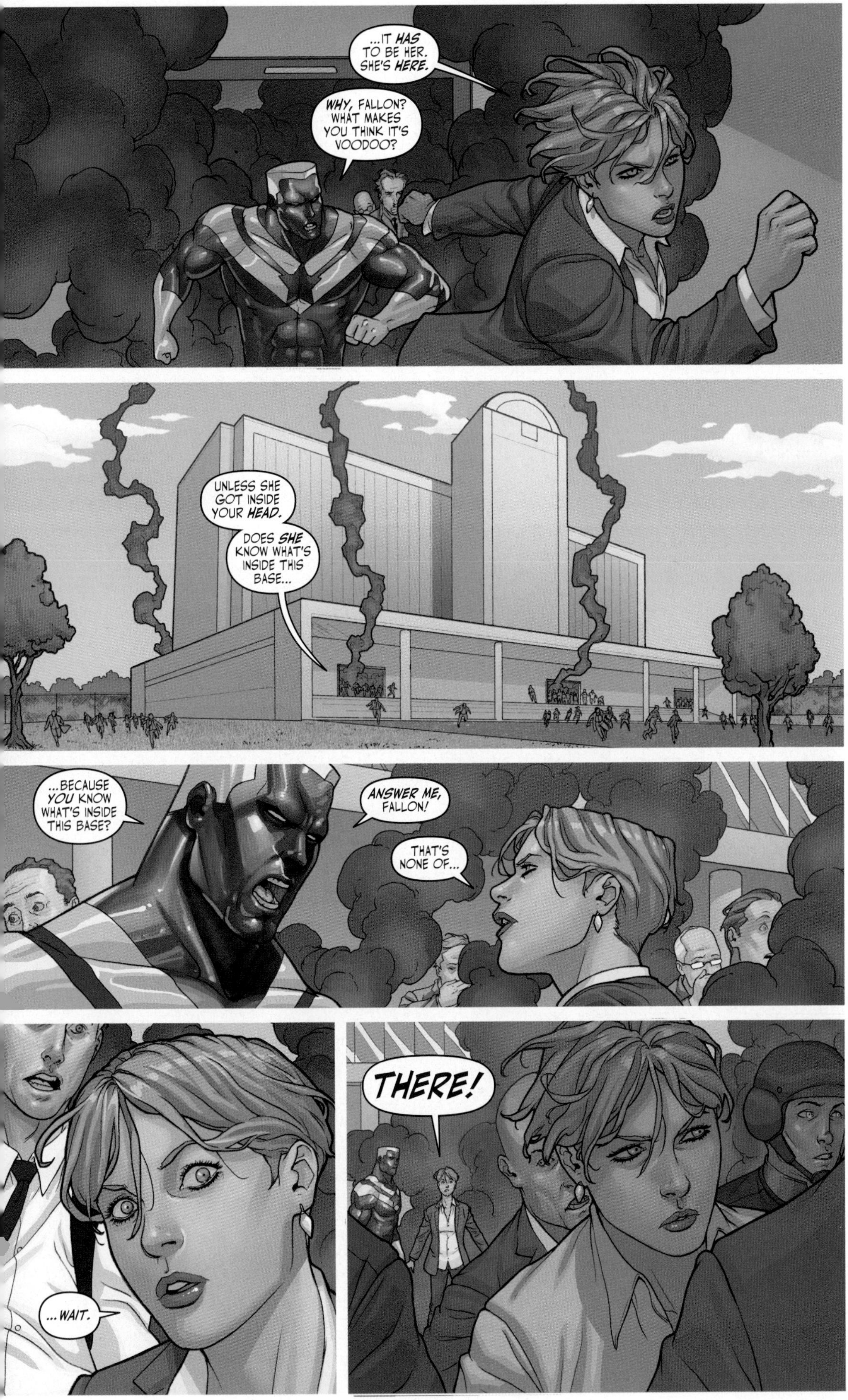
...IT HAS TO BE HER. SHE'S HERE.
WHY, FALLON? WHAT MAKES YOU THINK IT'S VOODOO?
UNLESS SHE GOT INSIDE YOUR HEAD.
DOES SHE KNOW WHAT'S INSIDE THIS BASE...
...BECAUSE YOU KNOW WHAT'S INSIDE THIS BASE?
ANSWER ME, FALLON!
THAT'S NONE OF...
...WAIT.
THERE!

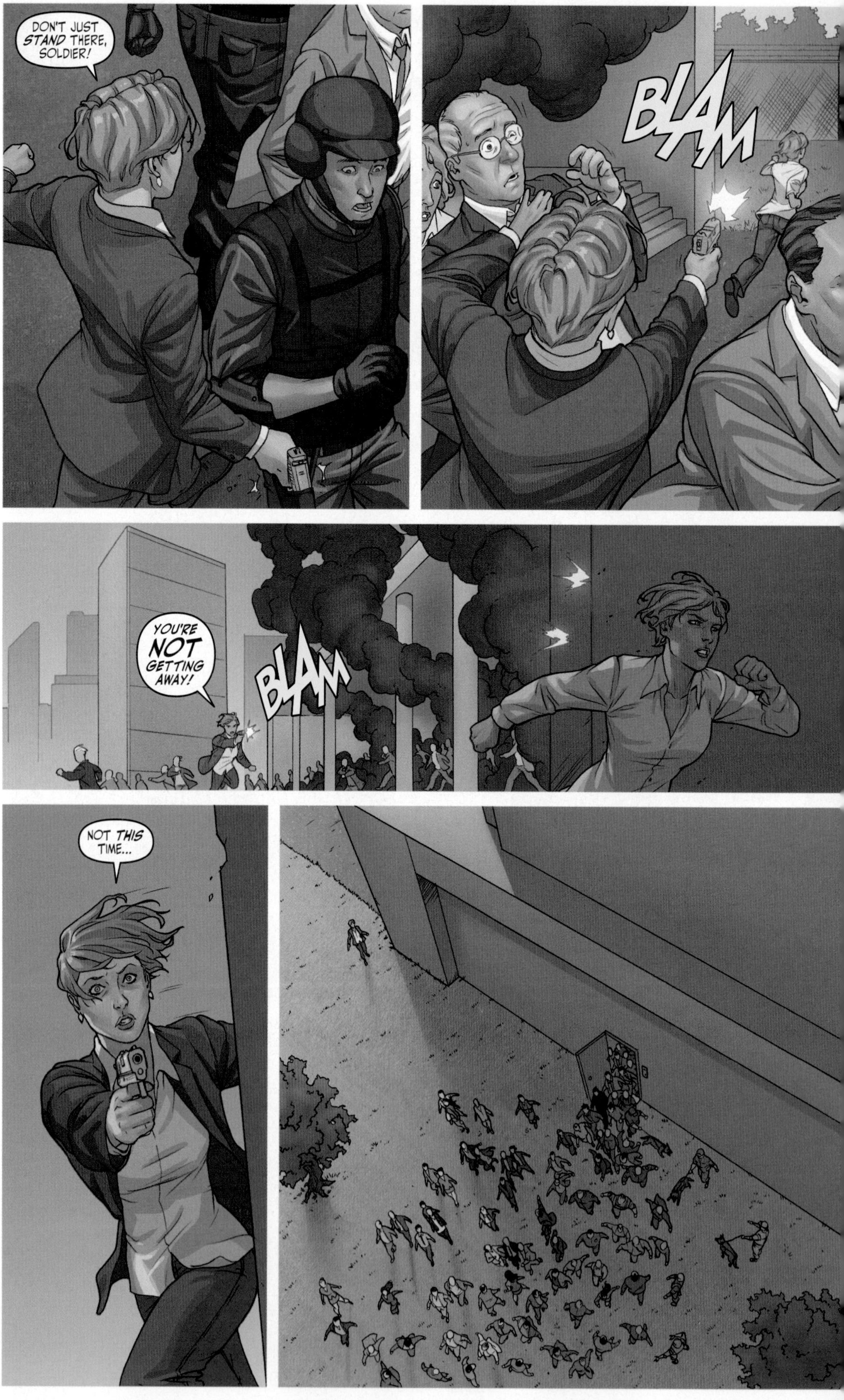
DON'T JUST STAND THERE, SOLDIER!
BLAM
YOU'RE NOT GETTING AWAY!
BLAM
NOT THIS TIME...

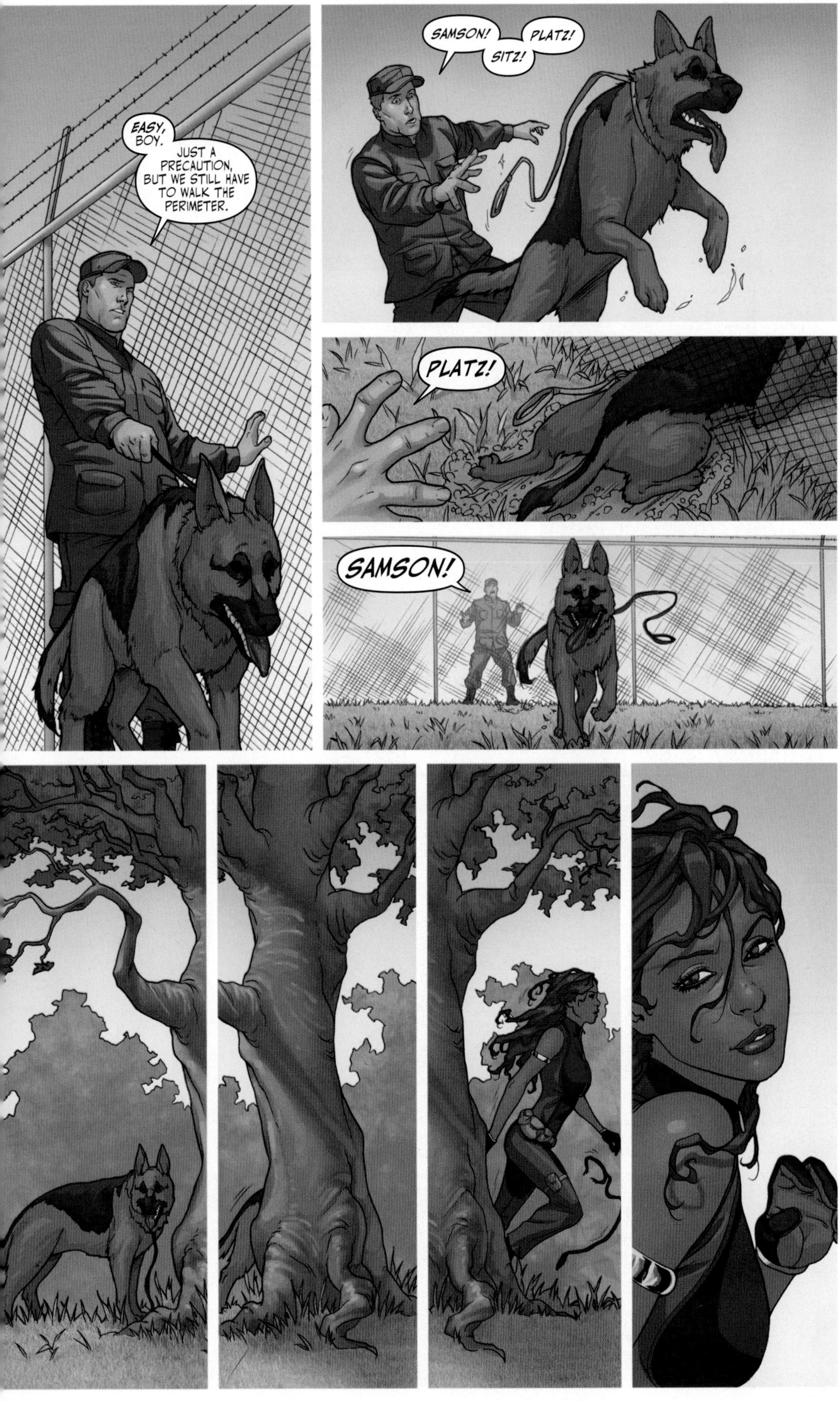
EASY, BOY.
JUST A PRECAUTION, BUT WE STILL HAVE TO WALK THE PERIMETER.
SAMSON!
SITZ!
PLATZ!
PLATZ!
SAMSON!

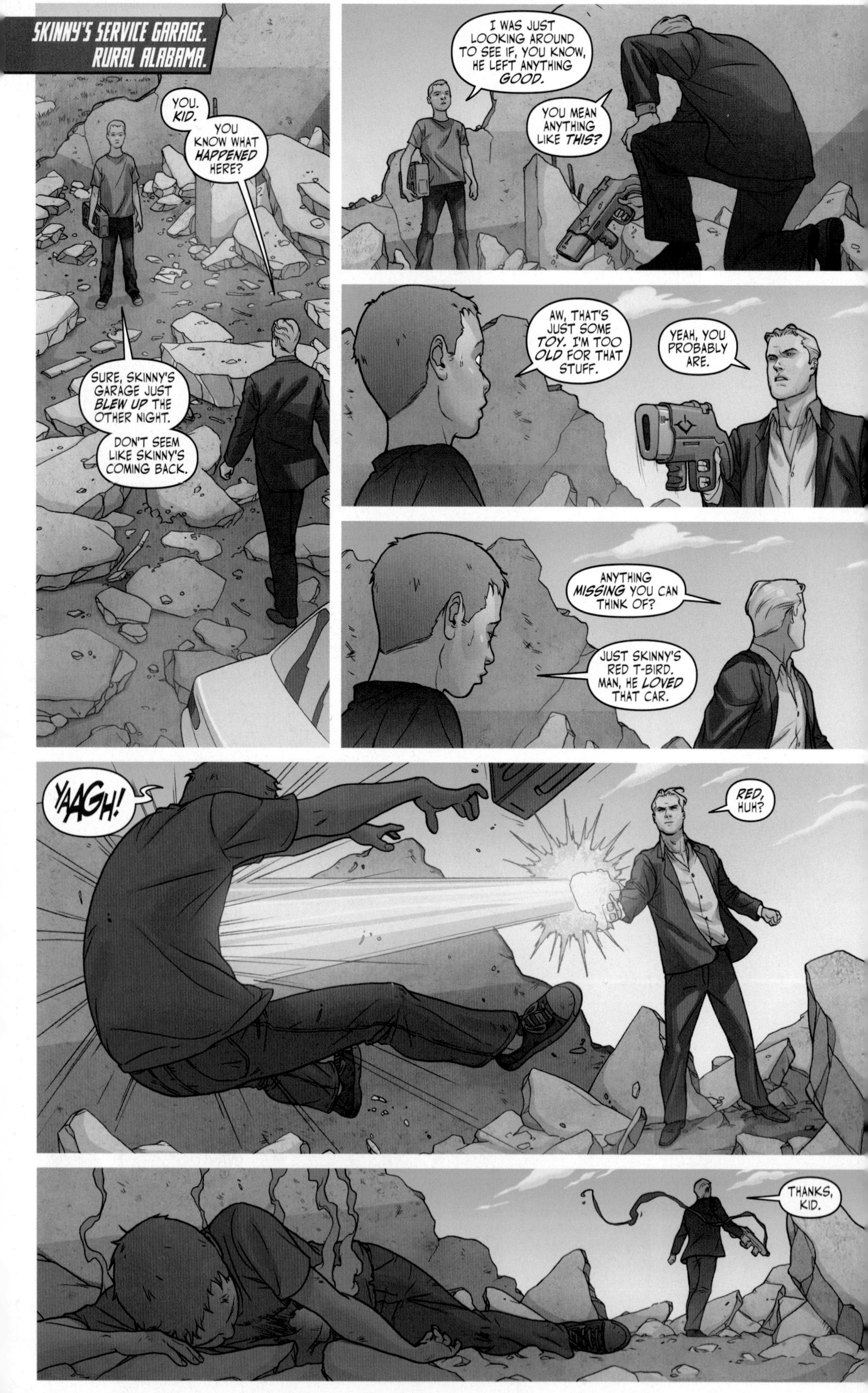
SKINNY'S SERVICE GARAGE. RURAL ALABAMA.
YOU. KID.
YOU KNOW WHAT HAPPENED HERE?
SURE, SKINNY'S GARAGE JUST BLEW UP THE OTHER NIGHT.
DON'T SEEM LIKE SKINNY'S COMING BACK.
I WAS JUST LOOKING AROUND TO SEE IF, YOU KNOW, HE LEFT ANYTHING GOOD.
YOU MEAN ANYTHING LIKE THIS?
AW, THAT'S JUST SOME TOY. I'M TOO OLD FOR THAT STUFF.
YEAH, YOU PROBABLY ARE.
ANYTHING MISSING YOU CAN THINK OF?
JUST SKINNY'S RED T-BIRD. MAN, HE LOVED THAT CAR.
YAAGH!
RED, HUH?
THANKS, KID.

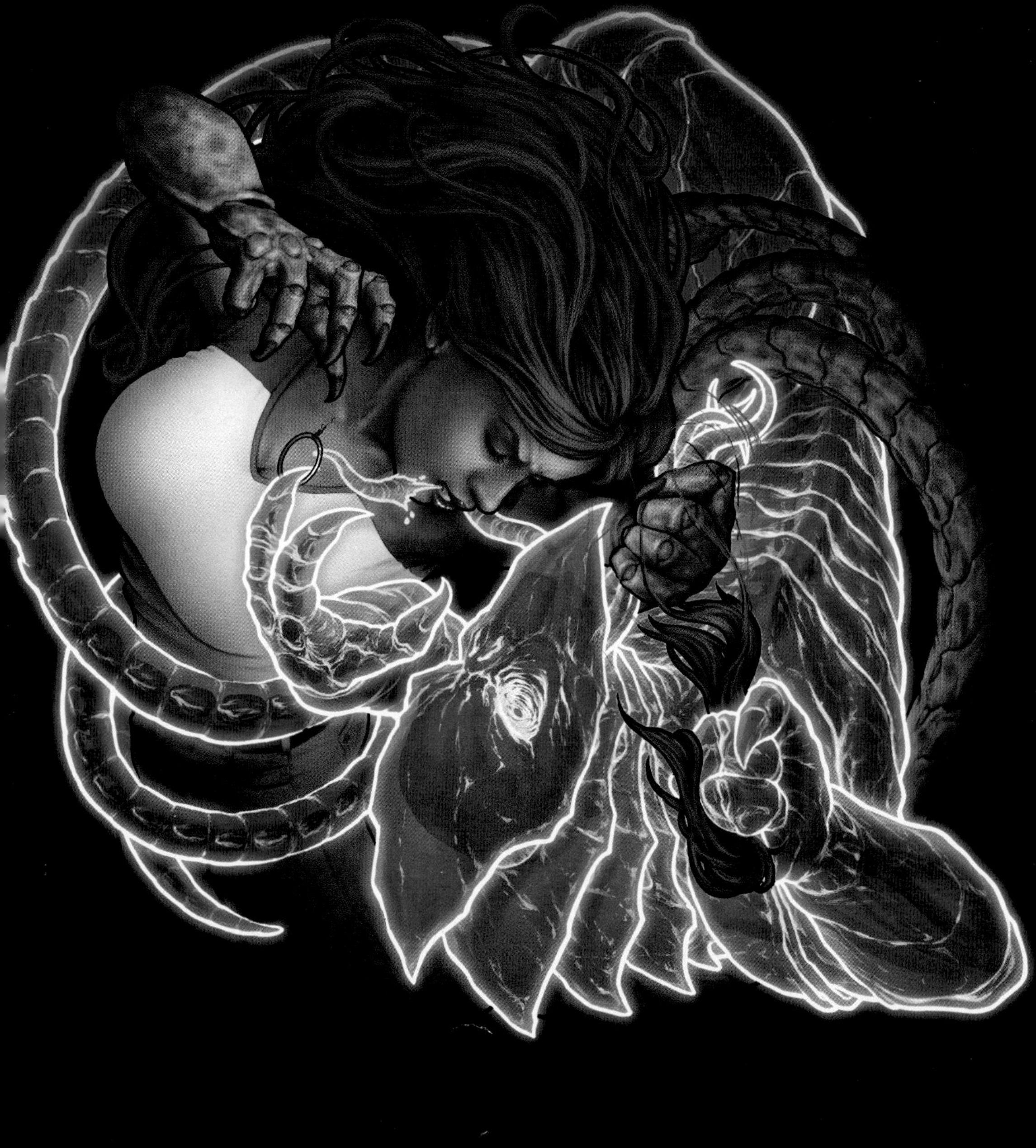

cover art by
JOHN TYLER CHRISTOPHER

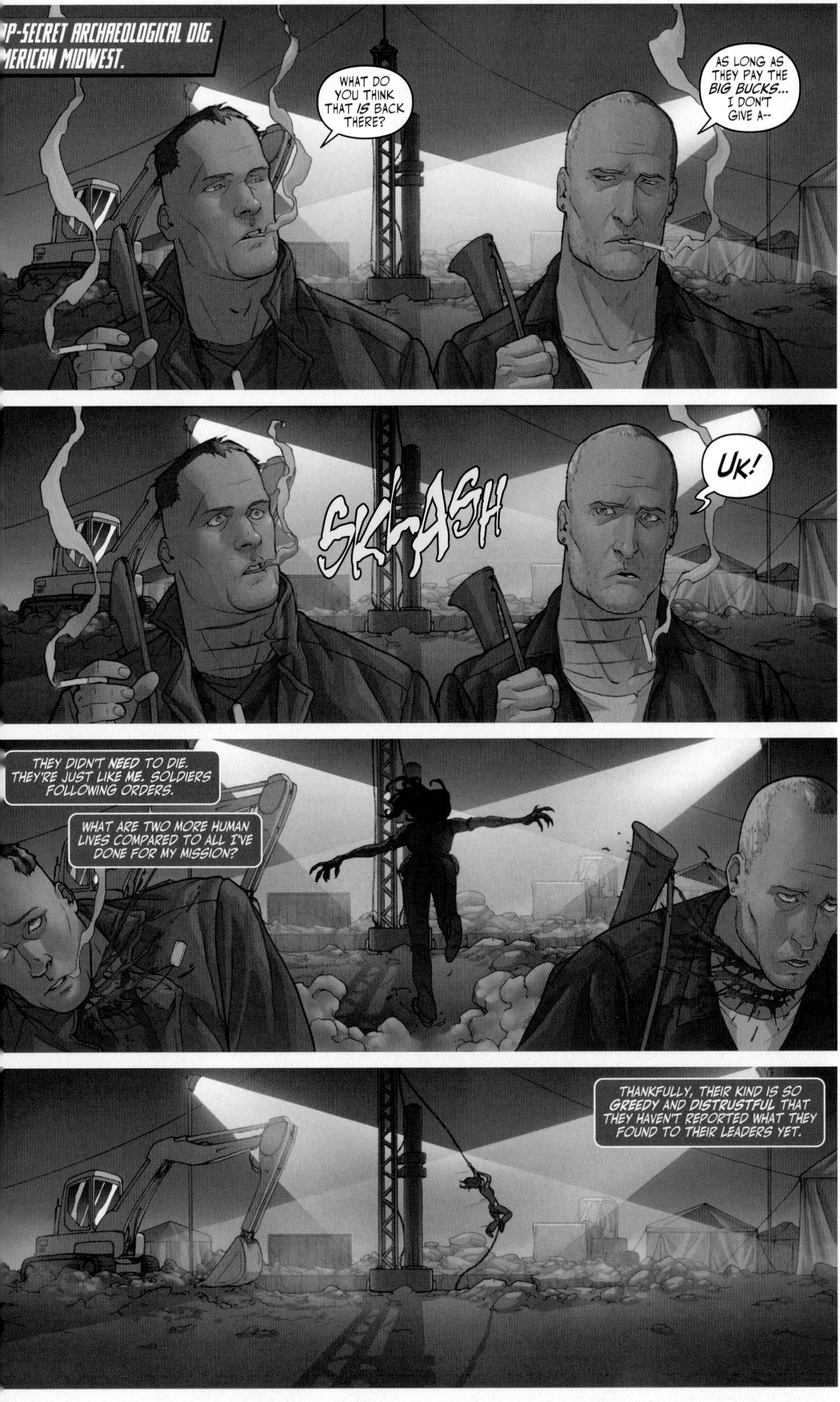
P-SECRET ARCHAEOLOGICAL DIG. MERICAN MIDWEST.
WHAT DO YOU THINK THAT IS BACK THERE?
AS LONG AS THEY PAY THE BIG BUCKS... I DON'T GIVE A--
SKLASH
UK!
THEY DIDN'T NEED TO DIE. THEY'RE JUST LIKE ME. SOLDIERS FOLLOWING ORDERS.
WHAT ARE TWO MORE HUMAN LIVES COMPARED TO ALL I'VE DONE FOR MY MISSION?
THANKFULLY, THEIR KIND IS SO GREEDY AND DISTRUSTFUL THAT THEY HAVEN'T REPORTED WHAT THEY FOUND TO THEIR LEADERS YET.

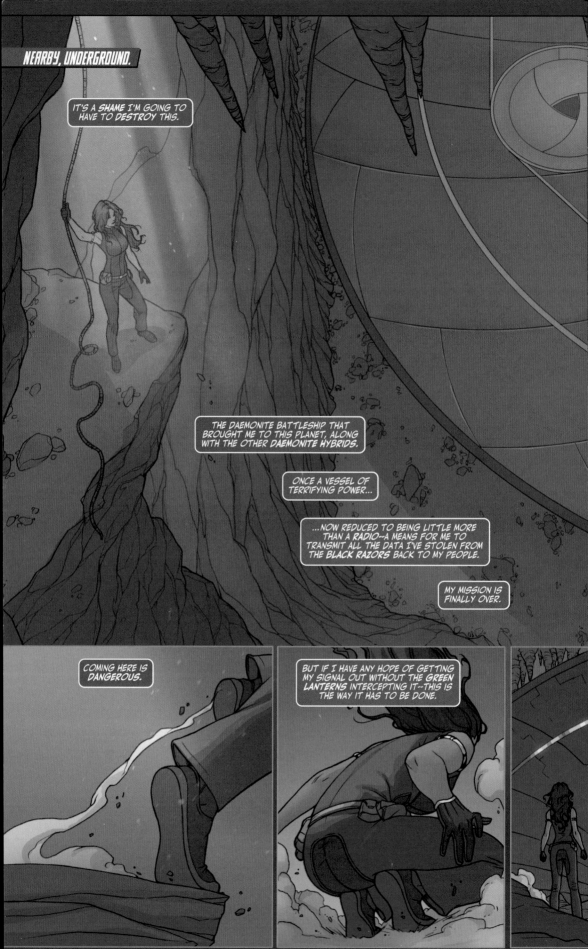

IT'S A **SHAME** I'M GOING TO HAVE TO **DESTROY** THIS.

THE DAEMONITE BATTLESHIP THAT BROUGHT ME TO THIS PLANET, ALONG WITH THE OTHER **DAEMONITE HYBRIDS.**

ONCE A VESSEL OF TERRIFYING POWER...

...NOW REDUCED TO BEING LITTLE MORE THAN A **RADIO**--A MEANS FOR ME TO TRANSMIT ALL THE DATA I'VE STOLEN FROM THE **BLACK RAZORS** BACK TO MY PEOPLE.

MY MISSION IS FINALLY OVER.

COMING HERE IS DANGEROUS.

BUT IF I HAVE ANY HOPE OF GETTING MY SIGNAL OUT WITHOUT THE **GREEN LANTERNS** INTERCEPTING IT--THIS IS THE WAY IT HAS TO BE DONE.

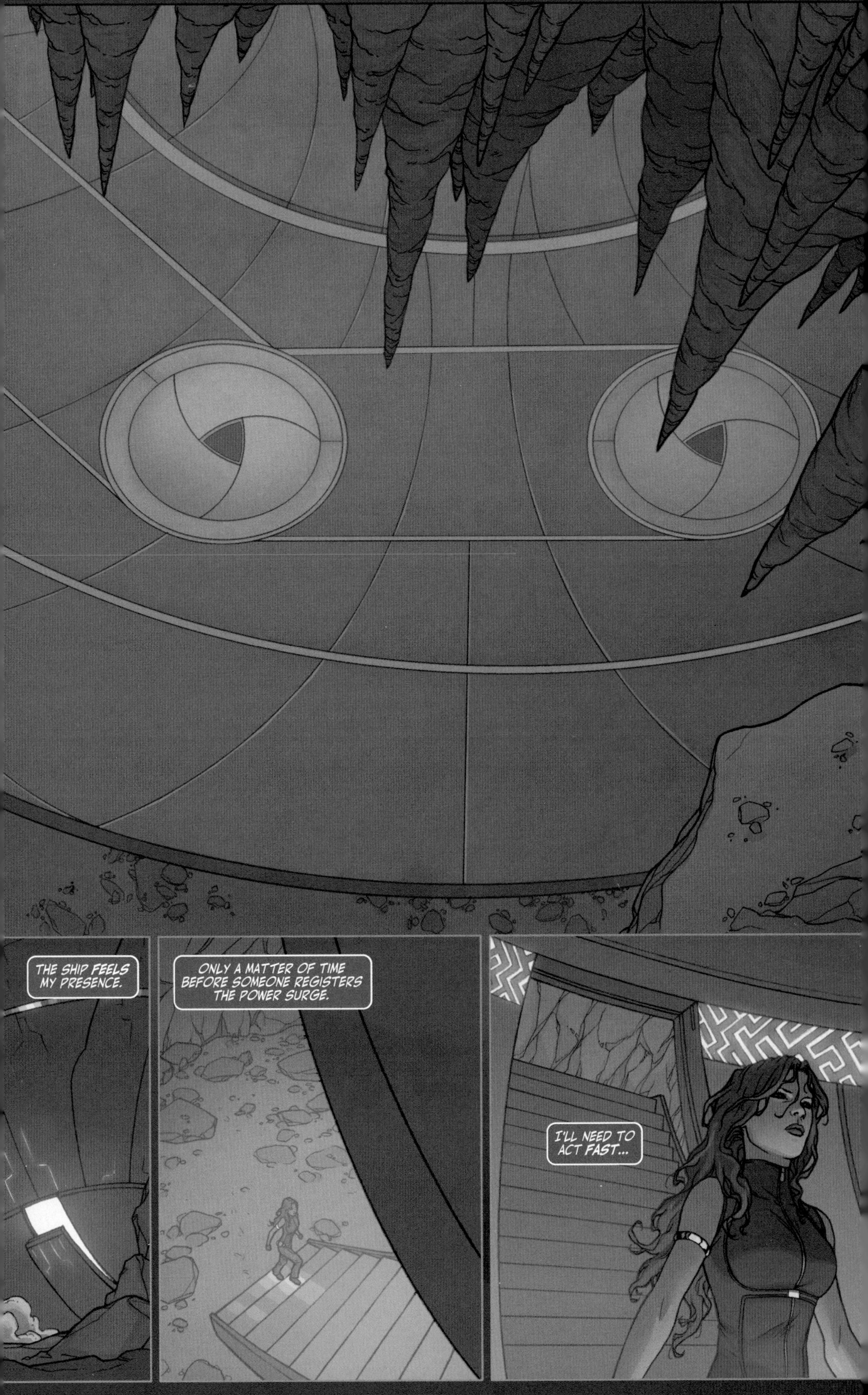
THE SHIP FEELS MY PRESENCE.
ONLY A MATTER OF TIME BEFORE SOMEONE REGISTERS THE POWER SURGE.
I'LL NEED TO ACT FAST...

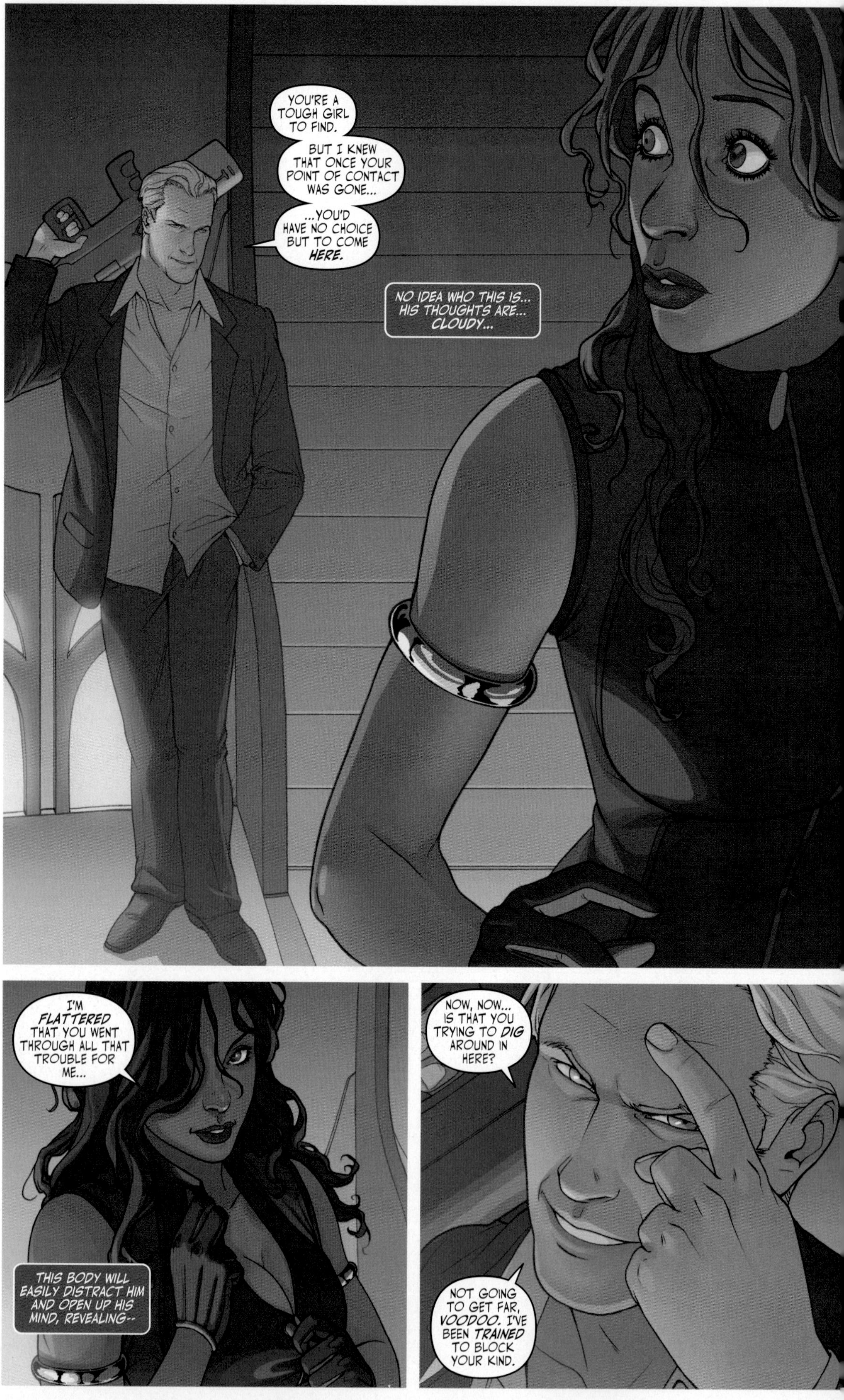
YOU'RE A TOUGH GIRL TO FIND.
BUT I KNEW THAT ONCE YOUR POINT OF CONTACT WAS GONE...
...YOU'D HAVE NO CHOICE BUT TO COME *HERE.*
NO IDEA WHO THIS IS... HIS THOUGHTS ARE... *CLOUDY...*
I'M *FLATTERED* THAT YOU WENT THROUGH ALL THAT TROUBLE FOR ME...
THIS BODY WILL EASILY DISTRACT HIM AND OPEN UP HIS MIND, REVEALING--
NOW, NOW... IS THAT YOU TRYING TO *DIG* AROUND IN HERE?
NOT GOING TO GET FAR, *VOODOO.* I'VE BEEN *TRAINED* TO BLOCK YOUR KIND.

YOU'RE A DAEMONITE?!

THAT'S AFFIRMATIVE, HYBRID.

MY IDENTITY WAS COMPROMISED, BUT I STILL COMPLETED THE MISSION. THERE WAS NO NEED TO SEND SOMEONE TO GET--

DON'T WORRY, VOODOO, I'M NOT HERE TO BRING YOU IN...

...I'M HERE TO KILL YOU.

YOU'RE A TRAITOR TO OUR CAUSE!

I'M A TRUE BELIEVER!

ONLY PURE-BLOOD DAEMONITES SHOULD BE REPRESENTING THE CAUSE. YOU HYBRIDS WERE A MISTAKE MADE BY THE COUNCIL...

THE HYBRIDS ARE AS MUCH A PART OF THE PROPHESY AS--

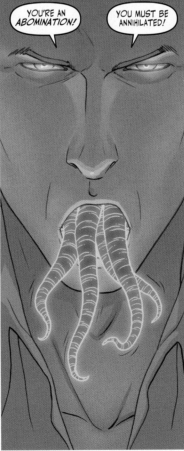

YOU'RE AN ABOMINATION!

YOU MUST BE ANNIHILATED!

YOU WILL NOT RUIN...

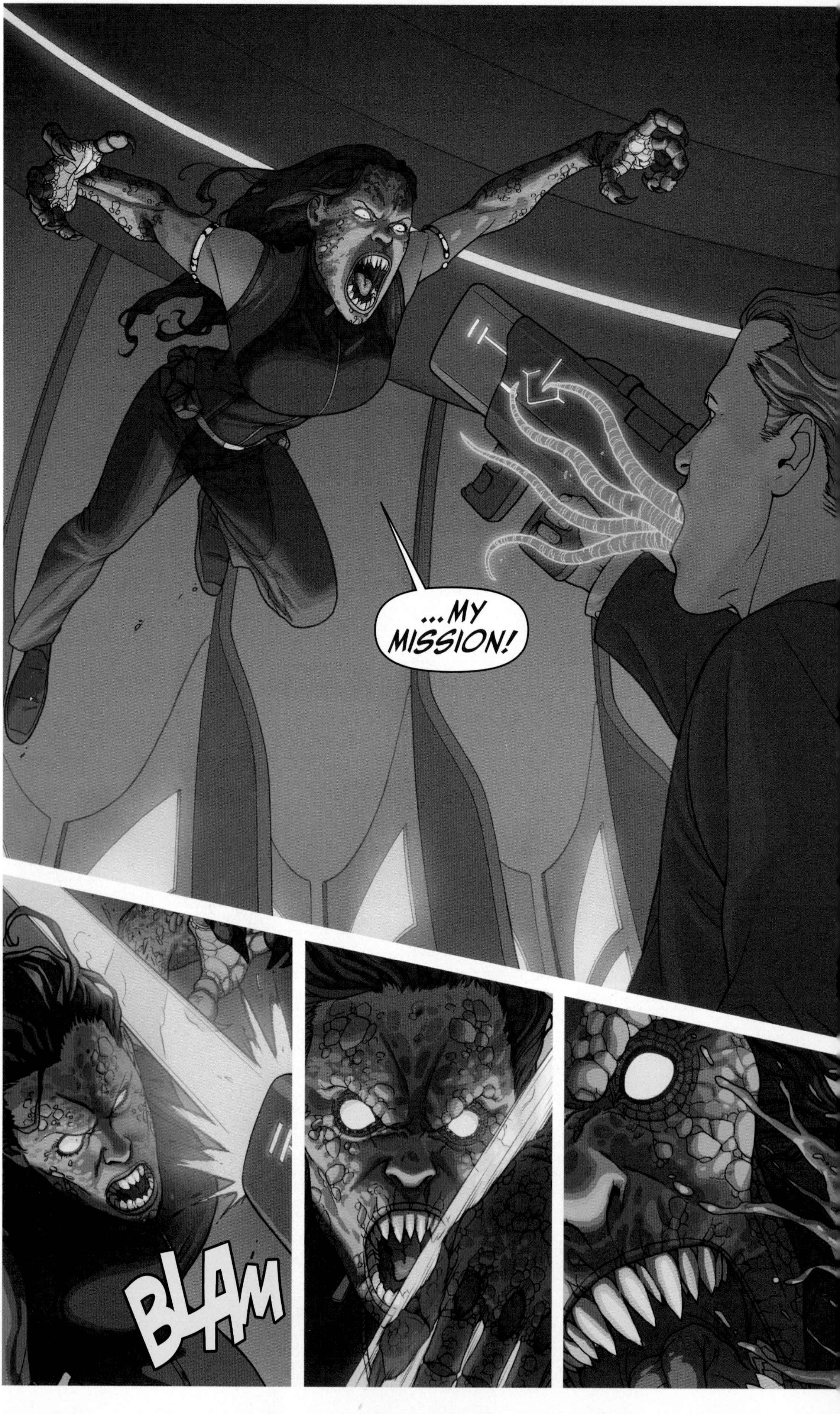
...MY MISSION!
BLAM

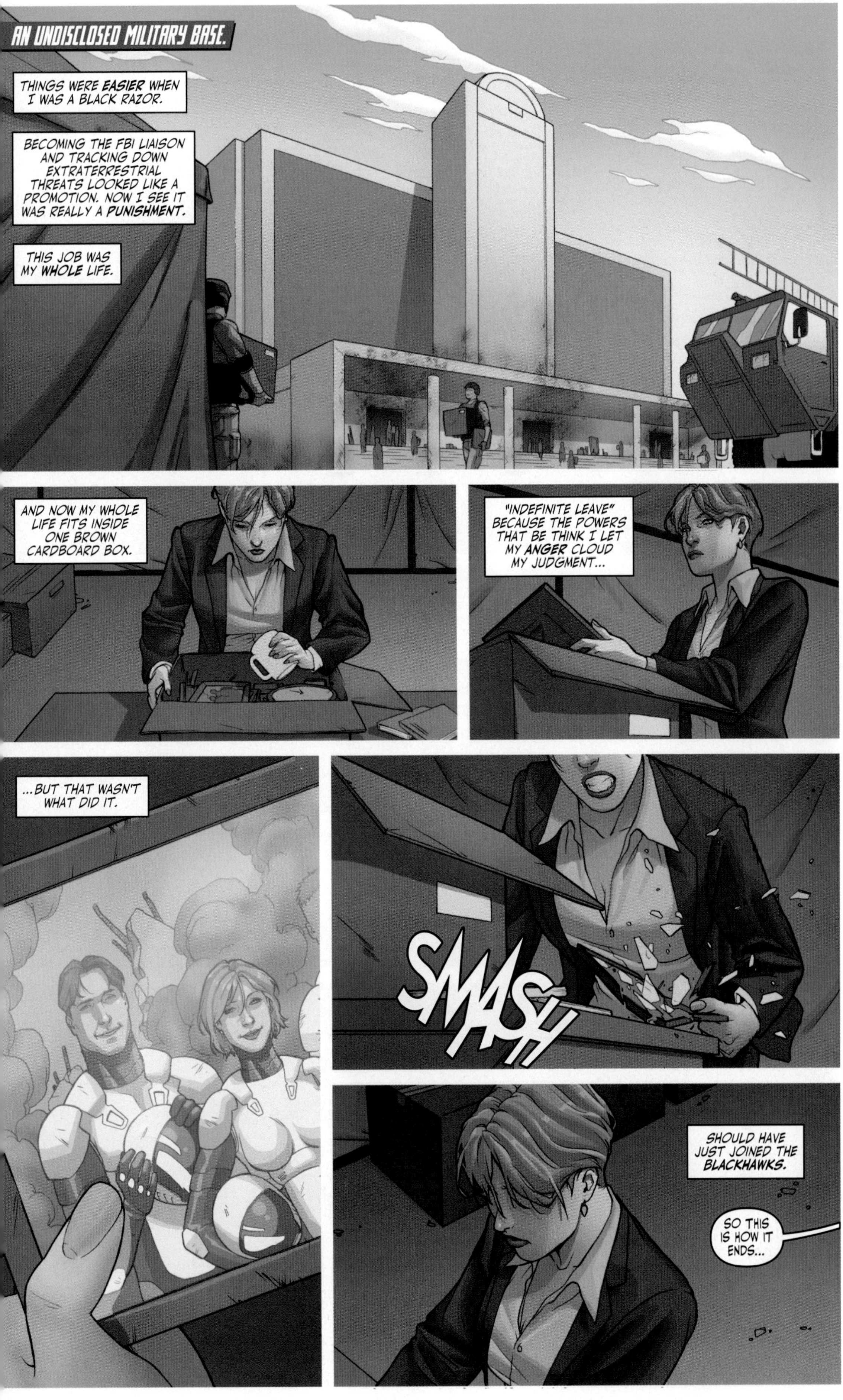
AN UNDISCLOSED MILITARY BASE.
THINGS WERE EASIER WHEN I WAS A BLACK RAZOR.
BECOMING THE FBI LIAISON AND TRACKING DOWN EXTRATERRESTRIAL THREATS LOOKED LIKE A PROMOTION. NOW I SEE IT WAS REALLY A PUNISHMENT.
THIS JOB WAS MY WHOLE LIFE.
AND NOW MY WHOLE LIFE FITS INSIDE ONE BROWN CARDBOARD BOX.
"INDEFINITE LEAVE" BECAUSE THE POWERS THAT BE THINK I LET MY ANGER CLOUD MY JUDGMENT...
...BUT THAT WASN'T WHAT DID IT.
SMASH
SHOULD HAVE JUST JOINED THE BLACKHAWKS.
SO THIS IS HOW IT ENDS...

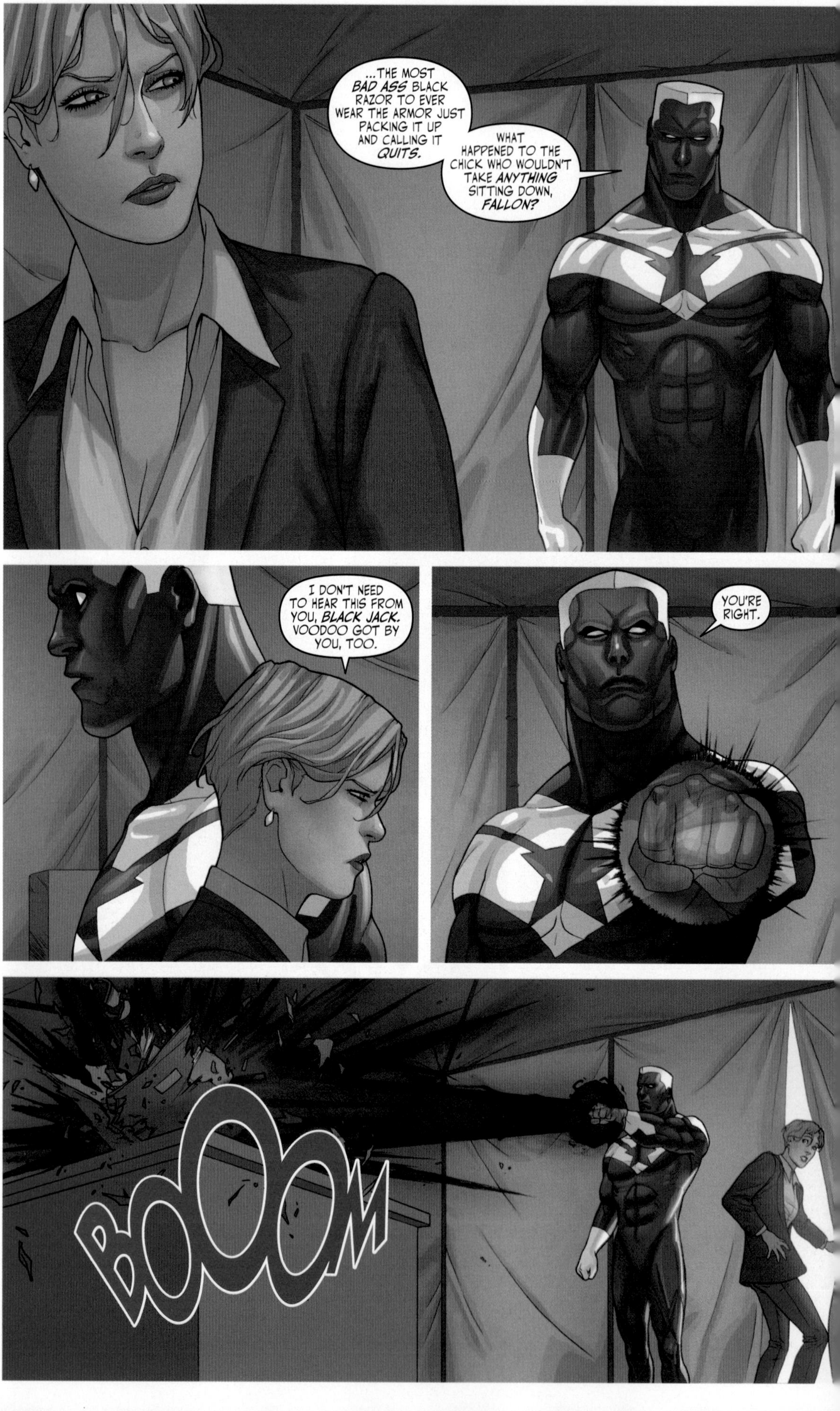
...THE MOST BAD ASS BLACK RAZOR TO EVER WEAR THE ARMOR JUST PACKING IT UP AND CALLING IT QUITS.
WHAT HAPPENED TO THE CHICK WHO WOULDN'T TAKE ANYTHING SITTING DOWN, FALLON?
I DON'T NEED TO HEAR THIS FROM YOU, BLACK JACK. VOODOO GOT BY YOU, TOO.
YOU'RE RIGHT.
BOOOOM

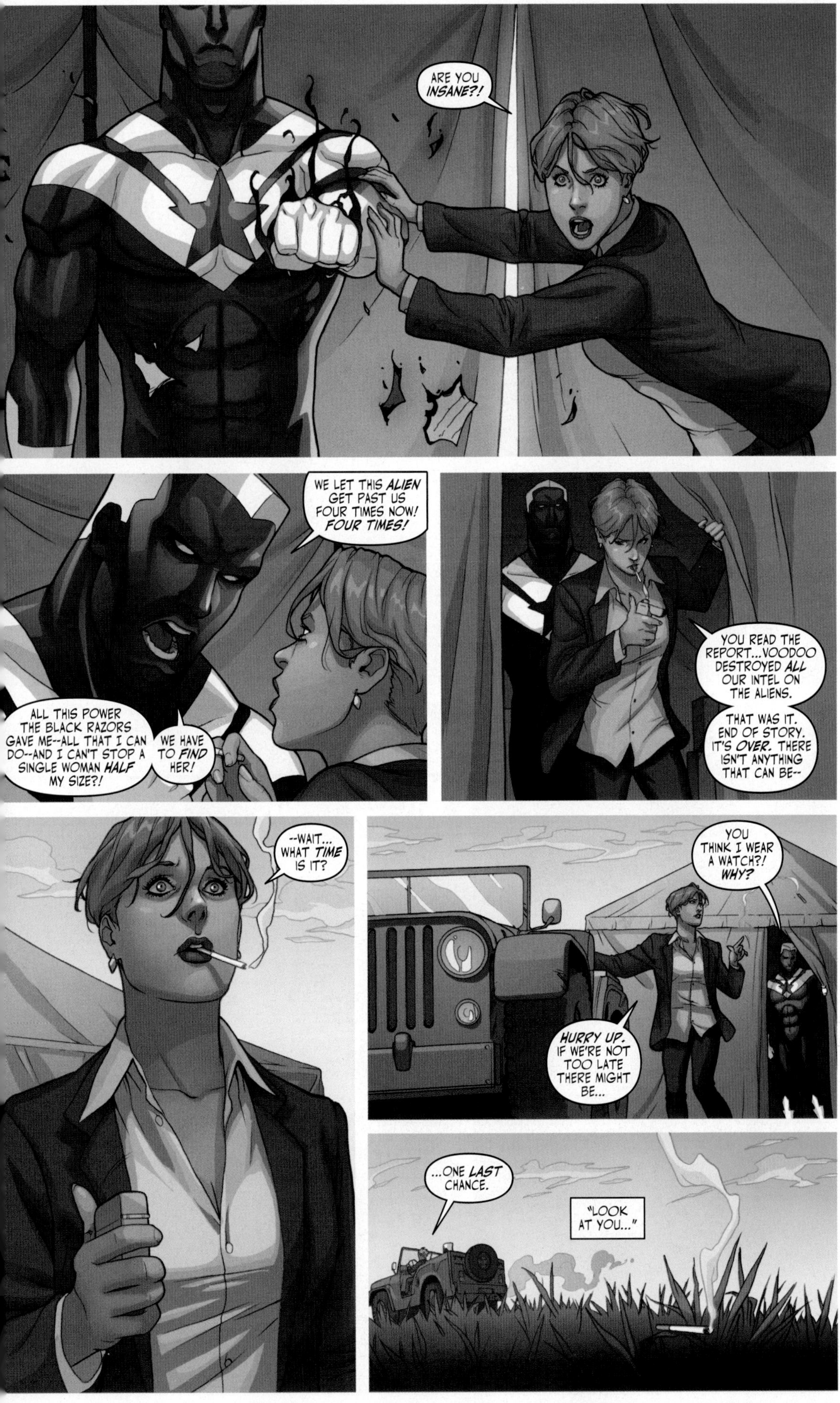
ARE YOU INSANE?!
WE LET THIS ALIEN GET PAST US FOUR TIMES NOW! FOUR TIMES!
ALL THIS POWER THE BLACK RAZORS GAVE ME--ALL THAT I CAN DO--AND I CAN'T STOP A SINGLE WOMAN HALF MY SIZE?!
WE HAVE TO FIND HER!
YOU READ THE REPORT...VOODOO DESTROYED ALL OUR INTEL ON THE ALIENS.
THAT WAS IT. END OF STORY. IT'S OVER. THERE ISN'T ANYTHING THAT CAN BE--
--WAIT... WHAT TIME IS IT?
YOU THINK I WEAR A WATCH?! WHY?
HURRY UP. IF WE'RE NOT TOO LATE THERE MIGHT BE...
...ONE LAST CHANCE.
"LOOK AT YOU..."

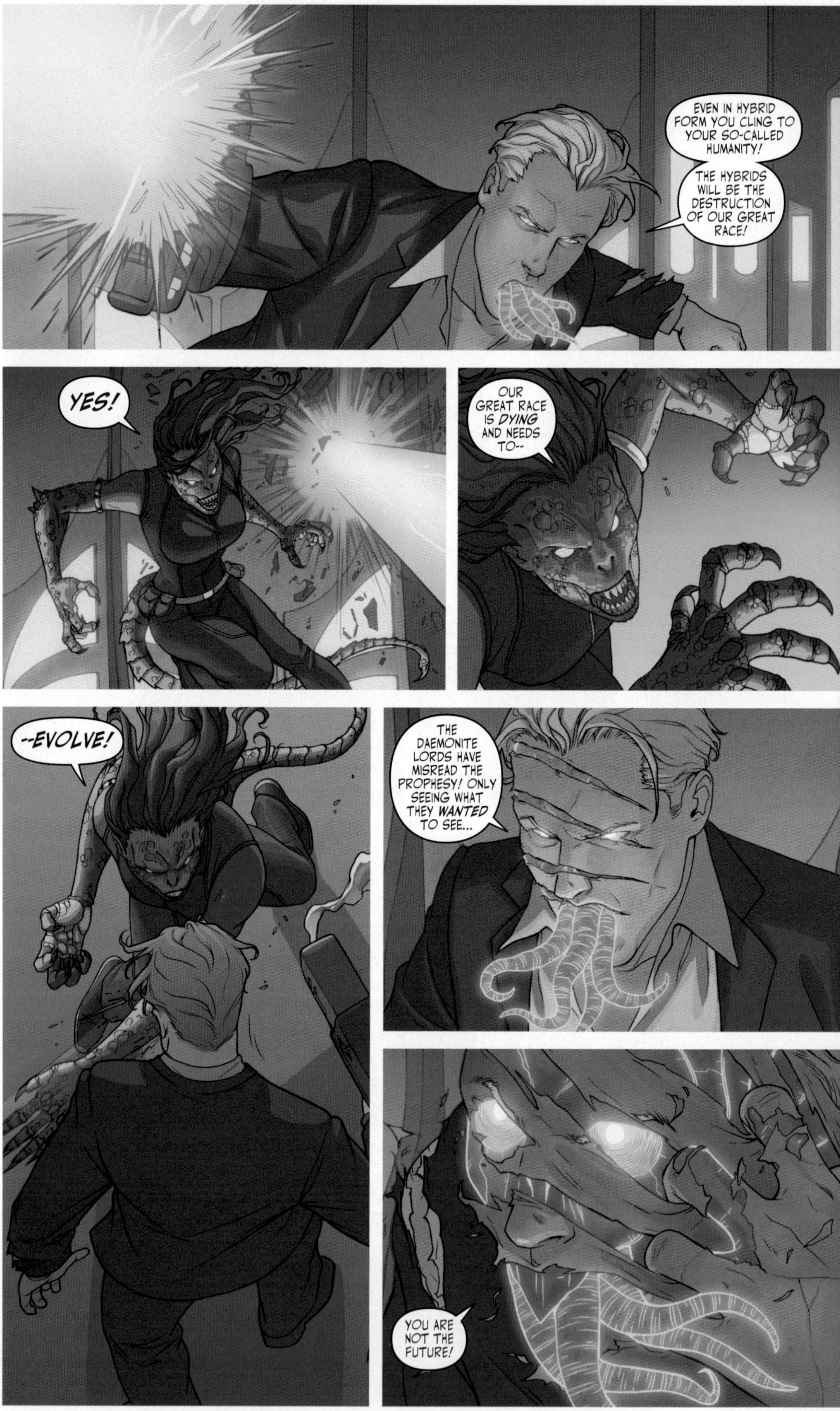
EVEN IN HYBRID FORM YOU CLING TO YOUR SO-CALLED HUMANITY!
THE HYBRIDS WILL BE THE DESTRUCTION OF OUR GREAT RACE!
YES!
OUR GREAT RACE IS *DYING* AND NEEDS TO--
--EVOLVE!
THE DAEMONITE LORDS HAVE MISREAD THE PROPHESY! ONLY SEEING WHAT THEY *WANTED* TO SEE...
YOU ARE NOT THE FUTURE!

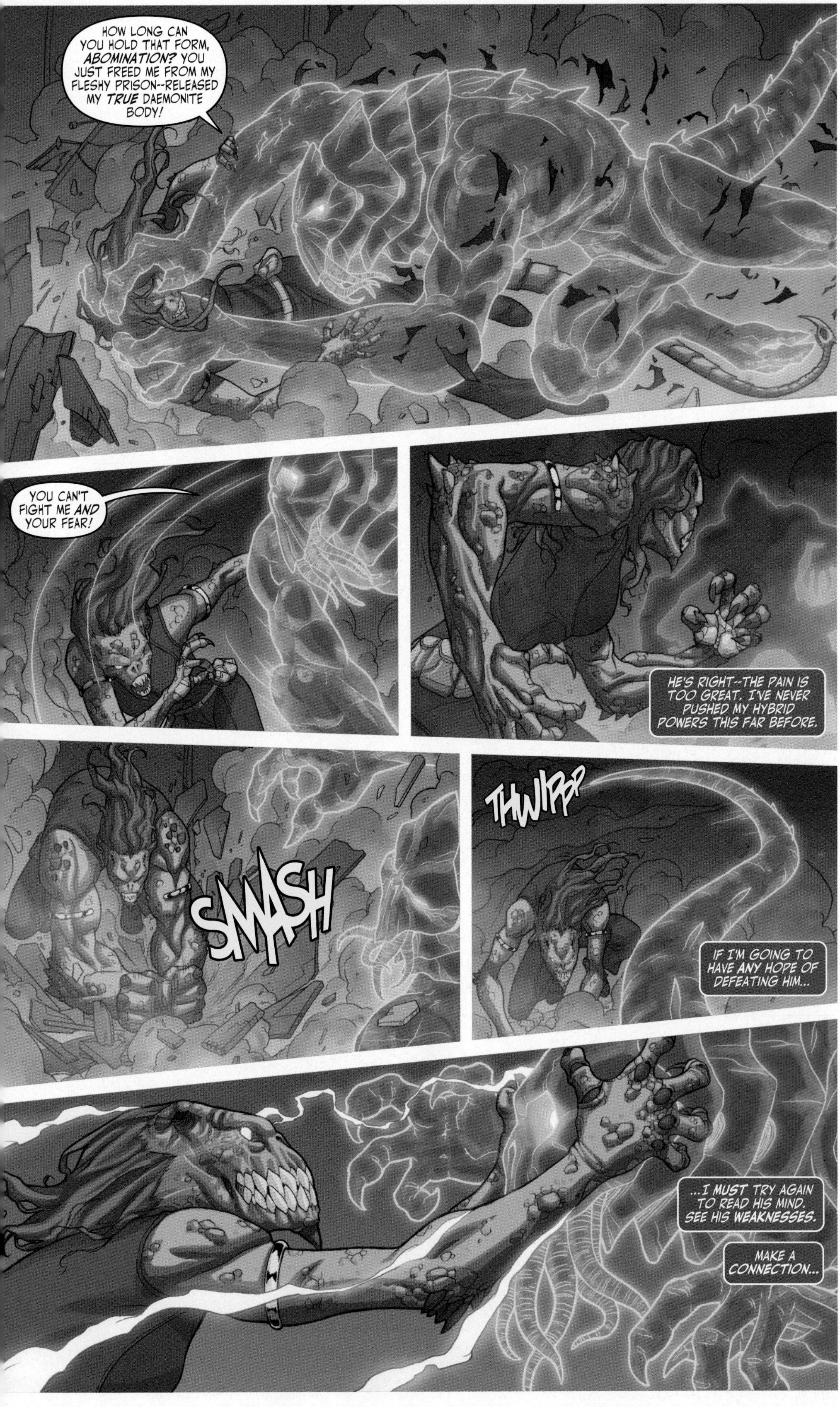
HOW LONG CAN YOU HOLD THAT FORM, ABOMINATION? YOU JUST FREED ME FROM MY FLESHY PRISON--RELEASED MY TRUE DAEMONITE BODY!
YOU CAN'T FIGHT ME AND YOUR FEAR!
HE'S RIGHT--THE PAIN IS TOO GREAT. I'VE NEVER PUSHED MY HYBRID POWERS THIS FAR BEFORE.
SMASH
THWIPP
IF I'M GOING TO HAVE ANY HOPE OF DEFEATING HIM...
...I MUST TRY AGAIN TO READ HIS MIND. SEE HIS WEAKNESSES.
MAKE A CONNECTION...

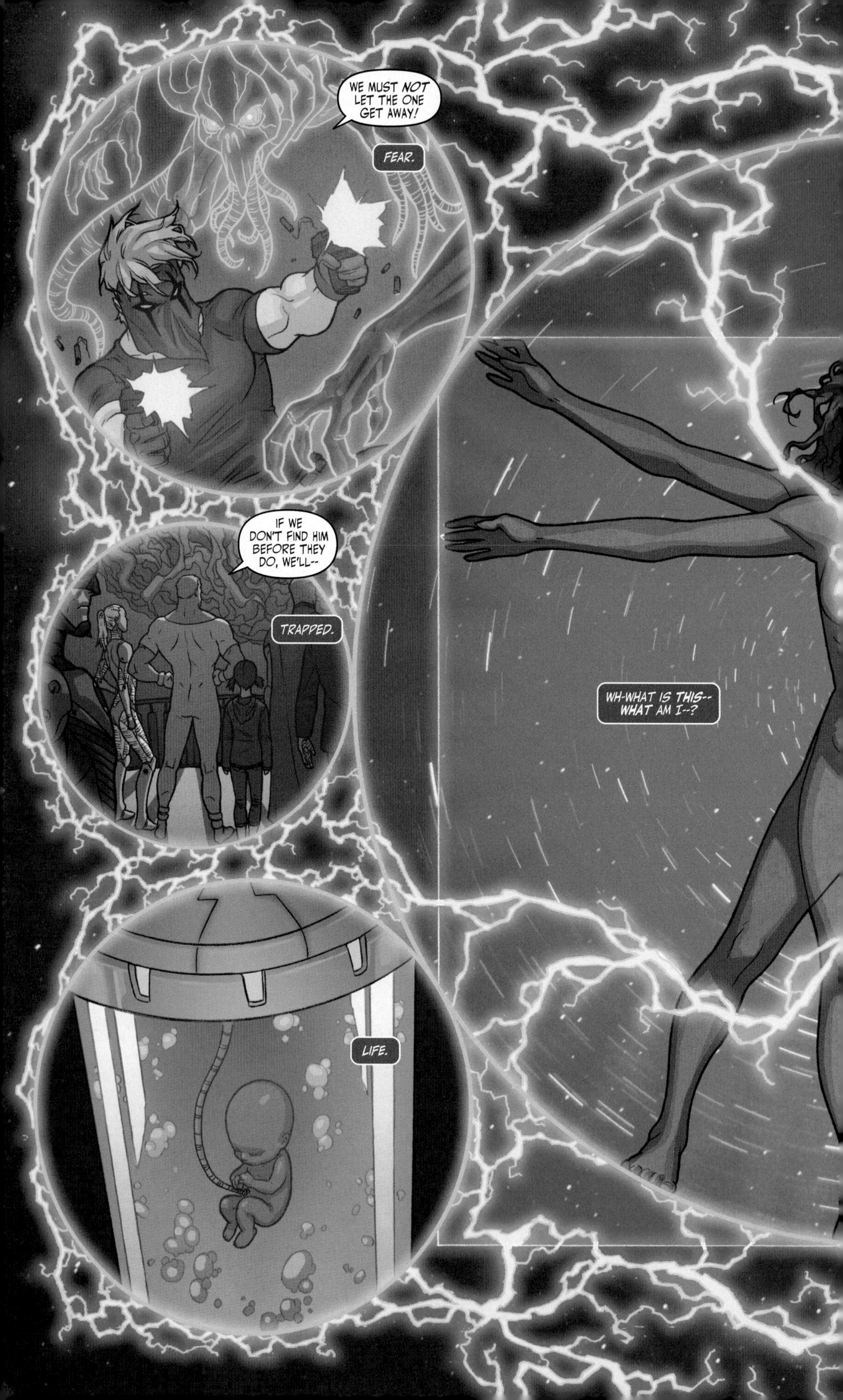
WE MUST NOT LET THE ONE GET AWAY!
FEAR.
IF WE DON'T FIND HIM BEFORE THEY DO, WE'LL--
TRAPPED.
LIFE.
WH-WHAT IS THIS-- WHAT AM I--?

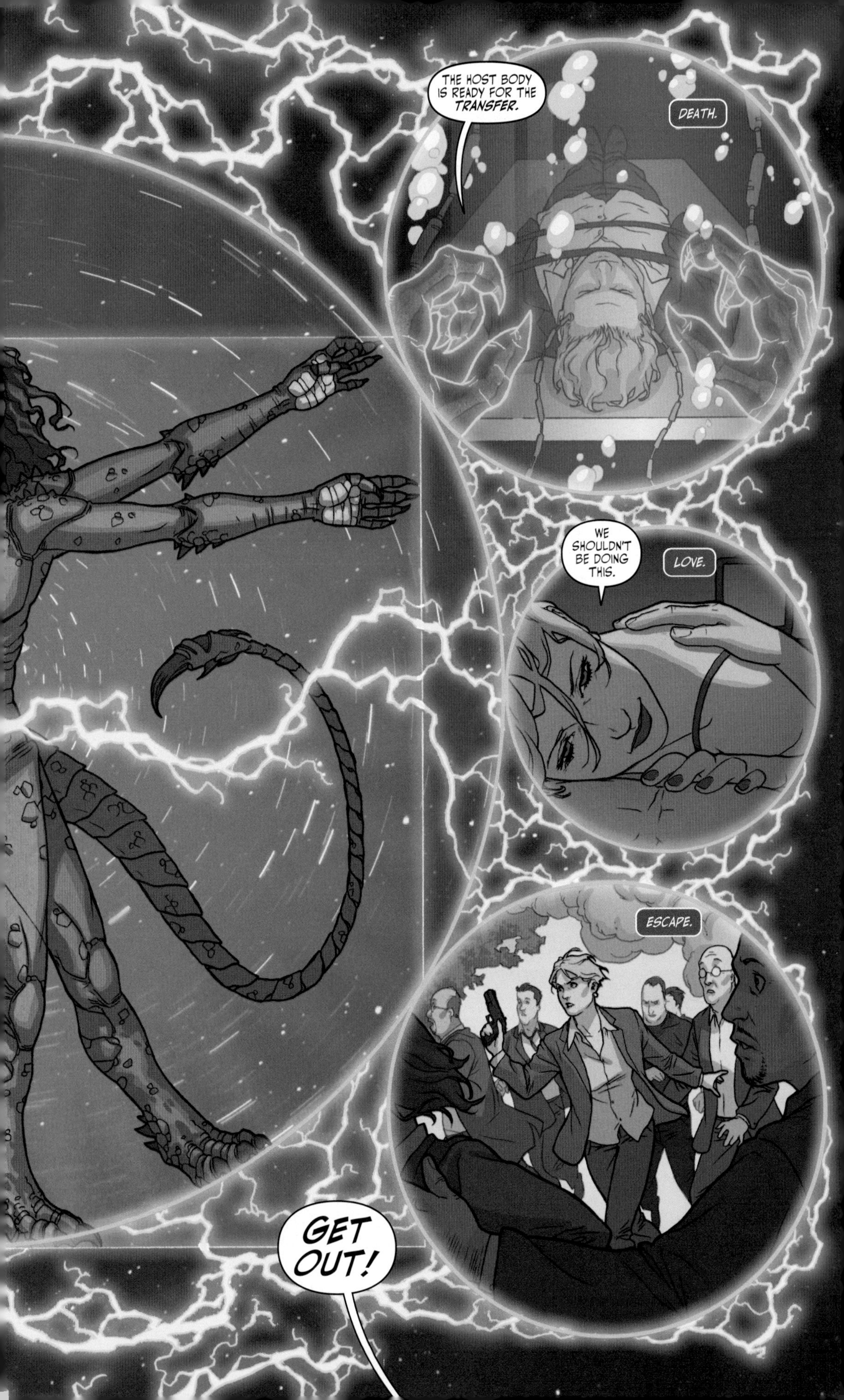
THE HOST BODY IS READY FOR THE TRANSFER.
DEATH.
WE SHOULDN'T BE DOING THIS.
LOVE.
ESCAPE.
GET OUT!

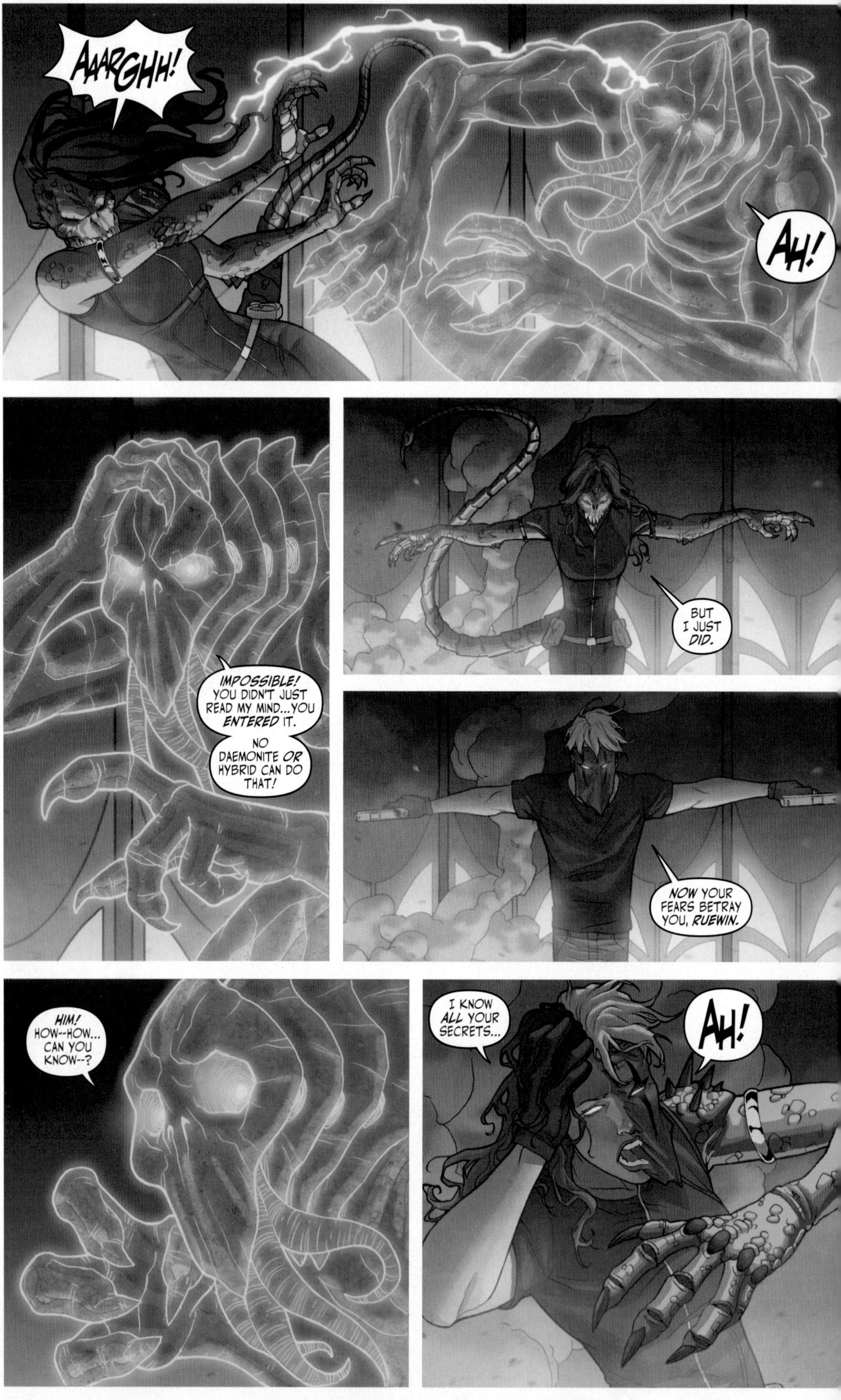
AAARGHH!
AH!
IMPOSSIBLE! YOU DIDN'T JUST READ MY MIND...YOU ENTERED IT.
NO DAEMONITE OR HYBRID CAN DO THAT!
BUT I JUST DID.
NOW YOUR FEARS BETRAY YOU, RUEWIN.
HIM! HOW--HOW... CAN YOU KNOW--?
I KNOW ALL YOUR SECRETS...
AH!

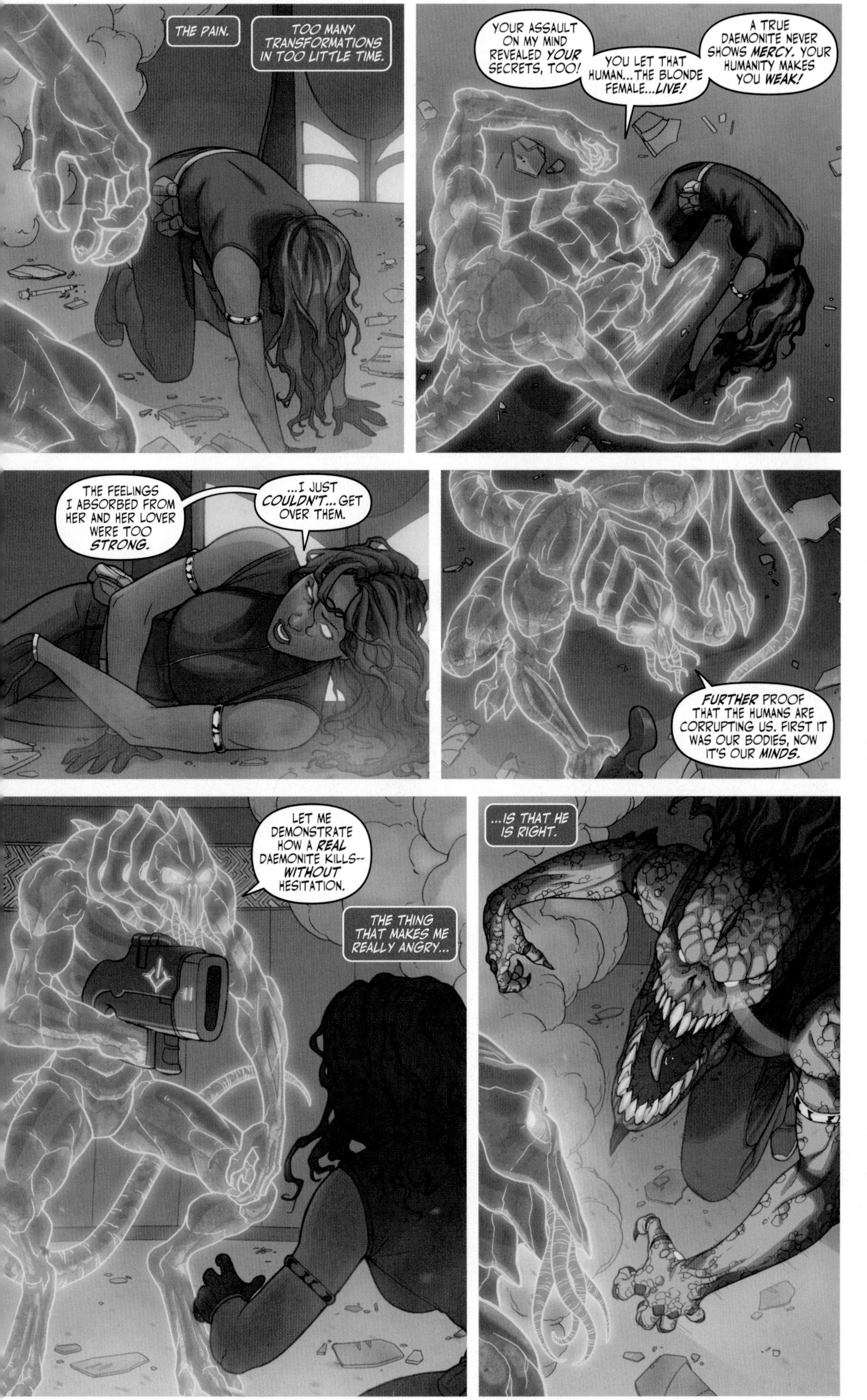
THE PAIN.
TOO MANY TRANSFORMATIONS IN TOO LITTLE TIME.
YOUR ASSAULT ON MY MIND REVEALED *YOUR* SECRETS, TOO!
YOU LET THAT HUMAN...THE BLONDE FEMALE...*LIVE!*
A TRUE DAEMONITE NEVER SHOWS *MERCY*. YOUR HUMANITY MAKES YOU *WEAK!*
THE FEELINGS I ABSORBED FROM HER AND HER LOVER WERE TOO *STRONG*.
...I JUST *COULDN'T*... GET OVER THEM.
FURTHER PROOF THAT THE HUMANS ARE CORRUPTING US. FIRST IT WAS OUR BODIES, NOW IT'S OUR *MINDS.*
LET ME DEMONSTRATE HOW A *REAL* DAEMONITE KILLS-- *WITHOUT* HESITATION.
THE THING THAT MAKES ME REALLY ANGRY...
...IS THAT HE IS RIGHT.

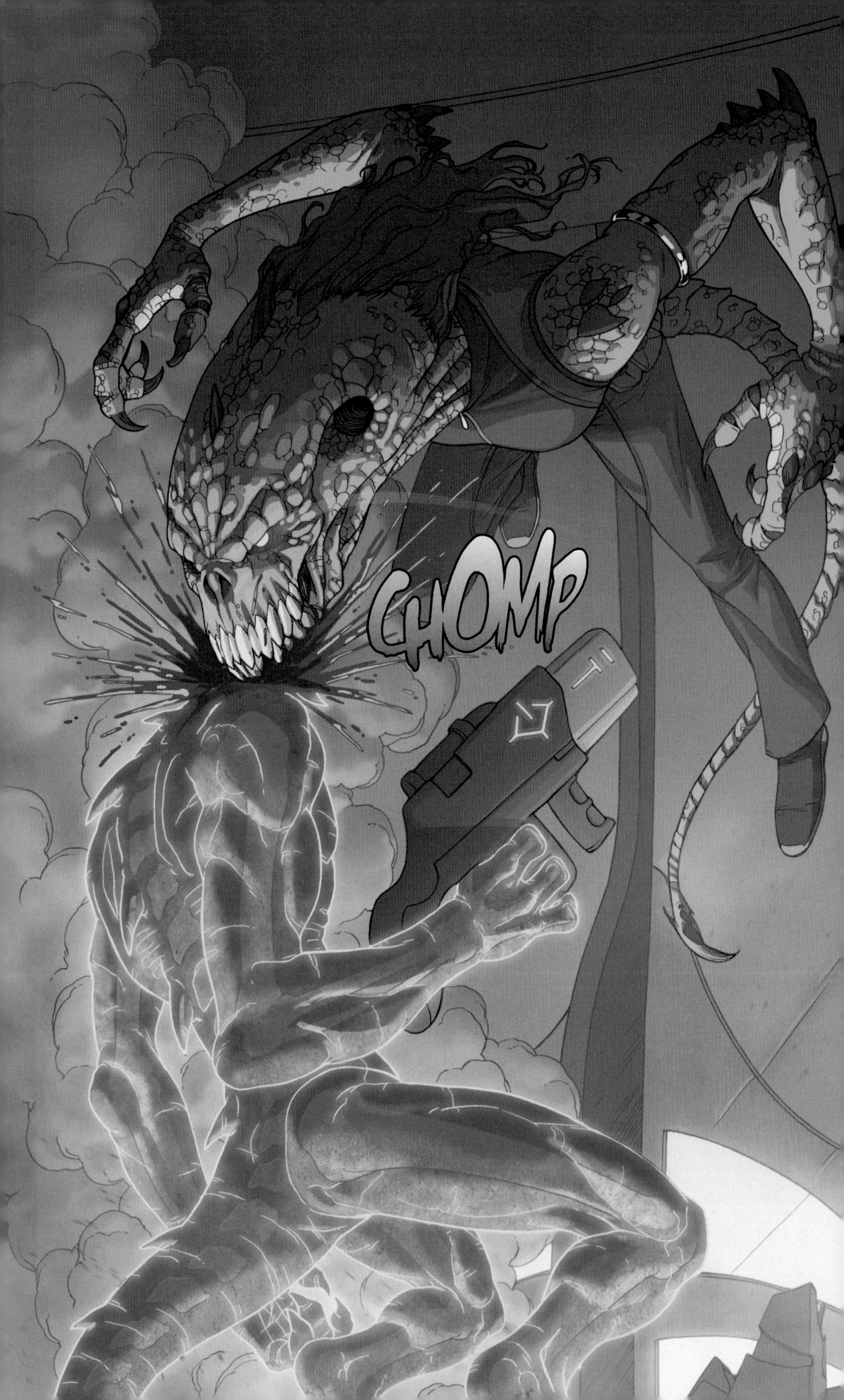
CHOMP

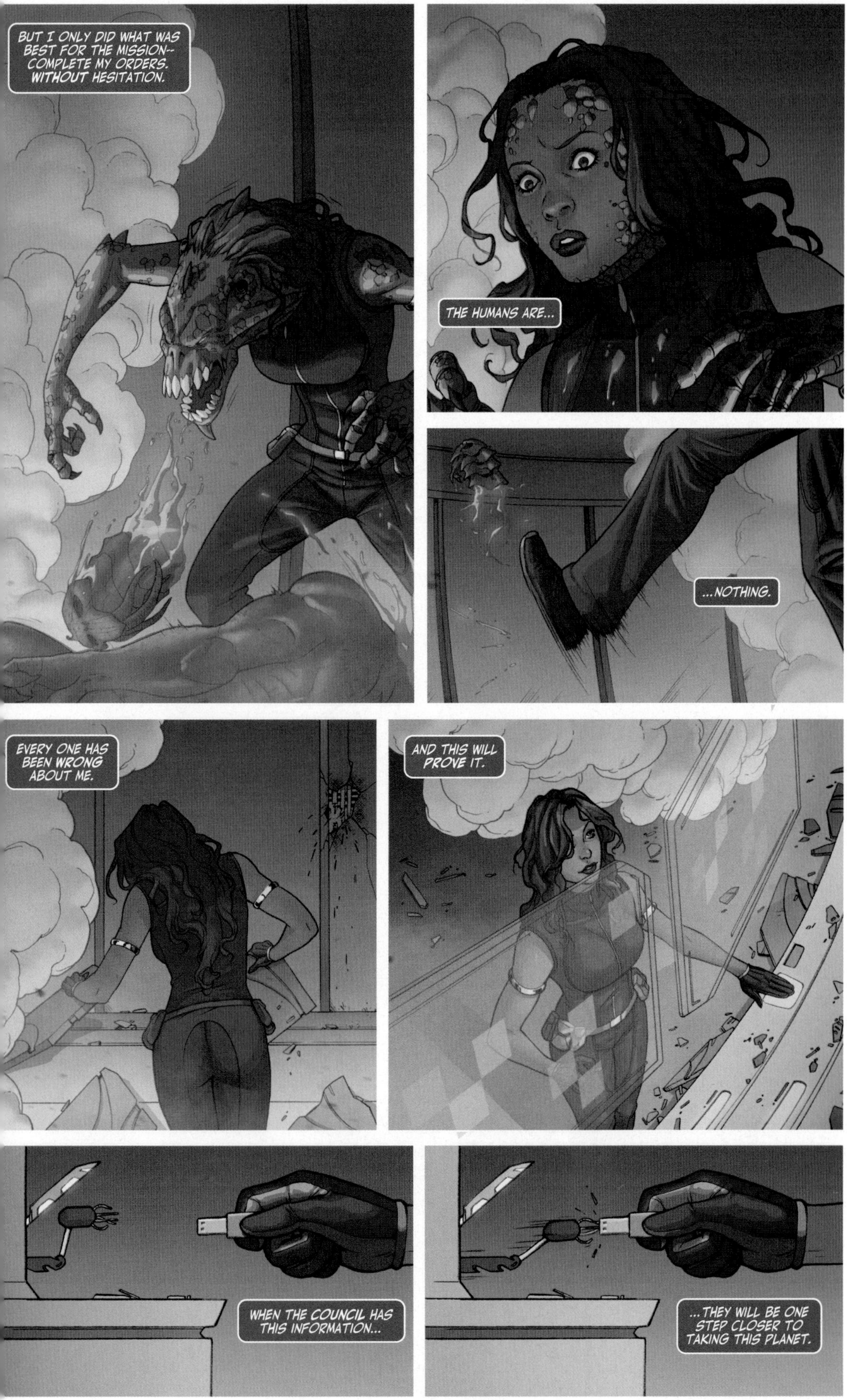
BUT I ONLY DID WHAT WAS BEST FOR THE MISSION-- COMPLETE MY ORDERS. WITHOUT HESITATION.
THE HUMANS ARE...
...NOTHING.
EVERY ONE HAS BEEN WRONG ABOUT ME.
AND THIS WILL PROVE IT.
WHEN THE COUNCIL HAS THIS INFORMATION...
...THEY WILL BE ONE STEP CLOSER TO TAKING THIS PLANET.

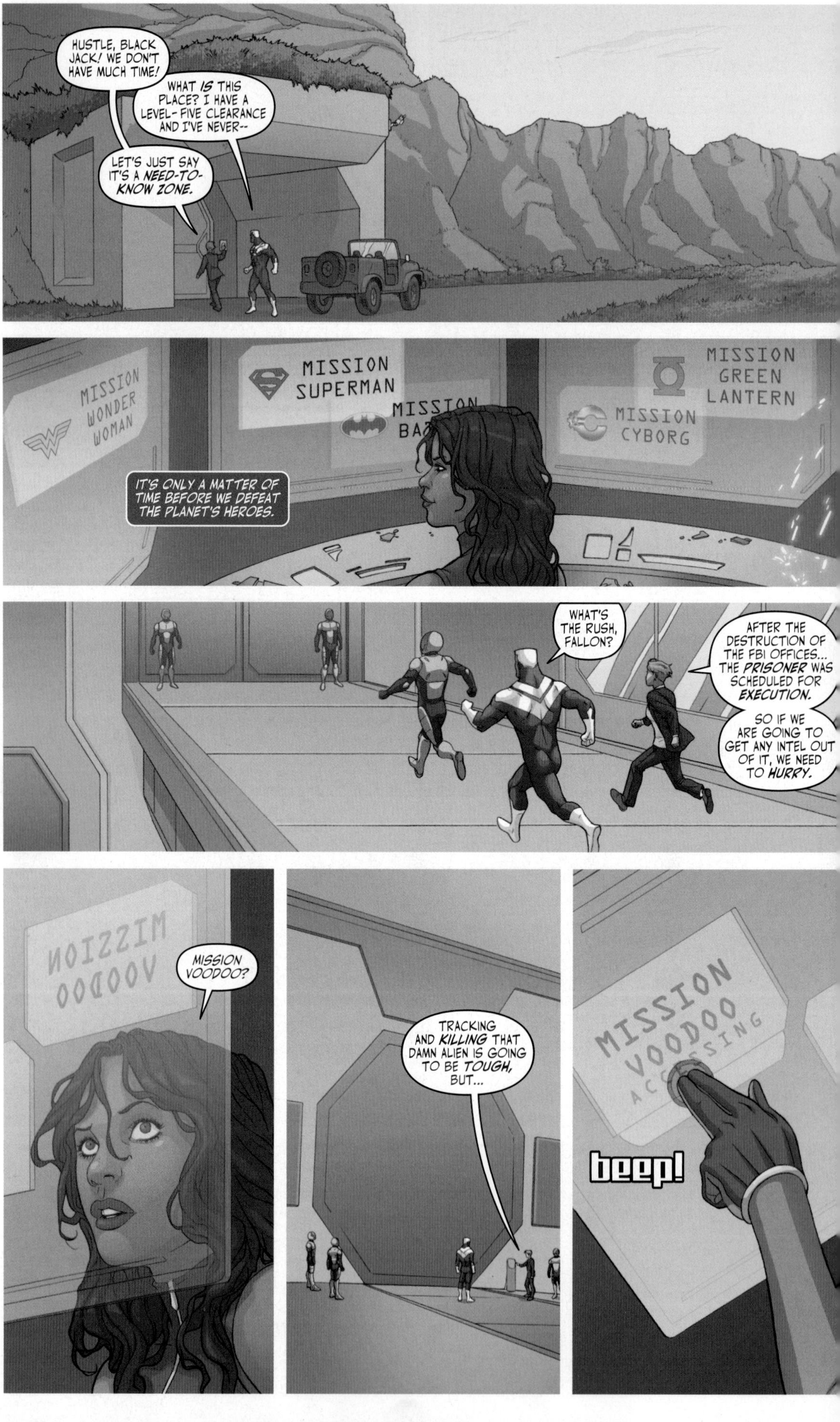
HUSTLE, BLACK JACK! WE DON'T HAVE MUCH TIME!
WHAT *IS* THIS PLACE? I HAVE A LEVEL-FIVE CLEARANCE AND I'VE NEVER--
LET'S JUST SAY IT'S A *NEED-TO-KNOW ZONE.*
MISSION WONDER WOMAN
MISSION SUPERMAN
MISSION BA
MISSION GREEN LANTERN
MISSION CYBORG
IT'S ONLY A MATTER OF TIME BEFORE WE DEFEAT THE PLANET'S HEROES.
WHAT'S THE RUSH, FALLON?
AFTER THE DESTRUCTION OF THE FBI OFFICES... THE ***PRISONER*** WAS SCHEDULED FOR ***EXECUTION.***
SO IF WE ARE GOING TO GET ANY INTEL OUT OF IT, WE NEED TO ***HURRY.***
MISSION VOODOO
MISSION VOODOO?
TRACKING AND ***KILLING*** THAT DAMN ALIEN IS GOING TO BE *TOUGH,* BUT...
MISSION VOODOO ACCESSING
beep!

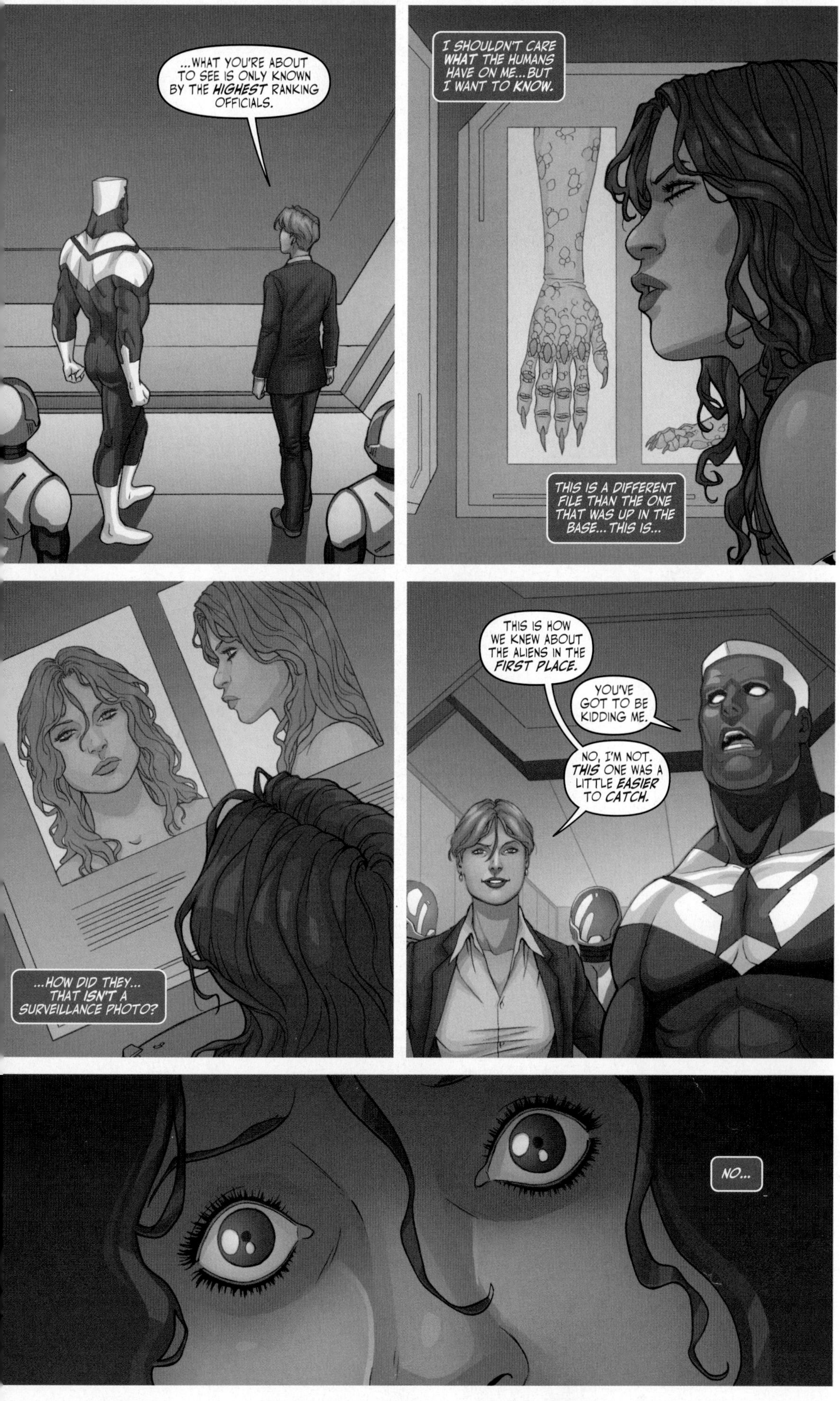
...WHAT YOU'RE ABOUT TO SEE IS ONLY KNOWN BY THE HIGHEST RANKING OFFICIALS.
I SHOULDN'T CARE WHAT THE HUMANS HAVE ON ME...BUT I WANT TO KNOW.
THIS IS A DIFFERENT FILE THAN THE ONE THAT WAS UP IN THE BASE... THIS IS...
...HOW DID THEY... THAT ISN'T A SURVEILLANCE PHOTO?
THIS IS HOW WE KNEW ABOUT THE ALIENS IN THE FIRST PLACE.
YOU'VE GOT TO BE KIDDING ME.
NO, I'M NOT. THIS ONE WAS A LITTLE EASIER TO CATCH.
NO...

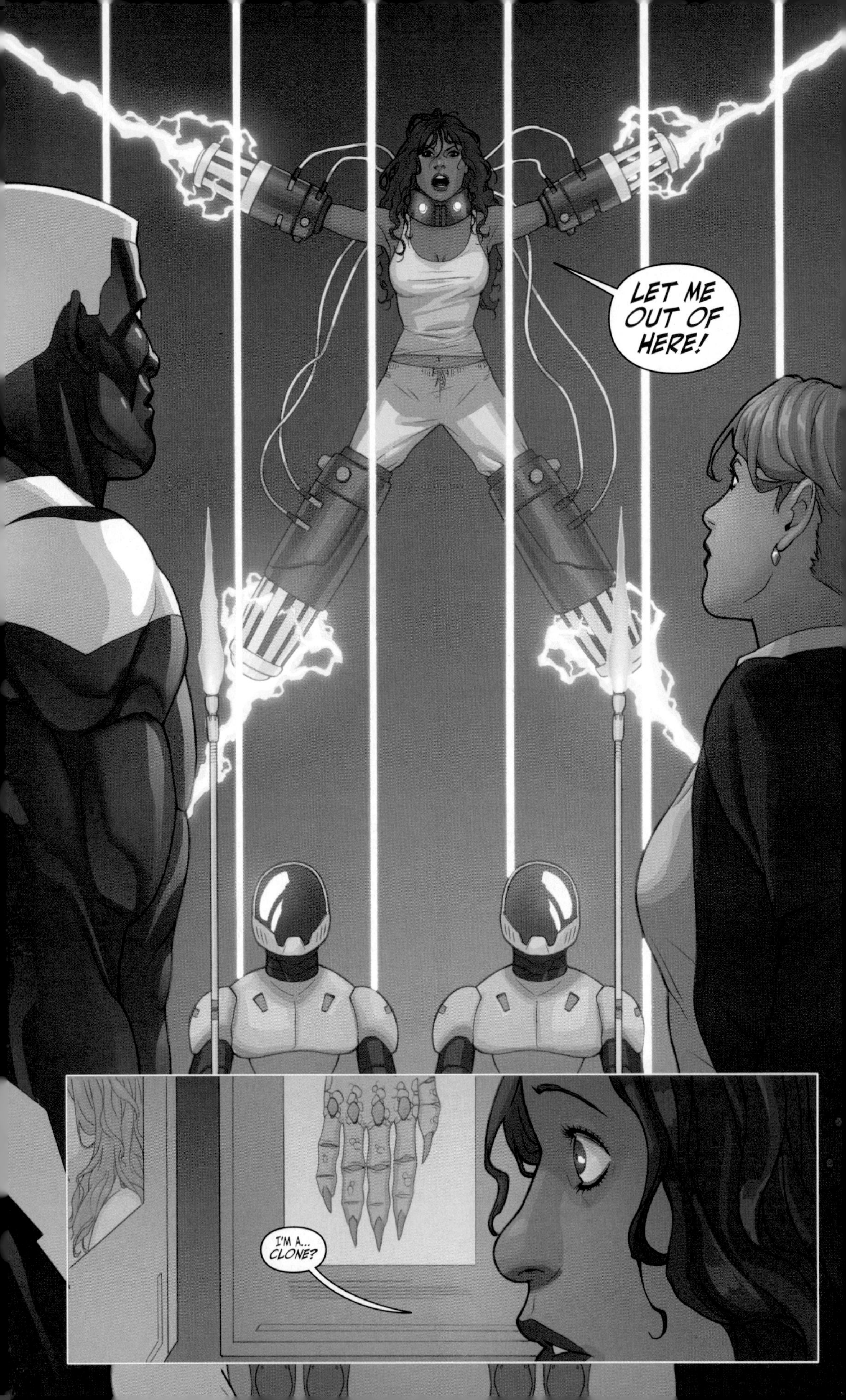
LET ME OUT OF HERE!
I'M A... CLONE?

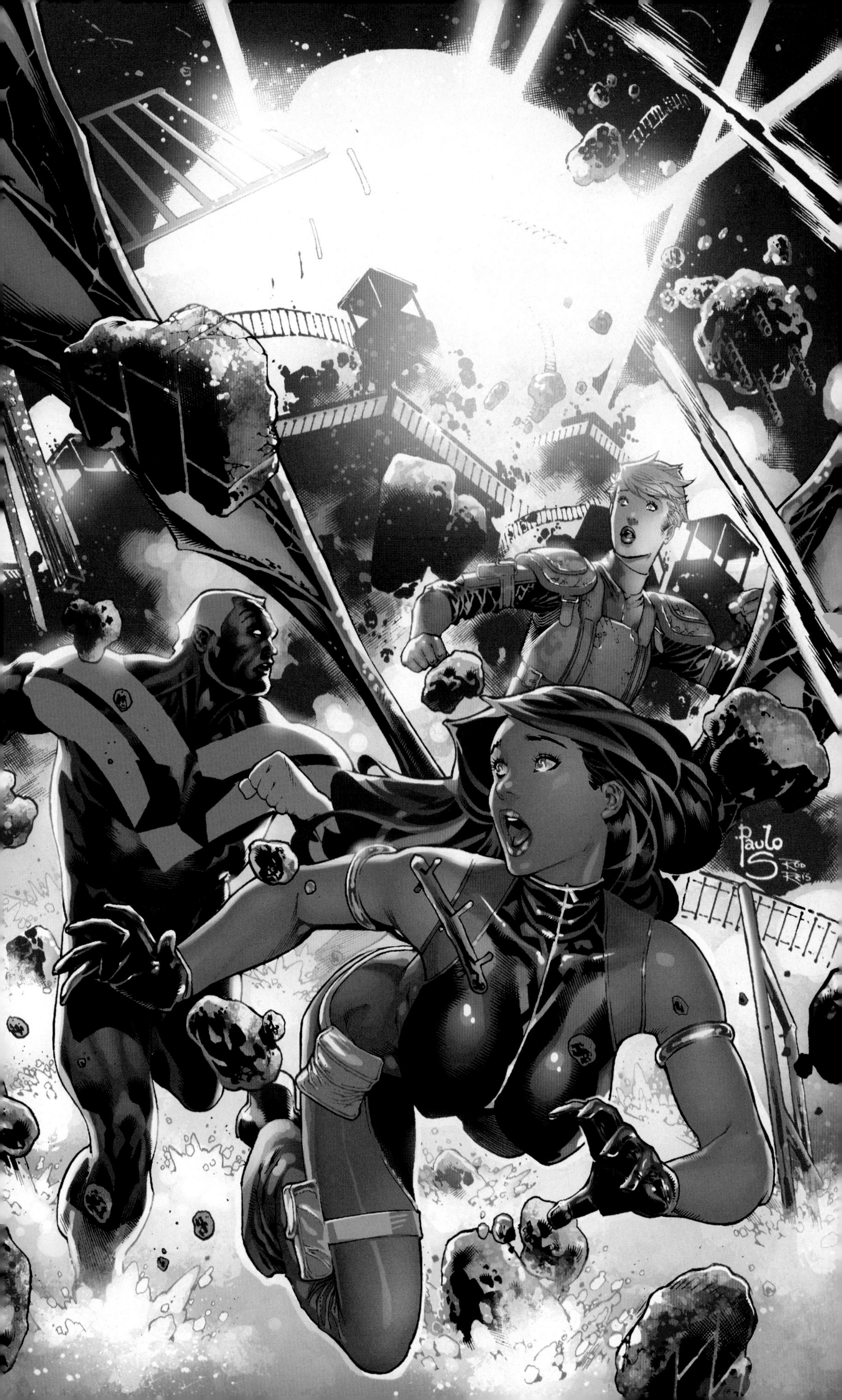
Paulo S
Rod Reis

cover art by

PAULO SIQUEIRA & ROD REIS

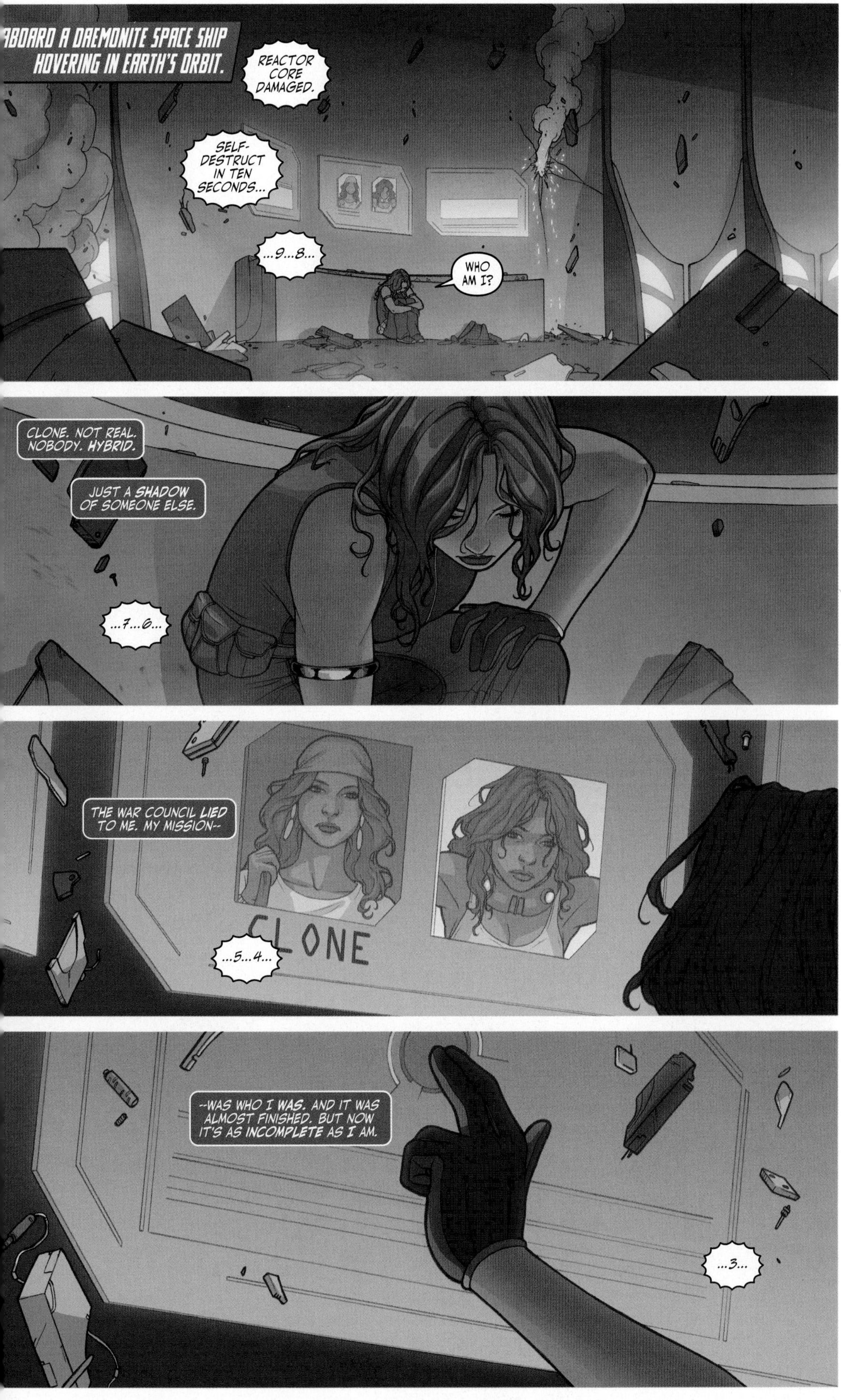
ABOARD A DAEMONITE SPACE SHIP HOVERING IN EARTH'S ORBIT.
REACTOR CORE DAMAGED.
SELF-DESTRUCT IN TEN SECONDS...
...9...8...
WHO AM I?
CLONE. NOT REAL. NOBODY. HYBRID.
JUST A SHADOW OF SOMEONE ELSE.
...7...6...
THE WAR COUNCIL LIED TO ME. MY MISSION--
CLONE
...5...4...
--WAS WHO I WAS. AND IT WAS ALMOST FINISHED. BUT NOW IT'S AS INCOMPLETE AS I AM.
...3...

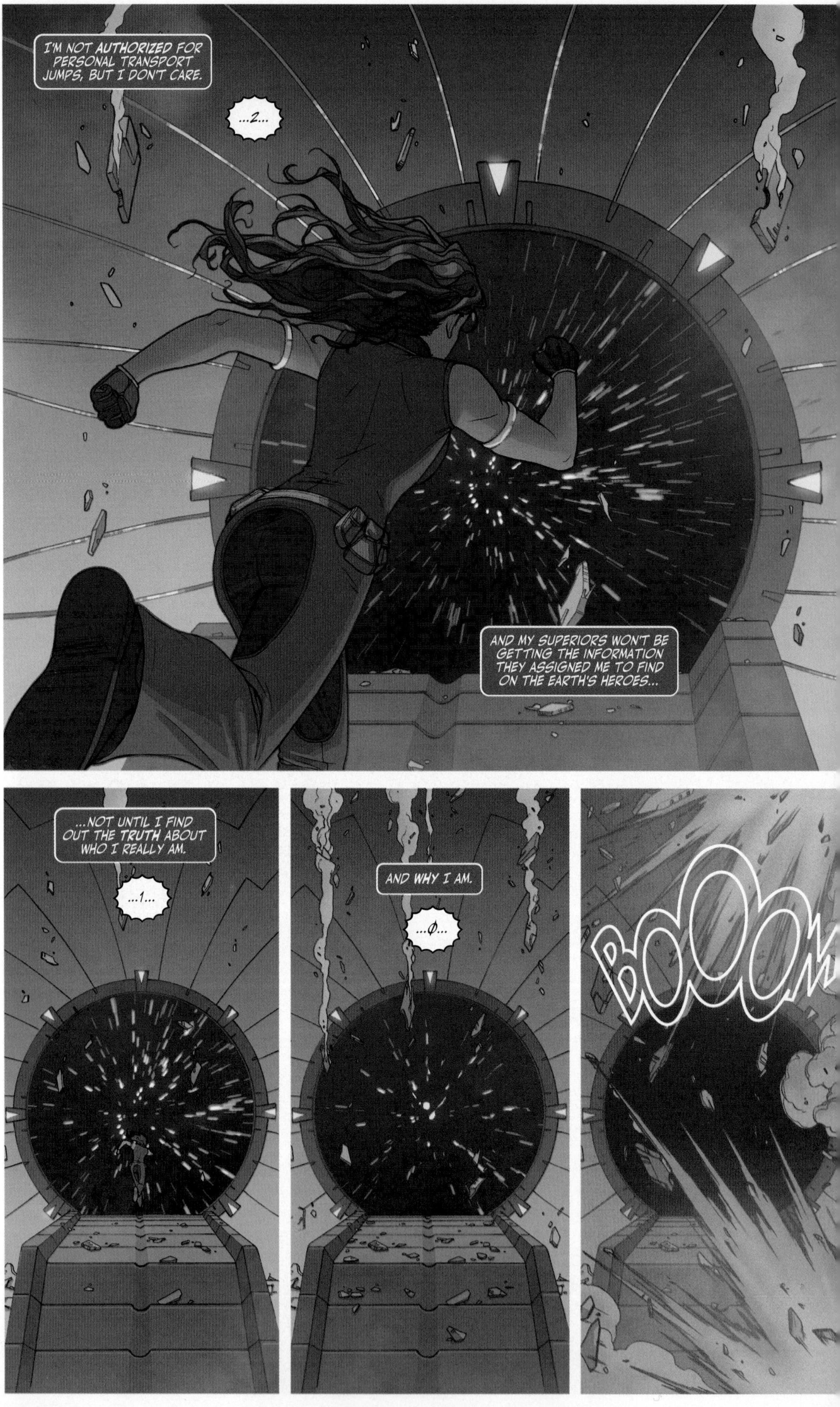
I'M NOT AUTHORIZED FOR PERSONAL TRANSPORT JUMPS, BUT I DON'T CARE.
...2...
AND MY SUPERIORS WON'T BE GETTING THE INFORMATION THEY ASSIGNED ME TO FIND ON THE EARTH'S HEROES...
...NOT UNTIL I FIND OUT THE TRUTH ABOUT WHO I REALLY AM.
...1...
AND WHY I AM.
...Ø...
BOOOM

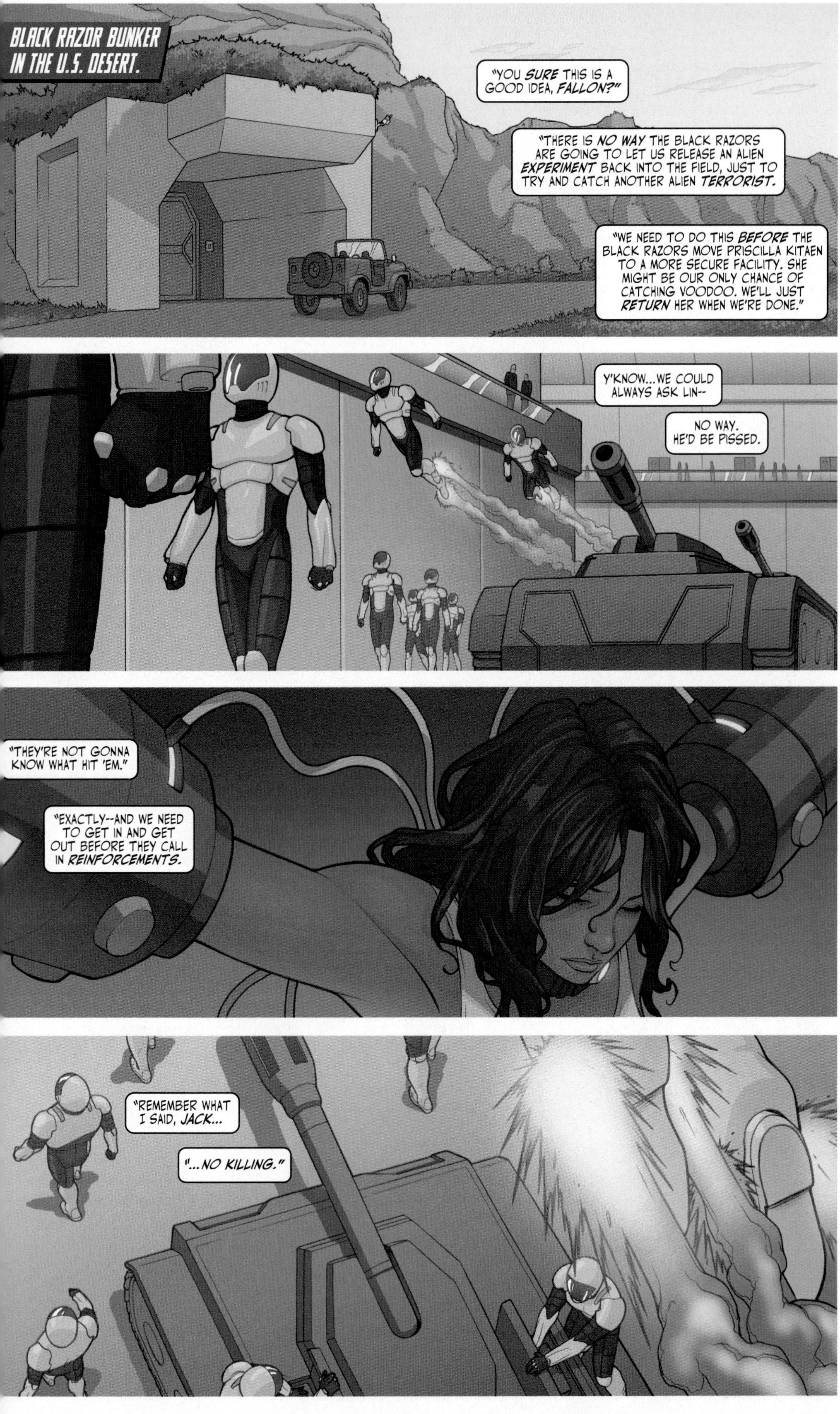
BLACK RAZOR BUNKER IN THE U.S. DESERT.
"YOU SURE THIS IS A GOOD IDEA, FALLON?"
"THERE IS NO WAY THE BLACK RAZORS ARE GOING TO LET US RELEASE AN ALIEN EXPERIMENT BACK INTO THE FIELD, JUST TO TRY AND CATCH ANOTHER ALIEN TERRORIST.
"WE NEED TO DO THIS BEFORE THE BLACK RAZORS MOVE PRISCILLA KITAEN TO A MORE SECURE FACILITY. SHE MIGHT BE OUR ONLY CHANCE OF CATCHING VOODOO. WE'LL JUST RETURN HER WHEN WE'RE DONE."
Y'KNOW...WE COULD ALWAYS ASK LIN--
NO WAY. HE'D BE PISSED.
"THEY'RE NOT GONNA KNOW WHAT HIT 'EM."
"EXACTLY--AND WE NEED TO GET IN AND GET OUT BEFORE THEY CALL IN REINFORCEMENTS.
"REMEMBER WHAT I SAID, JACK...
"...NO KILLING."

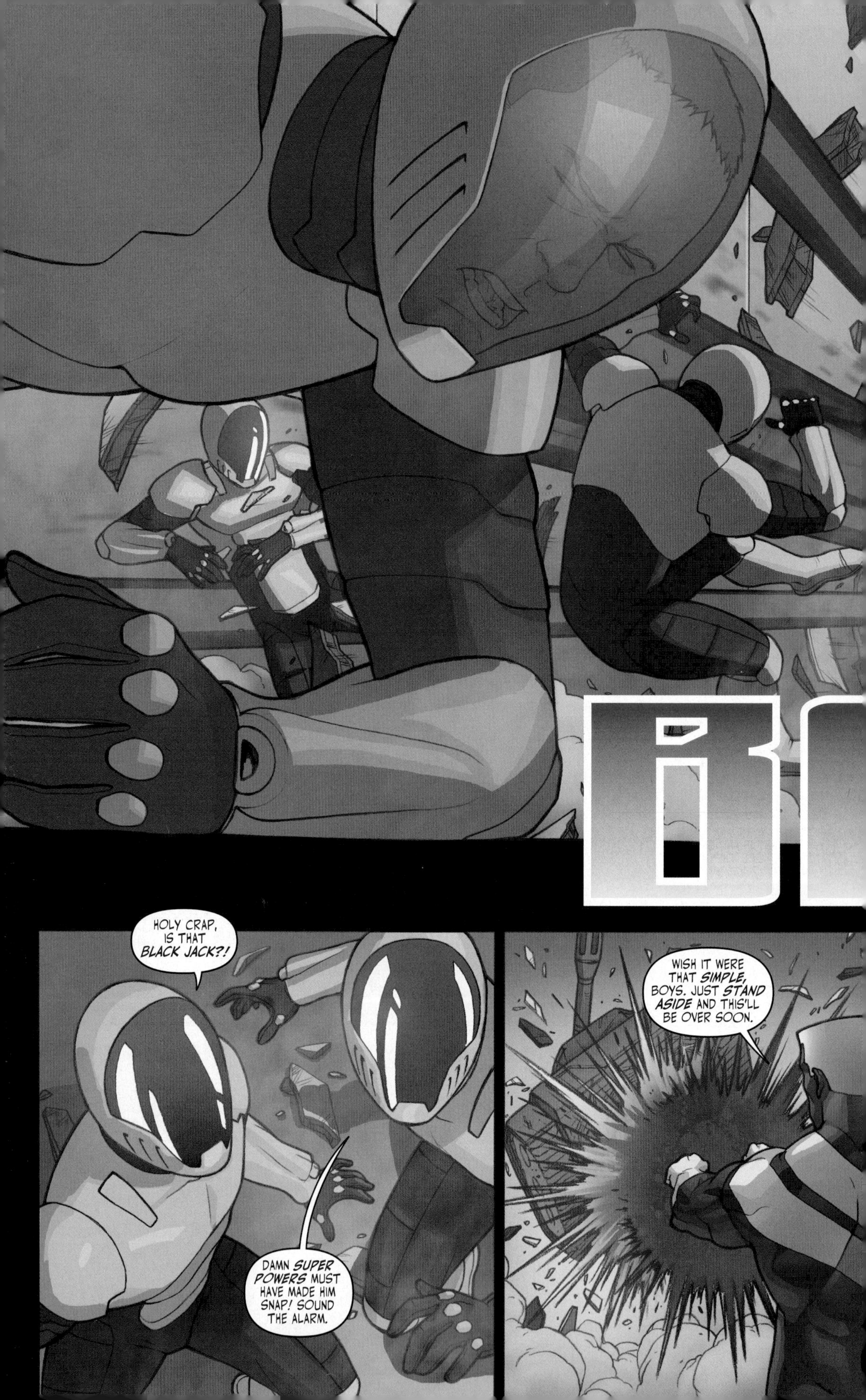
HOLY CRAP, IS THAT BLACK JACK?!
DAMN SUPER POWERS MUST HAVE MADE HIM SNAP! SOUND THE ALARM.
WISH IT WERE THAT SIMPLE, BOYS. JUST STAND ASIDE AND THIS'LL BE OVER SOON.

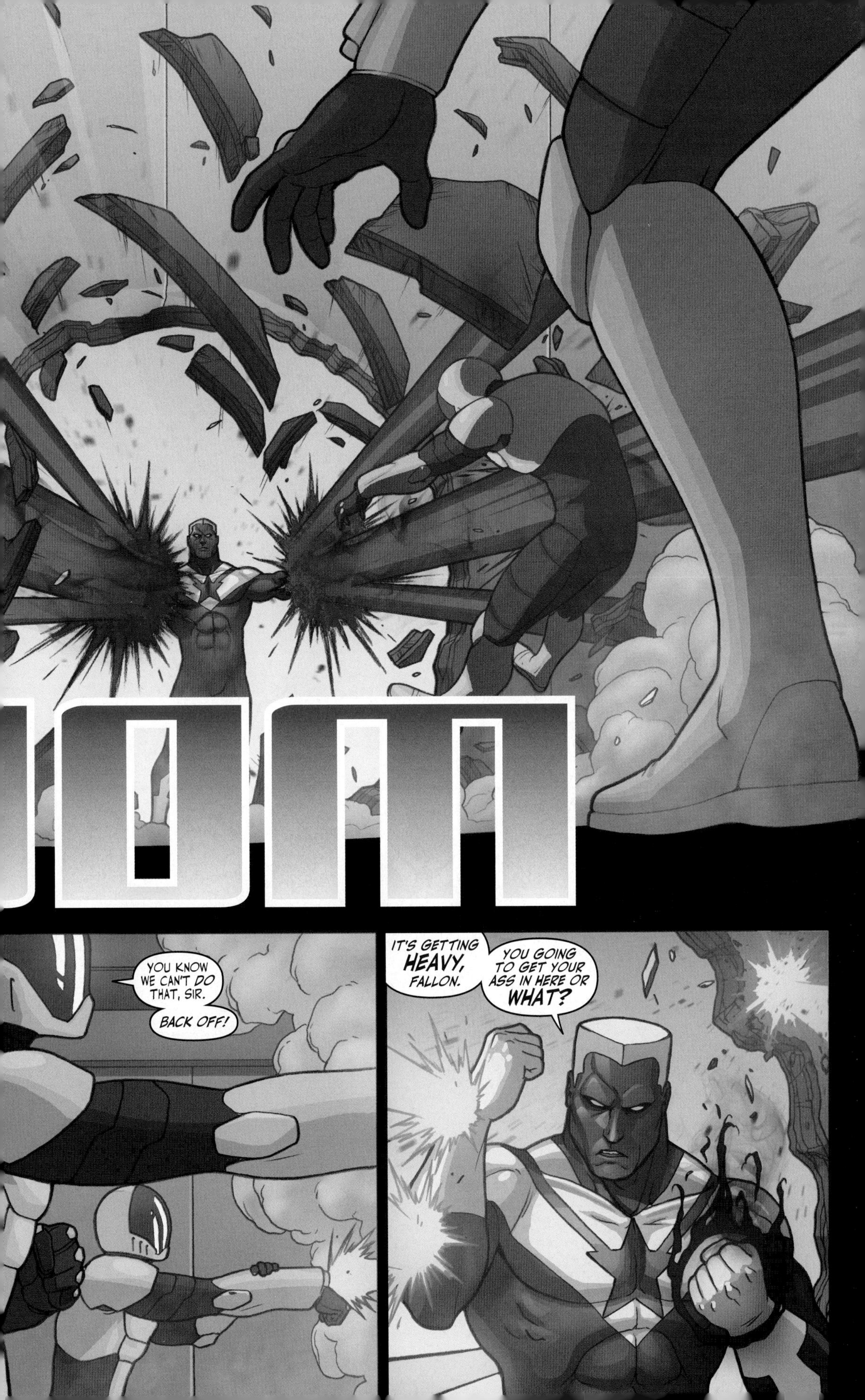
YOU KNOW WE CAN'T DO THAT, SIR.
BACK OFF!
IT'S GETTING HEAVY, FALLON.
YOU GOING TO GET YOUR ASS IN HERE OR WHAT?

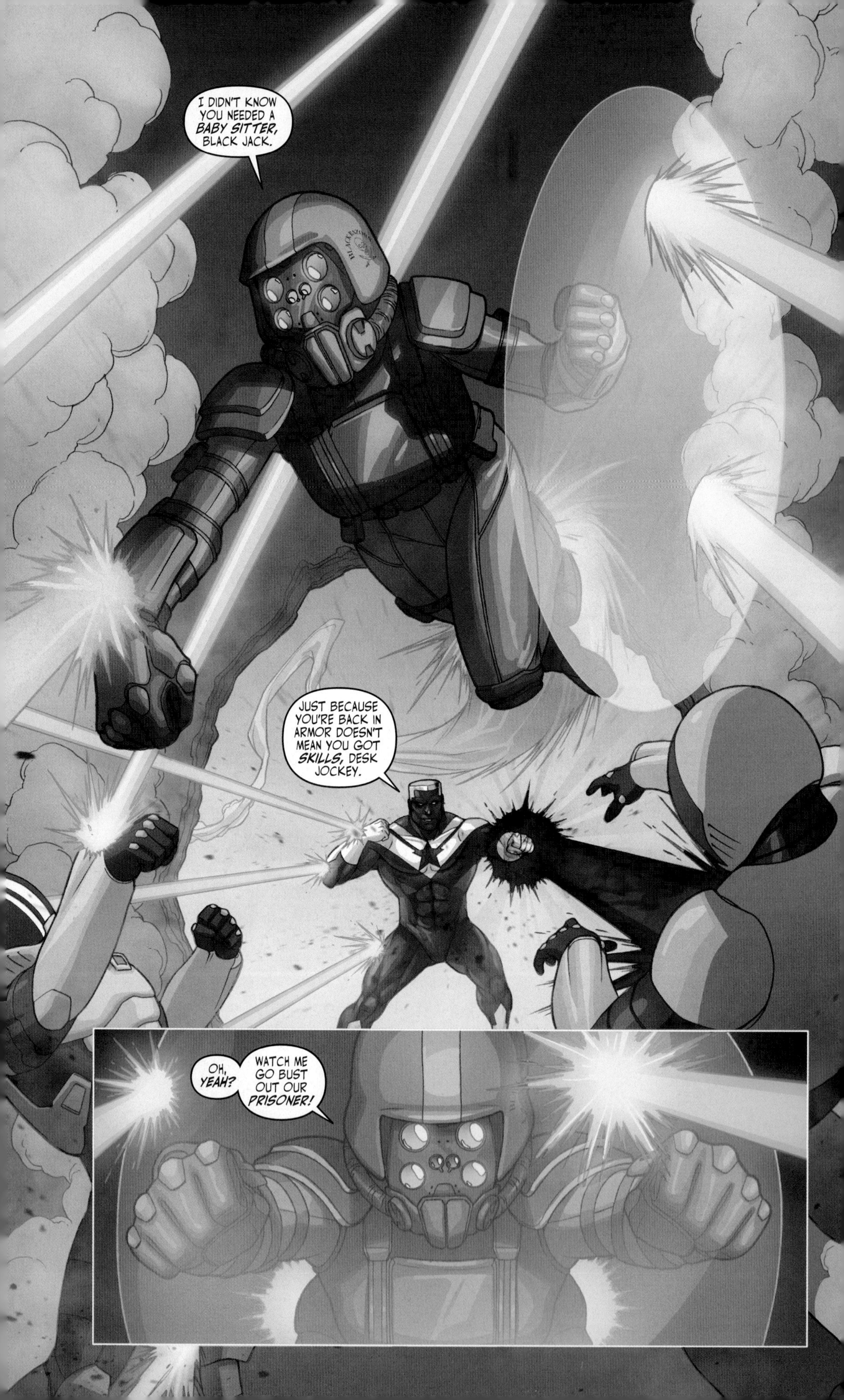
I DIDN'T KNOW YOU NEEDED A *BABY SITTER,* BLACK JACK.
JUST BECAUSE YOU'RE BACK IN ARMOR DOESN'T MEAN YOU GOT *SKILLS,* DESK JOCKEY.
OH, *YEAH?*
WATCH ME GO BUST OUT OUR *PRISONER!*

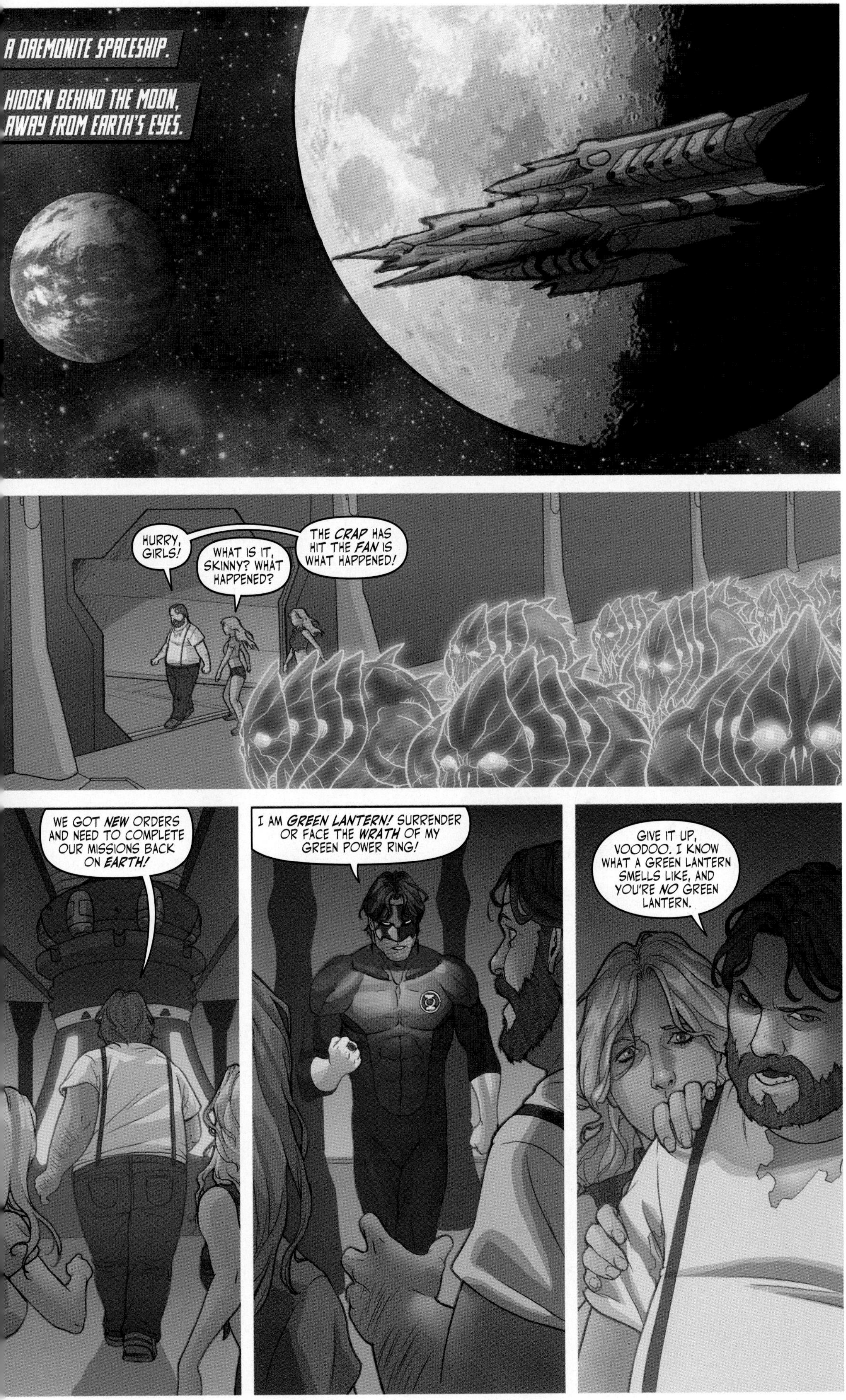
A DAEMONITE SPACESHIP.
HIDDEN BEHIND THE MOON, AWAY FROM EARTH'S EYES.
HURRY, GIRLS!
WHAT IS IT, SKINNY? WHAT HAPPENED?
THE CRAP HAS HIT THE FAN IS WHAT HAPPENED!
WE GOT NEW ORDERS AND NEED TO COMPLETE OUR MISSIONS BACK ON EARTH!
I AM GREEN LANTERN! SURRENDER OR FACE THE WRATH OF MY GREEN POWER RING!
GIVE IT UP, VOODOO. I KNOW WHAT A GREEN LANTERN SMELLS LIKE, AND YOU'RE NO GREEN LANTERN.

FINE.

WHAT ARE *YOU* DOING HERE? THE BOYS *UPSTAIRS* HAVE BEEN LOOKING FOR YOU.

YOU HEAR WHAT WENT DOWN YET?

HIS MIND TELLS ME *ALL* I NEED TO KNOW.

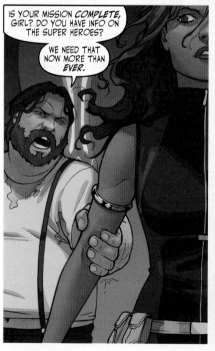

IS YOUR MISSION *COMPLETE*, GIRL? DO YOU HAVE INFO ON THE SUPER HEROES?

WE NEED THAT NOW MORE THAN *EVER*.

I REQUESTED AN AUDIENCE WITH THE *WAR COUNCIL*.

OH, THAT'S *RICH*. I KNEW YOU WOULD *FAIL*.

YOU *DUMMY!* YOU CAN'T GO RUNNING TO THE WAR COUNCIL THINKING THEY WILL *SAVE* YOU. THEY'RE STILL GONNA *PUNISH* YOU!

HA HA HA HA HA HA

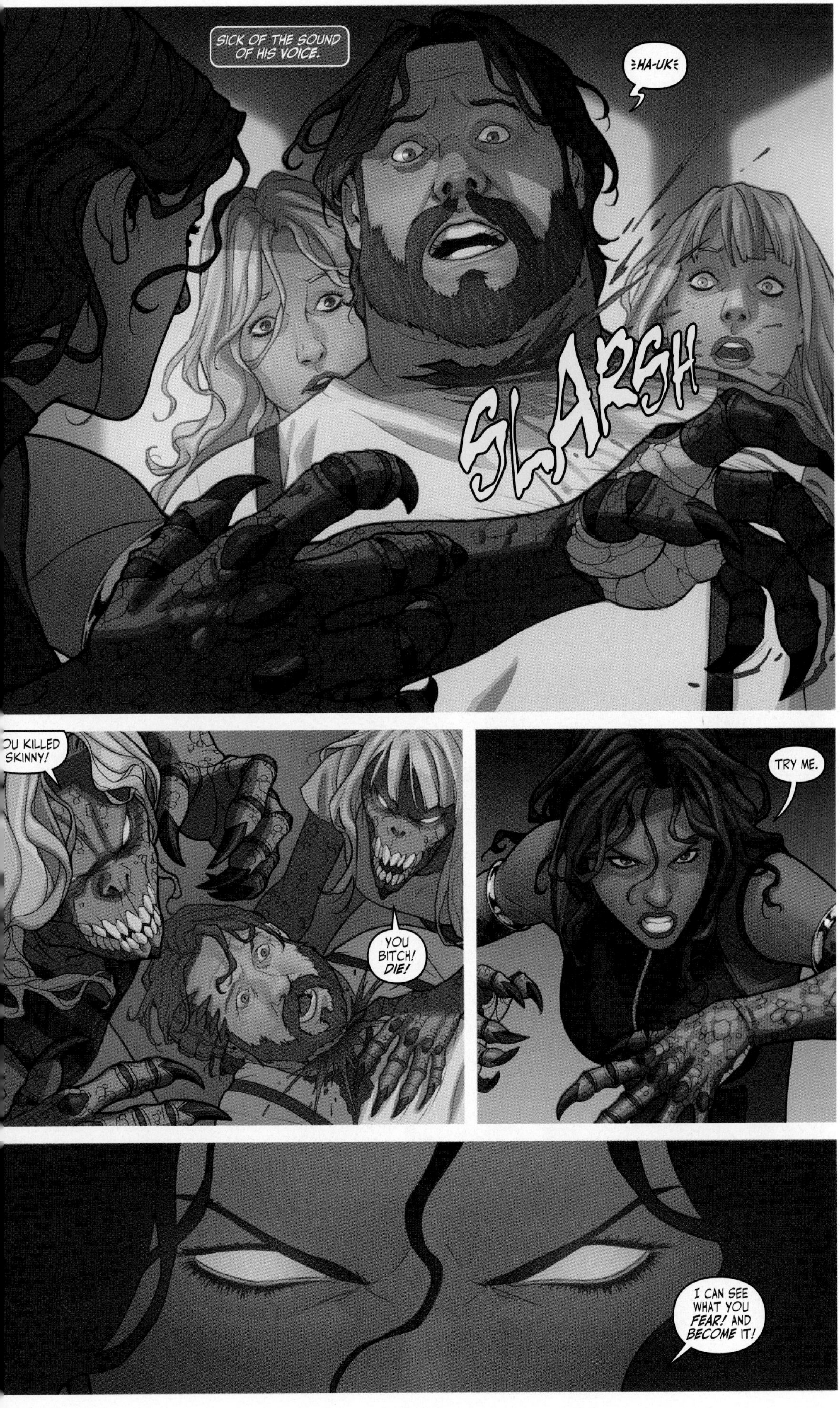
SICK OF THE SOUND OF HIS VOICE.
HA-UK
SLARSH
OU KILLED SKINNY!
YOU BITCH! DIE!
TRY ME.
I CAN SEE WHAT YOU FEAR! AND BECOME IT!

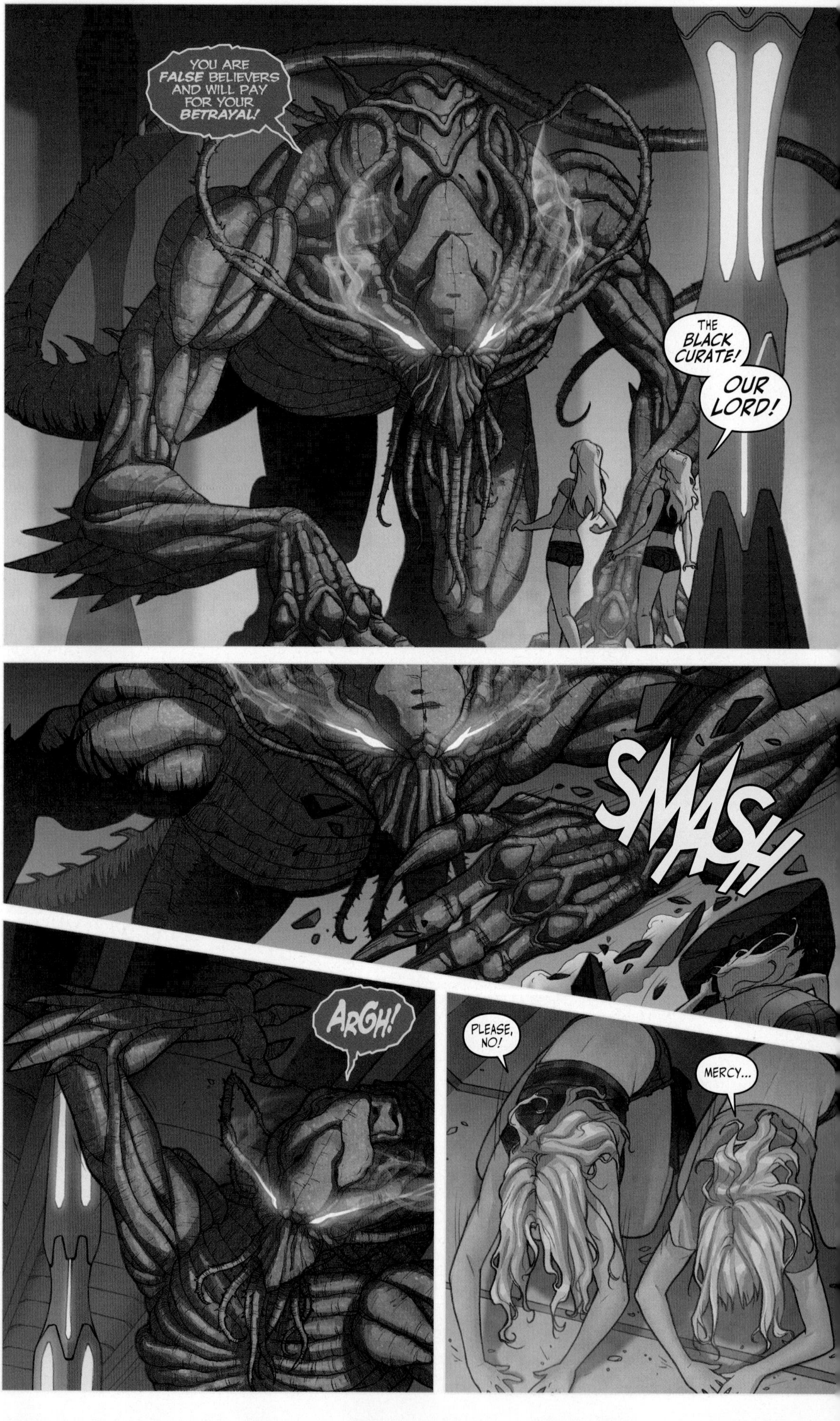
YOU ARE FALSE BELIEVERS AND WILL PAY FOR YOUR BETRAYAL!
THE BLACK CURATE!
OUR LORD!
SMASH
ARGH!
PLEASE, NO!
MERCY...

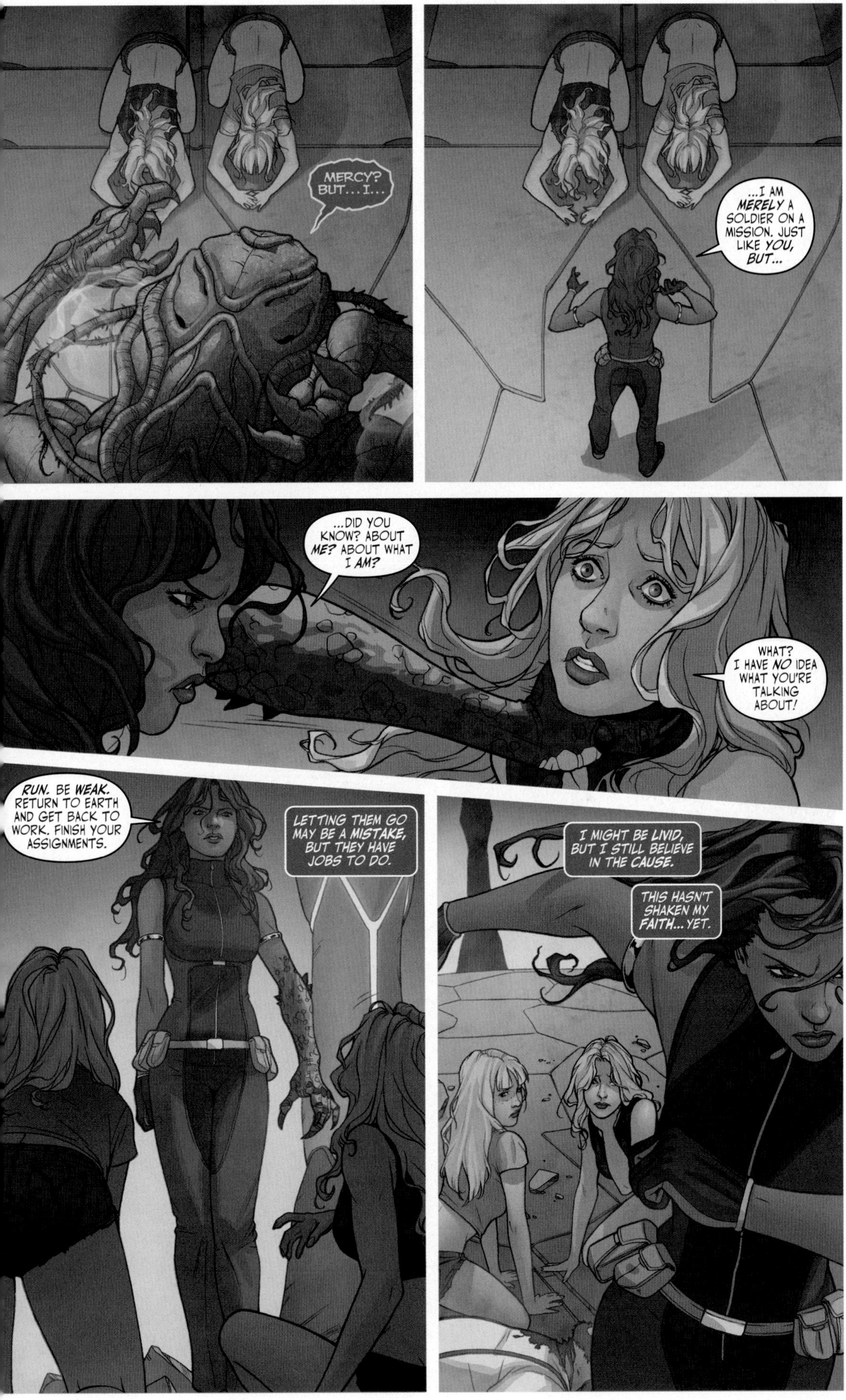
MERCY? BUT... I...
...I AM *MERELY* A SOLDIER ON A MISSION. JUST LIKE *YOU*, *BUT...*
...DID YOU KNOW? ABOUT *ME?* ABOUT WHAT *I AM?*
WHAT? I HAVE *NO* IDEA WHAT YOU'RE TALKING ABOUT!
RUN. BE *WEAK.* RETURN TO EARTH AND GET BACK TO WORK. FINISH YOUR ASSIGNMENTS.
LETTING THEM GO MAY BE A *MISTAKE*, BUT THEY HAVE JOBS TO DO.
I MIGHT BE *LIVID*, BUT I STILL BELIEVE IN THE *CAUSE*.
THIS HASN'T SHAKEN MY *FAITH*... YET.

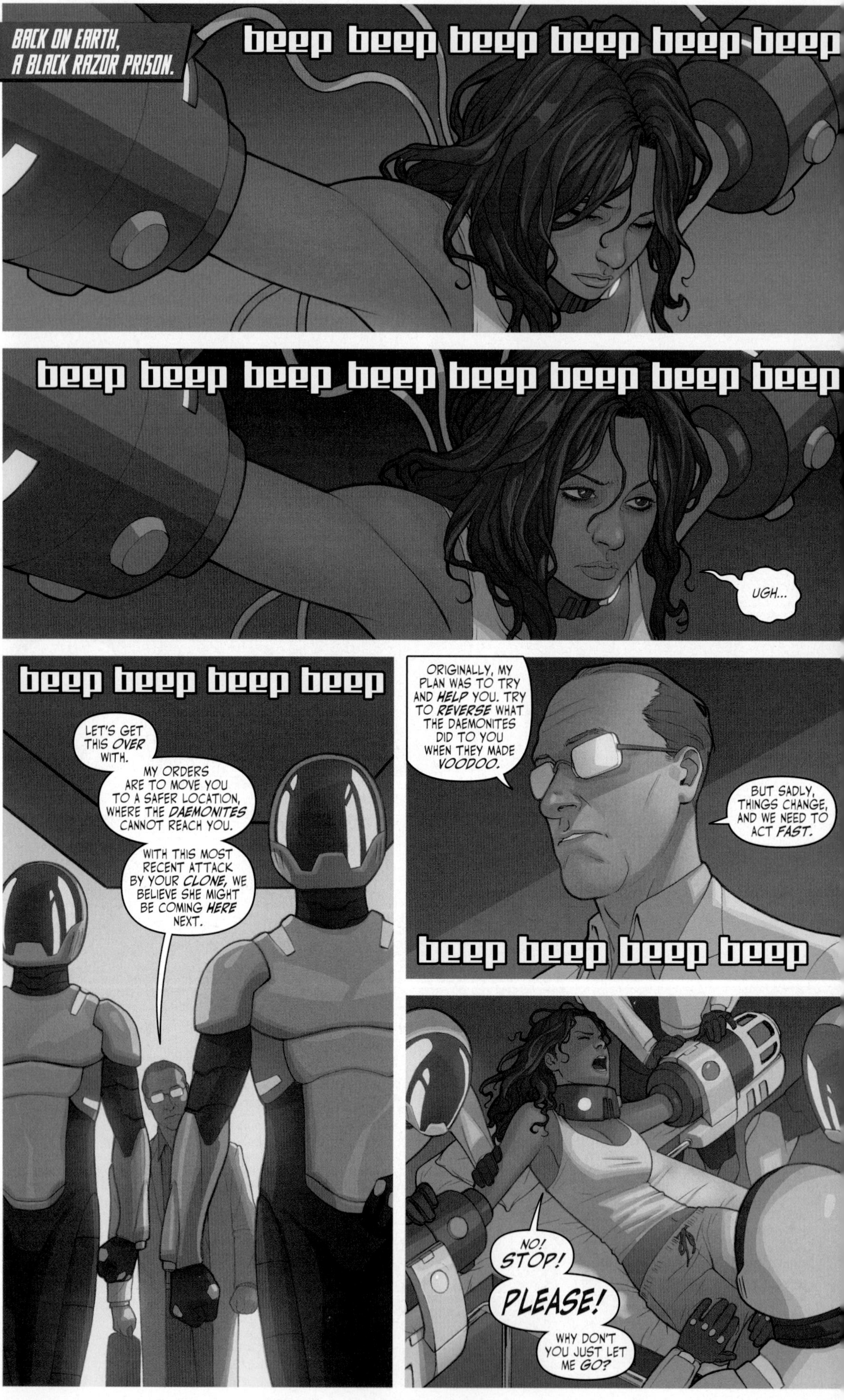
BACK ON EARTH, A BLACK RAZOR PRISON.
beep beep beep beep beep beep
beep beep beep beep beep beep beep beep
UGH...
beep beep beep beep
LET'S GET THIS OVER WITH.
MY ORDERS ARE TO MOVE YOU TO A SAFER LOCATION, WHERE THE DAEMONITES CANNOT REACH YOU.
WITH THIS MOST RECENT ATTACK BY YOUR CLONE, WE BELIEVE SHE MIGHT BE COMING HERE NEXT.
ORIGINALLY, MY PLAN WAS TO TRY AND HELP YOU. TRY TO REVERSE WHAT THE DAEMONITES DID TO YOU WHEN THEY MADE VOODOO.
BUT SADLY, THINGS CHANGE, AND WE NEED TO ACT FAST.
beep beep beep beep
NO! STOP!
PLEASE!
WHY DON'T YOU JUST LET ME GO?

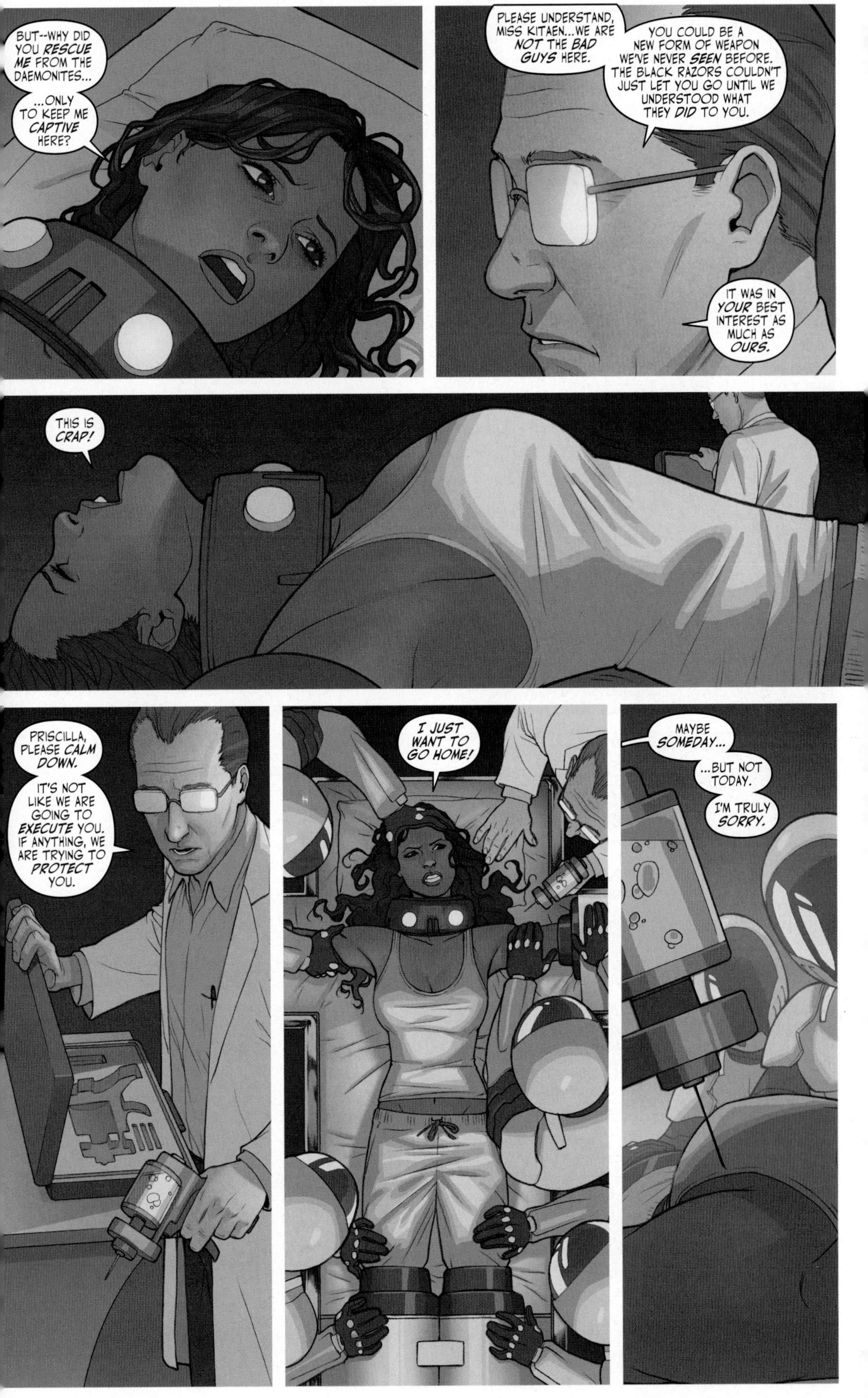
BUT--WHY DID YOU RESCUE ME FROM THE DAEMONITES...
...ONLY TO KEEP ME CAPTIVE HERE?
PLEASE UNDERSTAND, MISS KITAEN...WE ARE NOT THE BAD GUYS HERE.
YOU COULD BE A NEW FORM OF WEAPON WE'VE NEVER SEEN BEFORE. THE BLACK RAZORS COULDN'T JUST LET YOU GO UNTIL WE UNDERSTOOD WHAT THEY DID TO YOU.
IT WAS IN YOUR BEST INTEREST AS MUCH AS OURS.
THIS IS CRAP!
PRISCILLA, PLEASE CALM DOWN.
IT'S NOT LIKE WE ARE GOING TO EXECUTE YOU. IF ANYTHING, WE ARE TRYING TO PROTECT YOU.
I JUST WANT TO GO HOME!
MAYBE SOMEDAY...
...BUT NOT TODAY.
I'M TRULY SORRY.

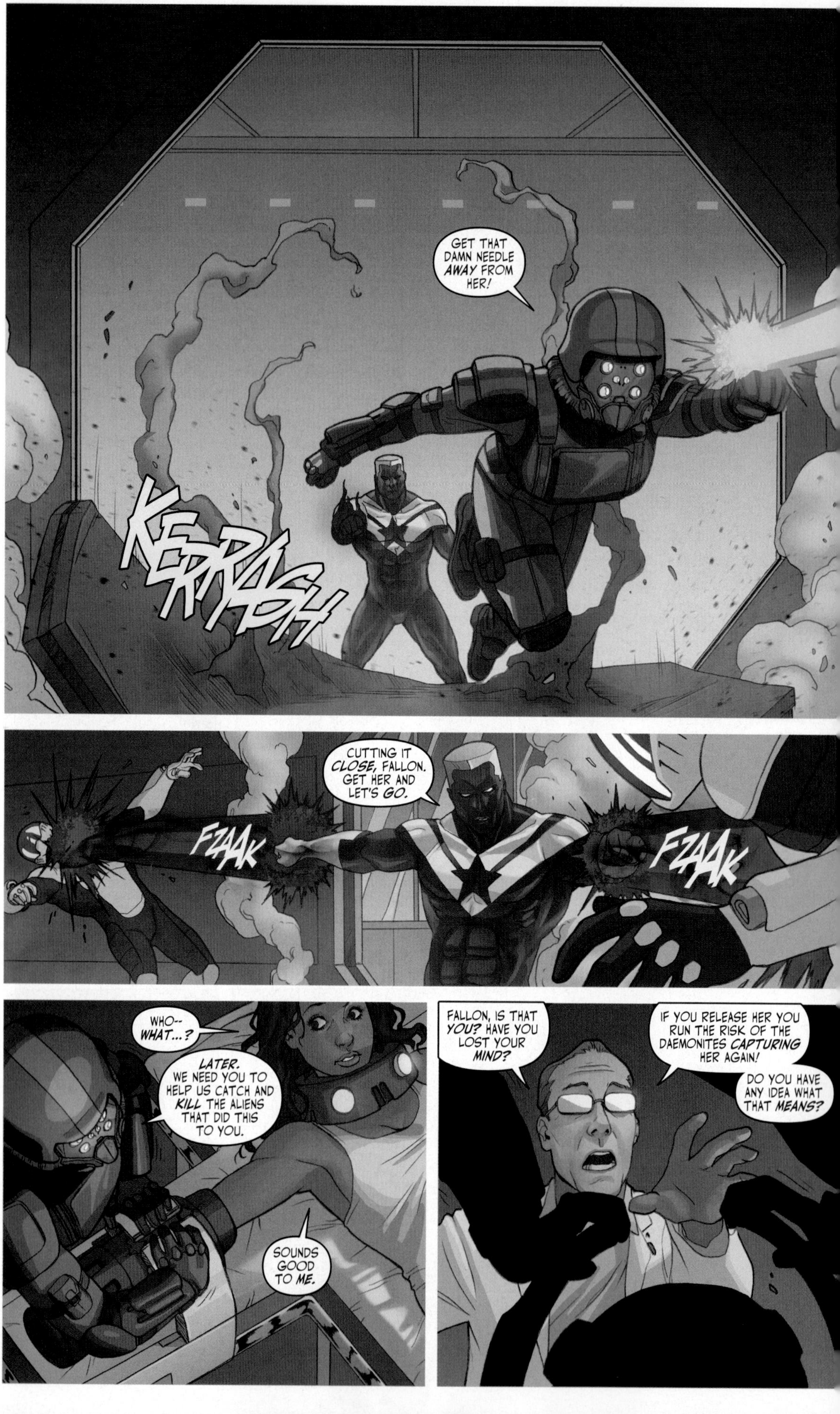
GET THAT DAMN NEEDLE AWAY FROM HER!
KERRASH
CUTTING IT CLOSE, FALLON. GET HER AND LET'S GO.
FZAAK
FZAAK
WHO-- WHAT...?
LATER. WE NEED YOU TO HELP US CATCH AND KILL THE ALIENS THAT DID THIS TO YOU.
SOUNDS GOOD TO ME.
FALLON, IS THAT YOU? HAVE YOU LOST YOUR MIND?
IF YOU RELEASE HER YOU RUN THE RISK OF THE DAEMONITES CAPTURING HER AGAIN!
DO YOU HAVE ANY IDEA WHAT THAT MEANS?

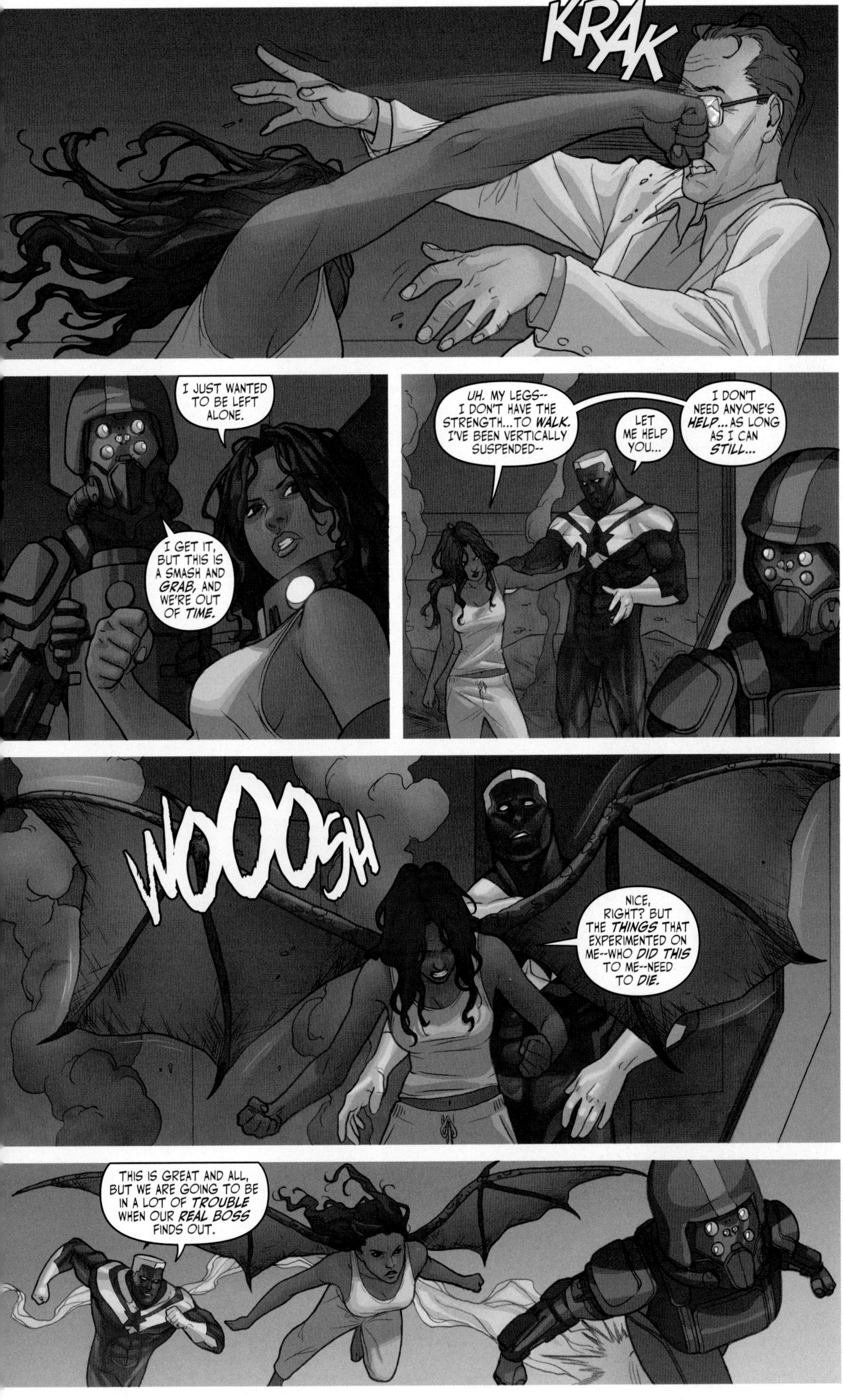
KRAK
I JUST WANTED TO BE LEFT ALONE.
I GET IT, BUT THIS IS A SMASH AND GRAB, AND WE'RE OUT OF TIME.
UH. MY LEGS-- I DON'T HAVE THE STRENGTH...TO WALK. I'VE BEEN VERTICALLY SUSPENDED--
LET ME HELP YOU...
I DON'T NEED ANYONE'S HELP... AS LONG AS I CAN STILL...
WOOOSH
NICE, RIGHT? BUT THE THINGS THAT EXPERIMENTED ON ME--WHO DID THIS TO ME--NEED TO DIE.
THIS IS GREAT AND ALL, BUT WE ARE GOING TO BE IN A LOT OF TROUBLE WHEN OUR REAL BOSS FINDS OUT.

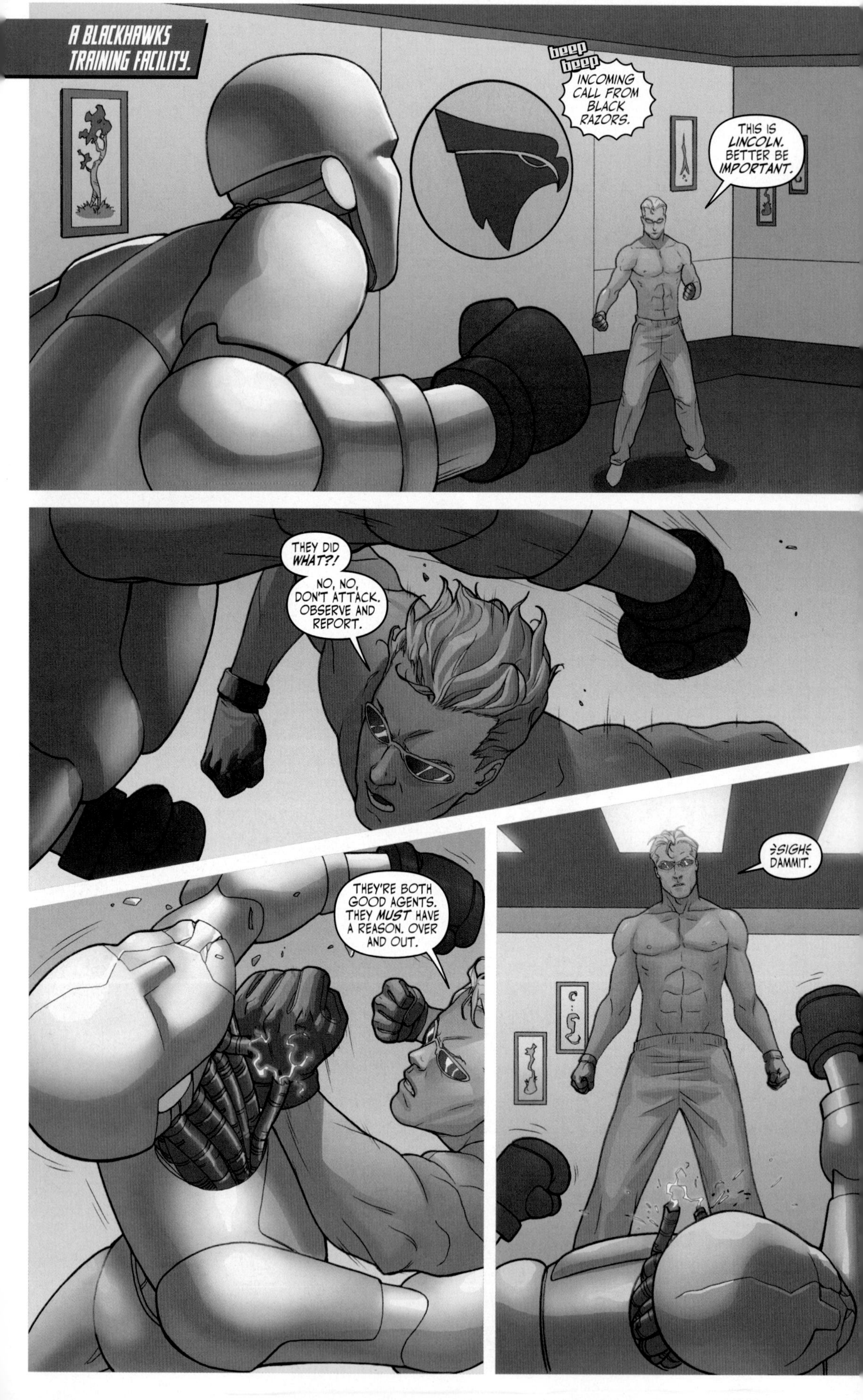
A BLACKHAWKS TRAINING FACILITY.
beep beep
INCOMING CALL FROM BLACK RAZORS.
THIS IS LINCOLN. BETTER BE IMPORTANT.
THEY DID WHAT?!
NO, NO, DON'T ATTACK. OBSERVE AND REPORT.
THEY'RE BOTH GOOD AGENTS. THEY MUST HAVE A REASON. OVER AND OUT.
SIGH
DAMMIT.

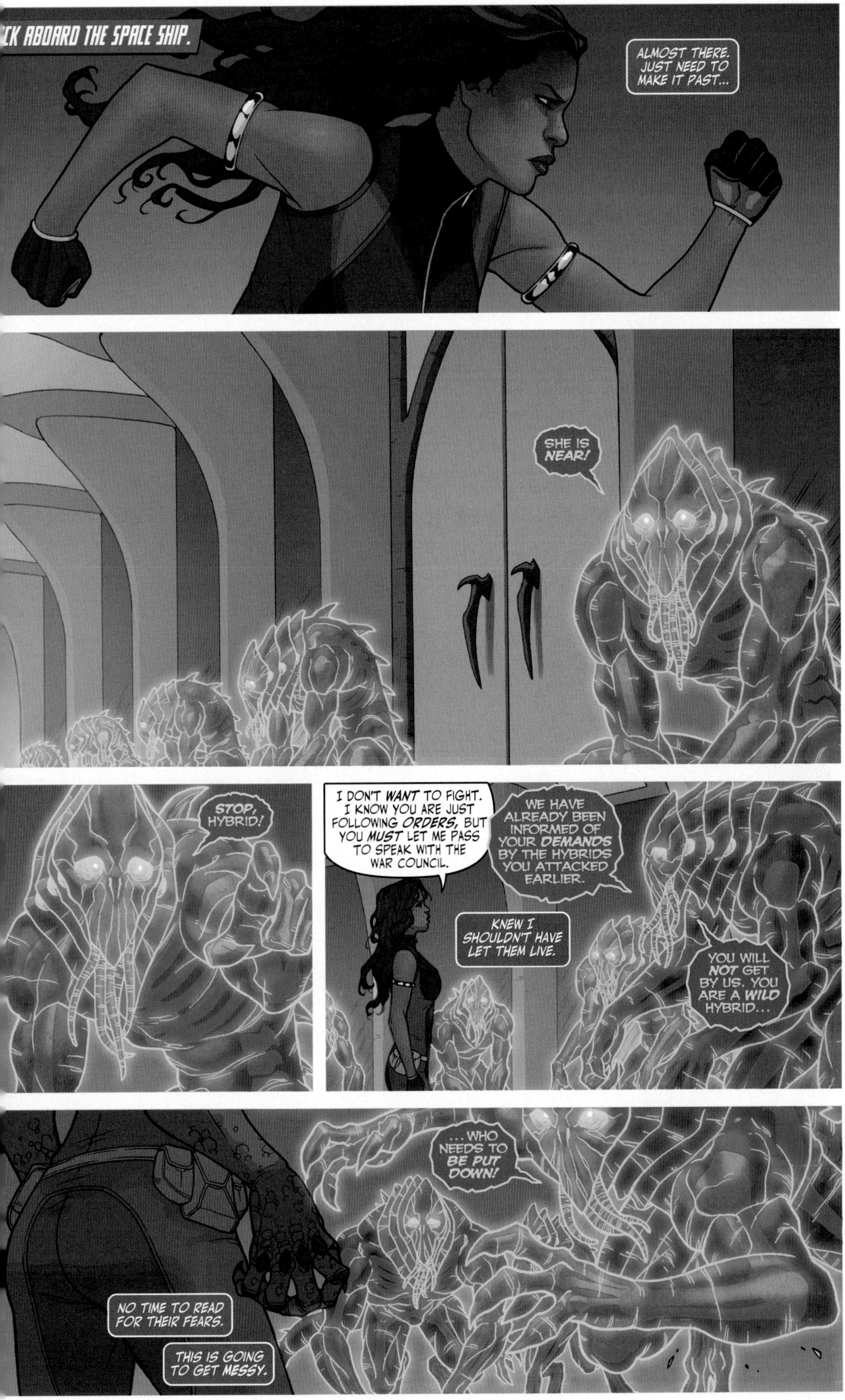
CK ABOARD THE SPACE SHIP.
ALMOST THERE. JUST NEED TO MAKE IT PAST...
SHE IS NEAR!
STOP, HYBRID!
I DON'T WANT TO FIGHT. I KNOW YOU ARE JUST FOLLOWING ORDERS, BUT YOU MUST LET ME PASS TO SPEAK WITH THE WAR COUNCIL.
WE HAVE ALREADY BEEN INFORMED OF YOUR DEMANDS BY THE HYBRIDS YOU ATTACKED EARLIER.
KNEW I SHOULDN'T HAVE LET THEM LIVE.
YOU WILL NOT GET BY US. YOU ARE A WILD HYBRID...
...WHO NEEDS TO BE PUT DOWN!
NO TIME TO READ FOR THEIR FEARS.
THIS IS GOING TO GET MESSY.

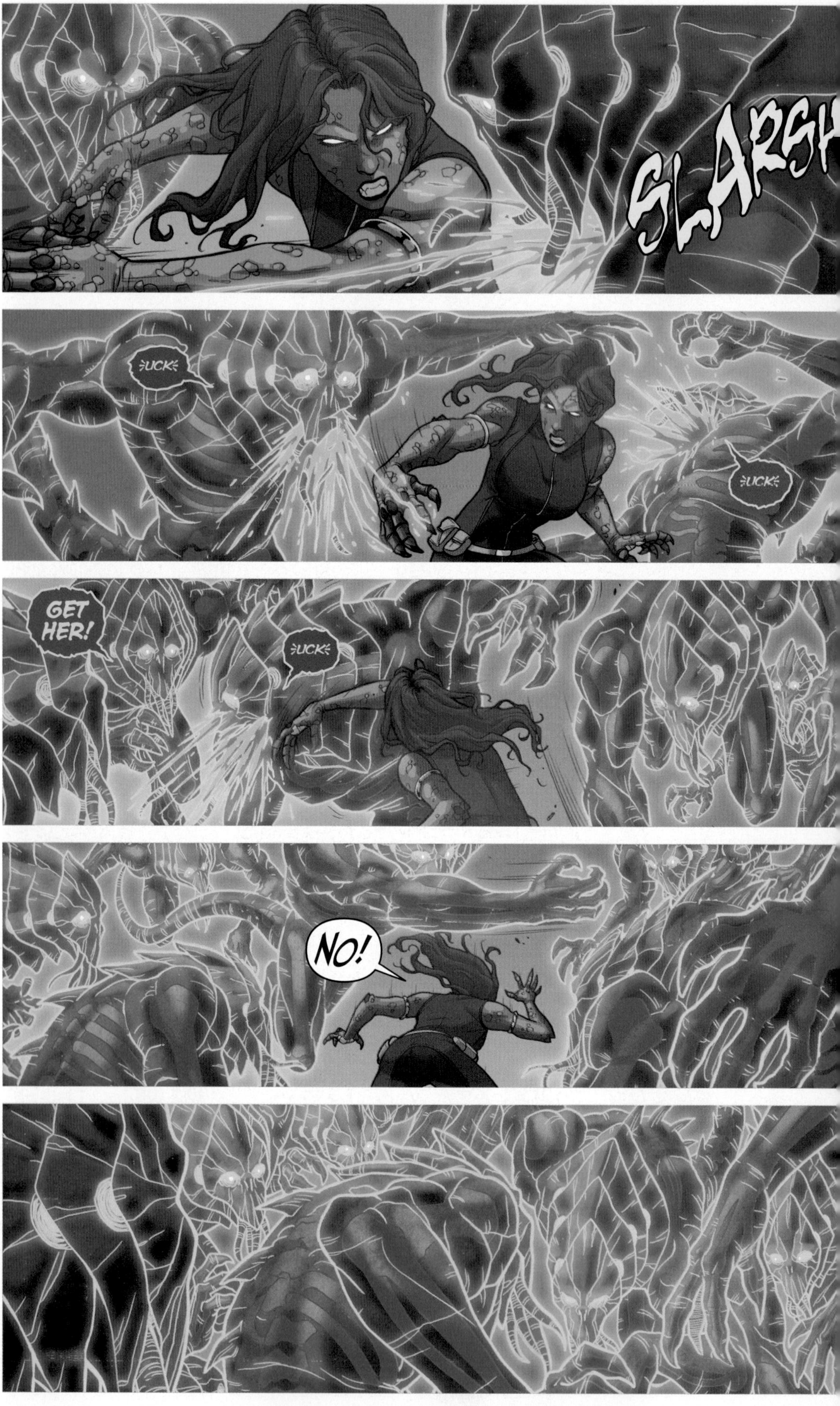
SLARSH
UCK
UCK
GET HER!
UCK
NO!

WITH THE *DESTRUCTION* OF *CARVER'S* SHIP... ...OUR PLANS ARE IN *DANGER,* MY LORDS.

AND WITH THE *FALLEN* ONE FREE FROM THE *STORMWATCH'S* IMPRISONMENT... ...WE CAN NO LONGER *AFFORD* TO KEEP HIDING IN THE SHADOWS, FOR THE HUMANS *HAVE* TO KNOW THAT SOMETHING IS COMING.

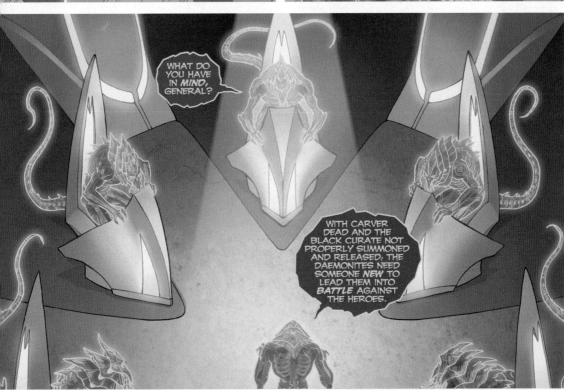

WHAT DO YOU HAVE IN *MIND,* GENERAL?

WITH CARVER DEAD AND THE BLACK CURATE NOT PROPERLY SUMMONED AND RELEASED, THE DAEMONITES NEED SOMEONE *NEW* TO LEAD THEM INTO *BATTLE* AGAINST THE HEROES.

OBVIOUSLY MY *FIRST* SUGGESTION WOULD BE SOMEONE SUCH AS *MYS--*

SMACK

UG!

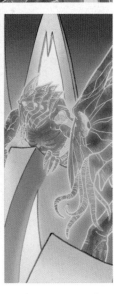

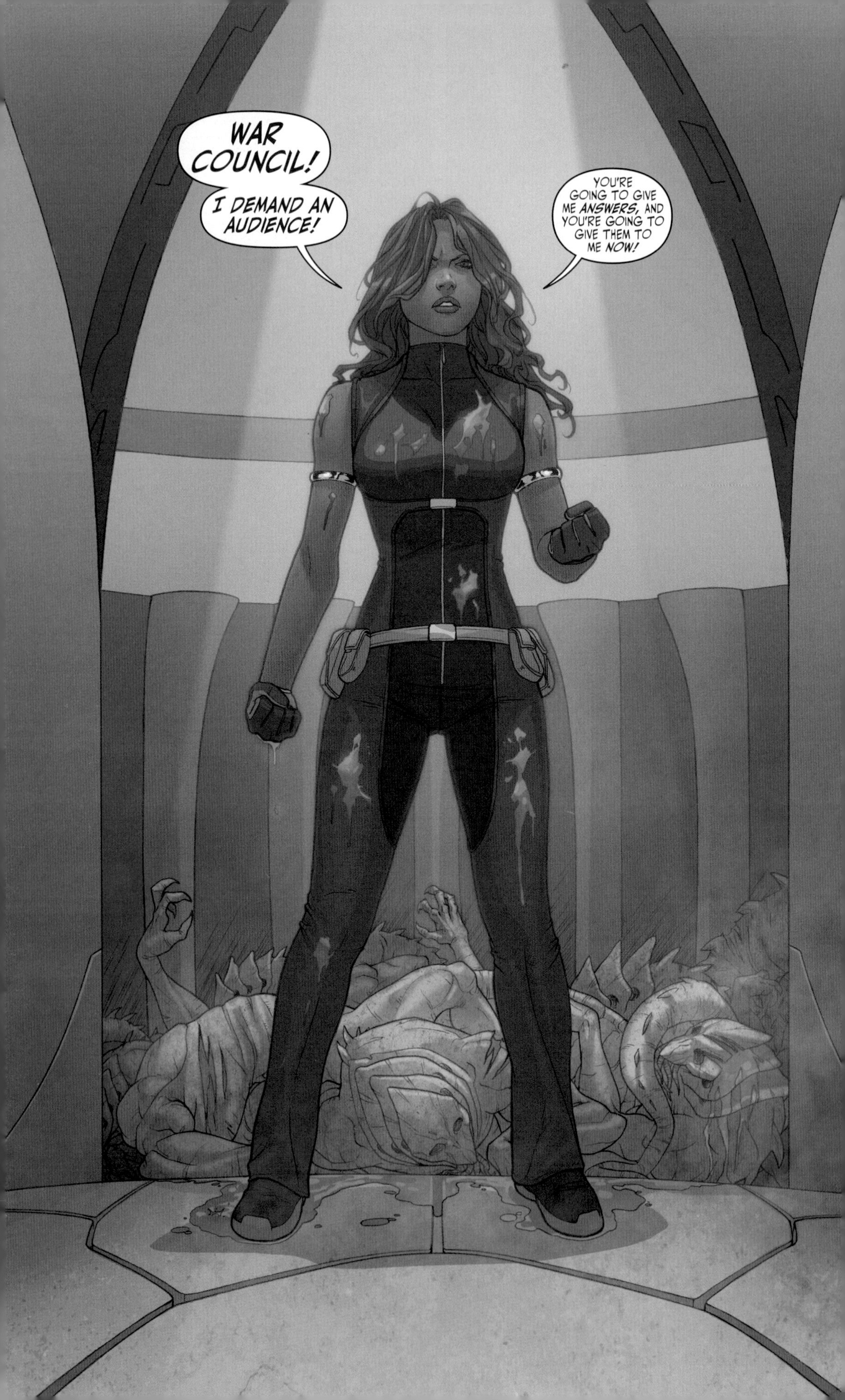
WAR COUNCIL!
I DEMAND AN AUDIENCE!
YOU'RE GOING TO GIVE ME ANSWERS, AND YOU'RE GOING TO GIVE THEM TO ME NOW!

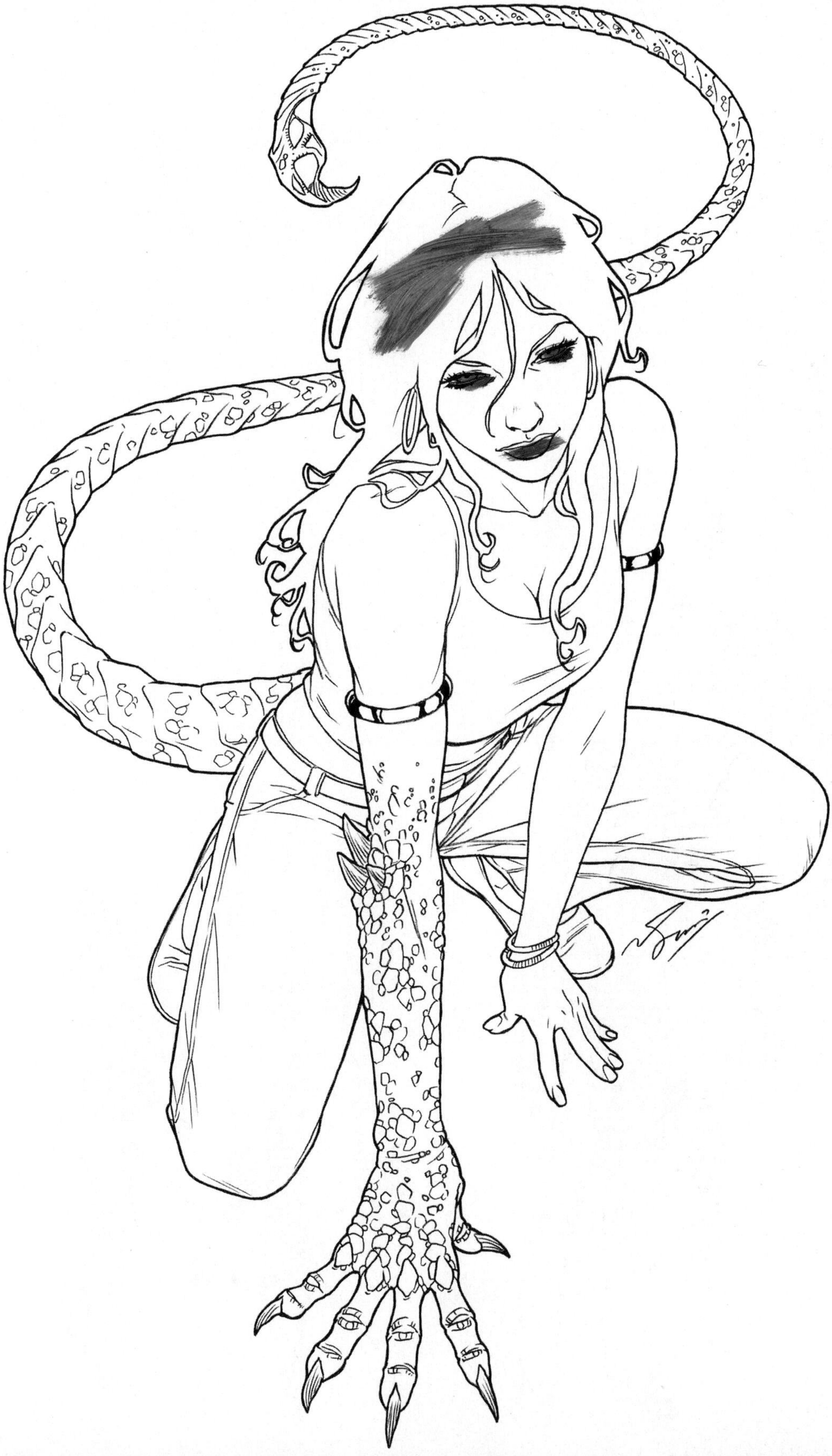

VOODOO

CHARACTER SKETCHES BY SAMI BASRI

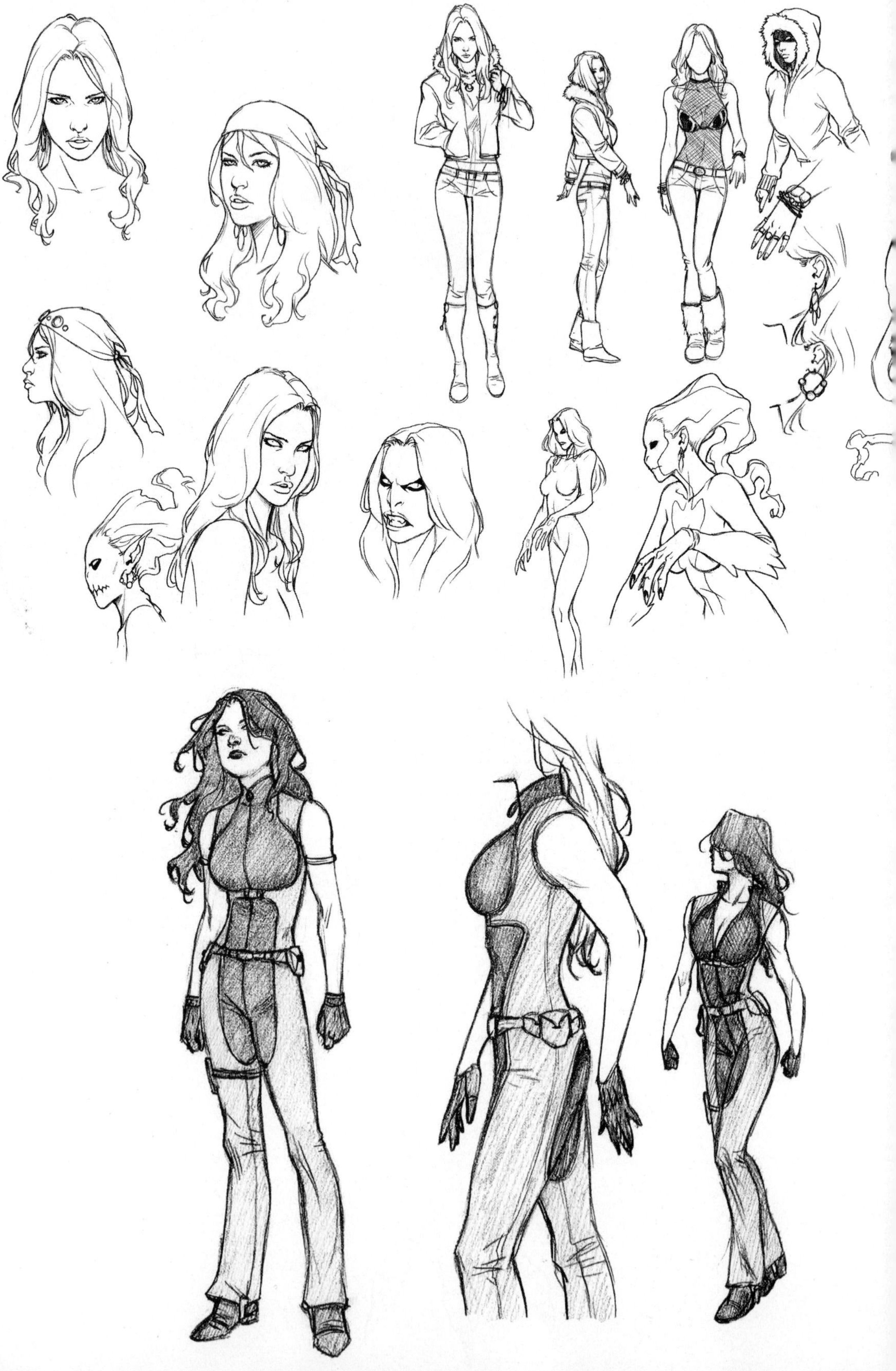

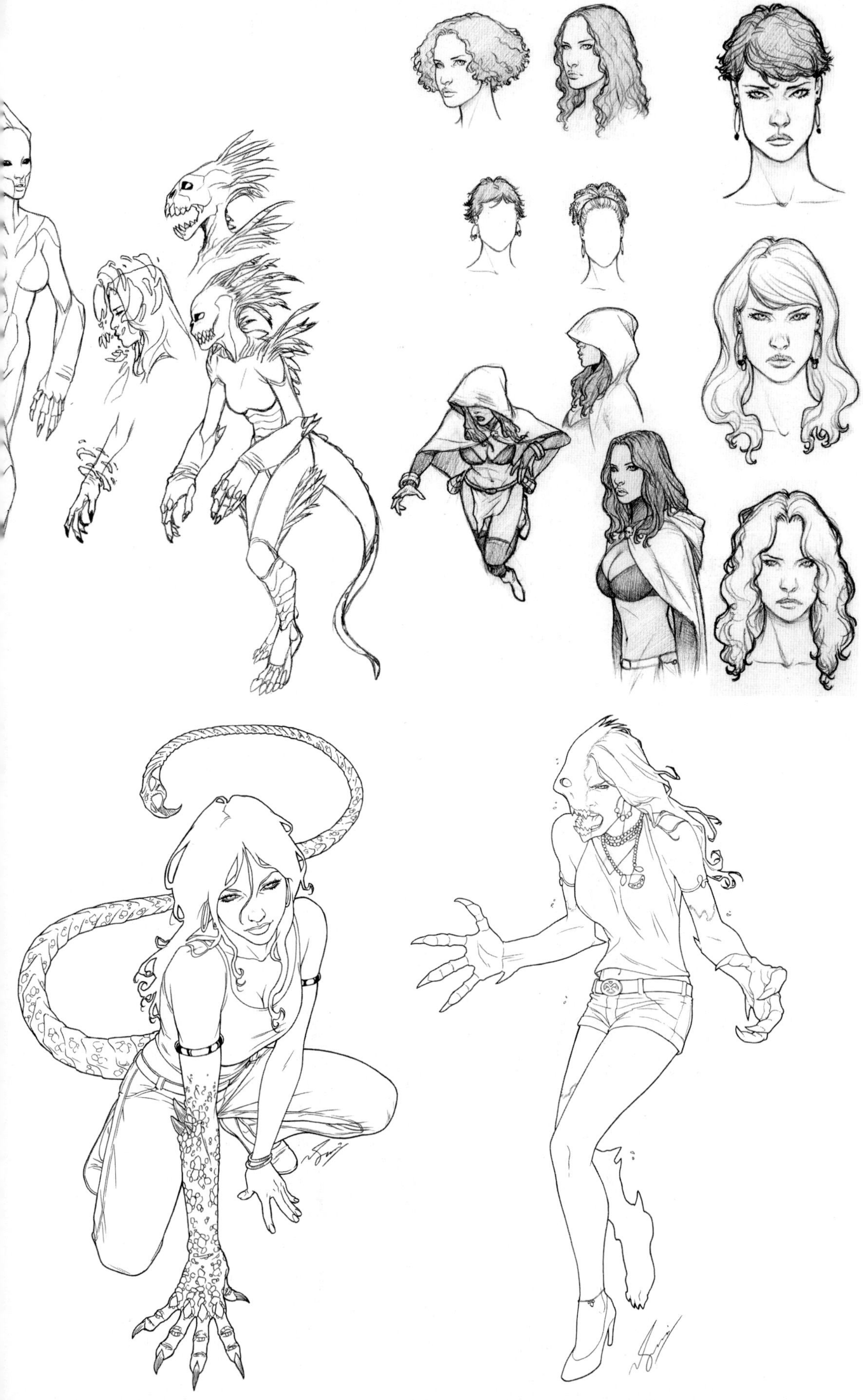

VOODOO

BLACK RAZOR CHARACTER SKETCHES BY SAMI BASRI

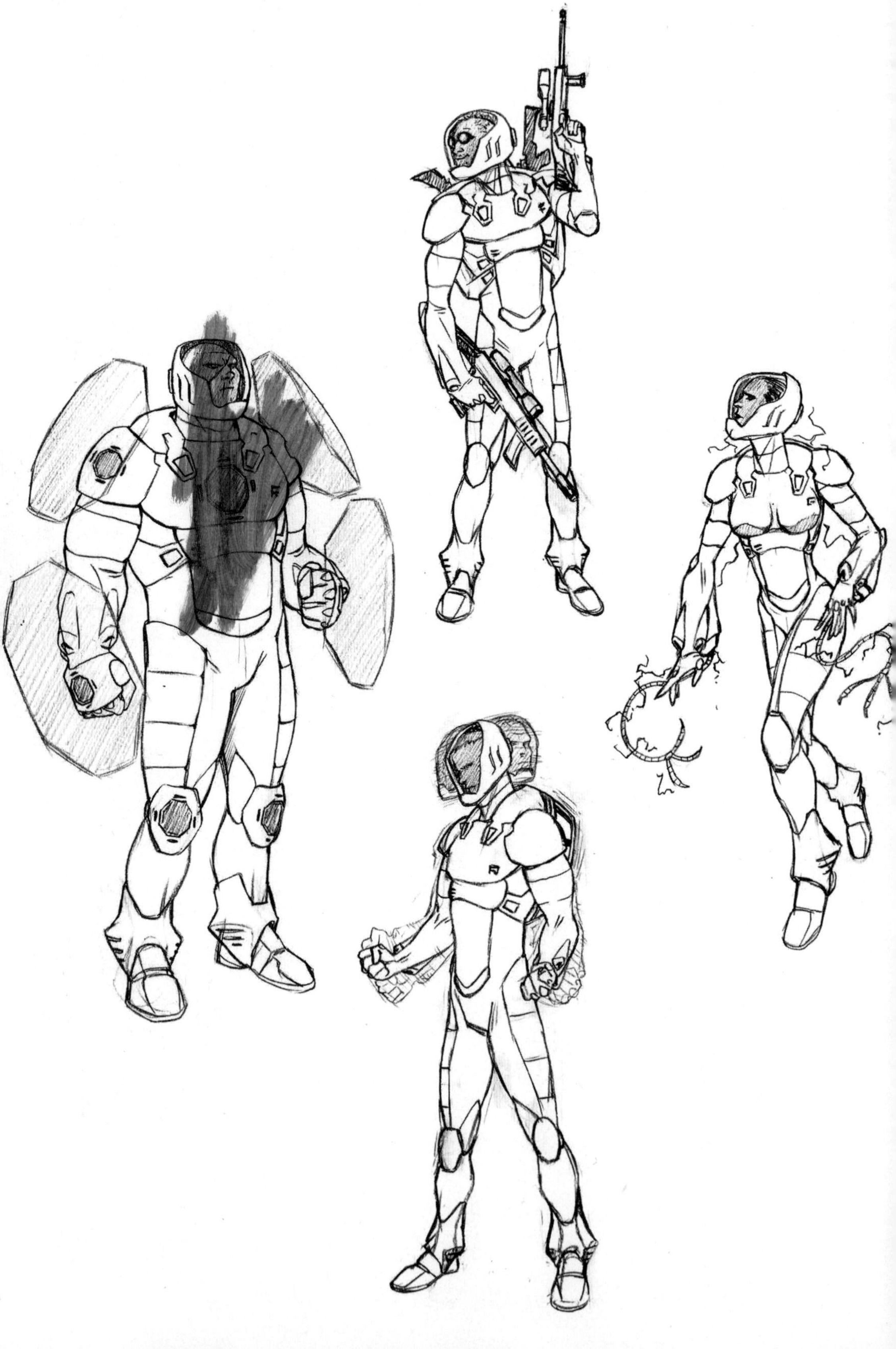

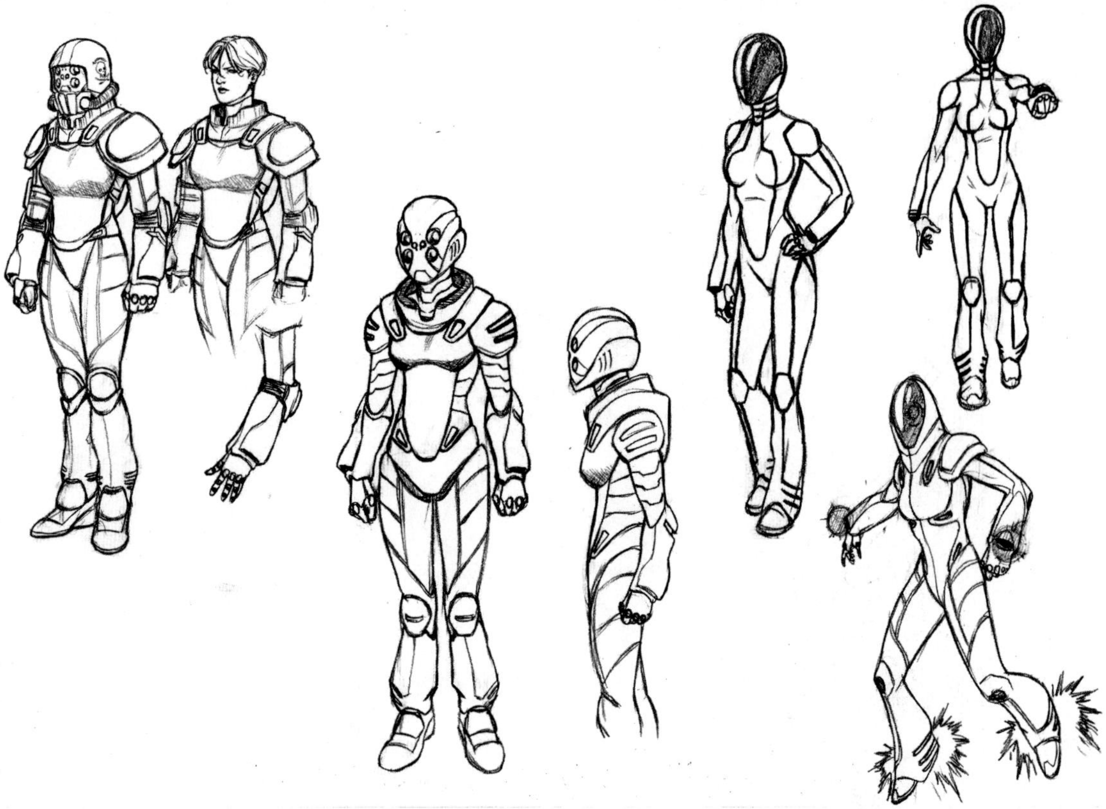

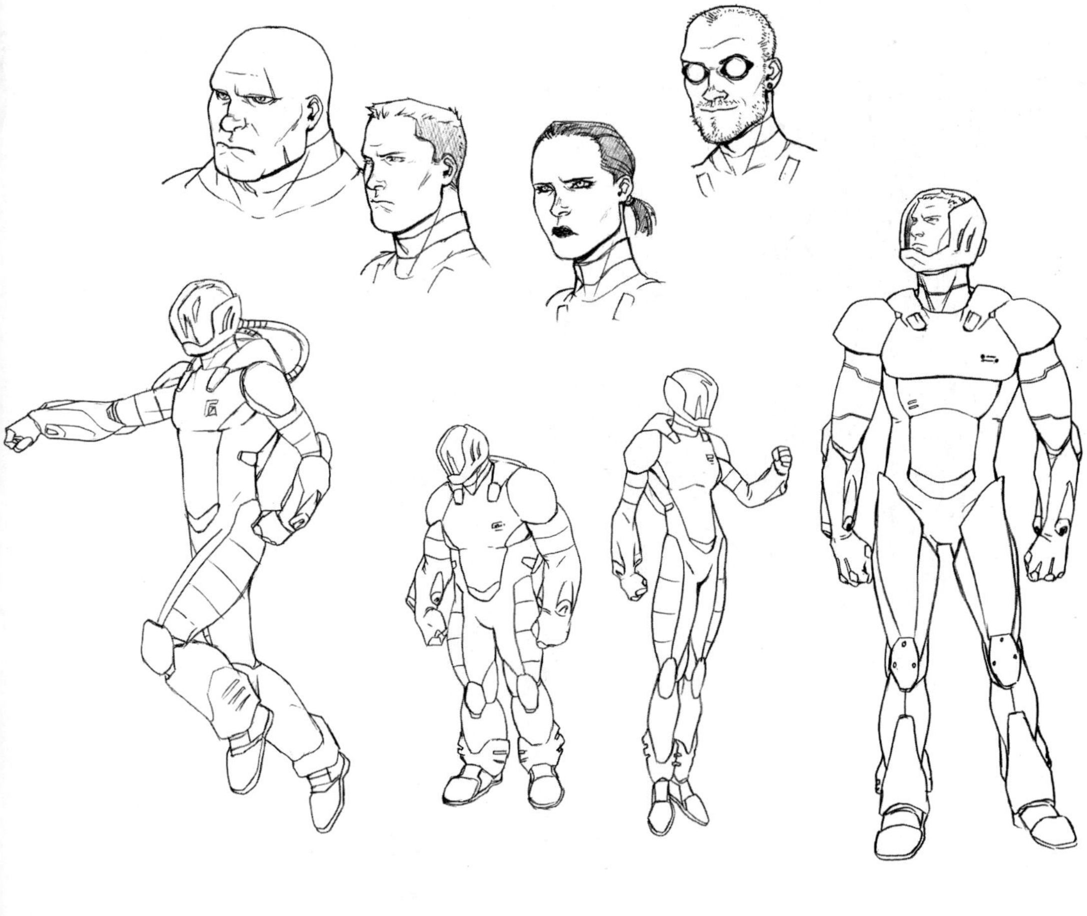

VOODOO

INITIAL COVER SKETCH BY SAMI BASRI

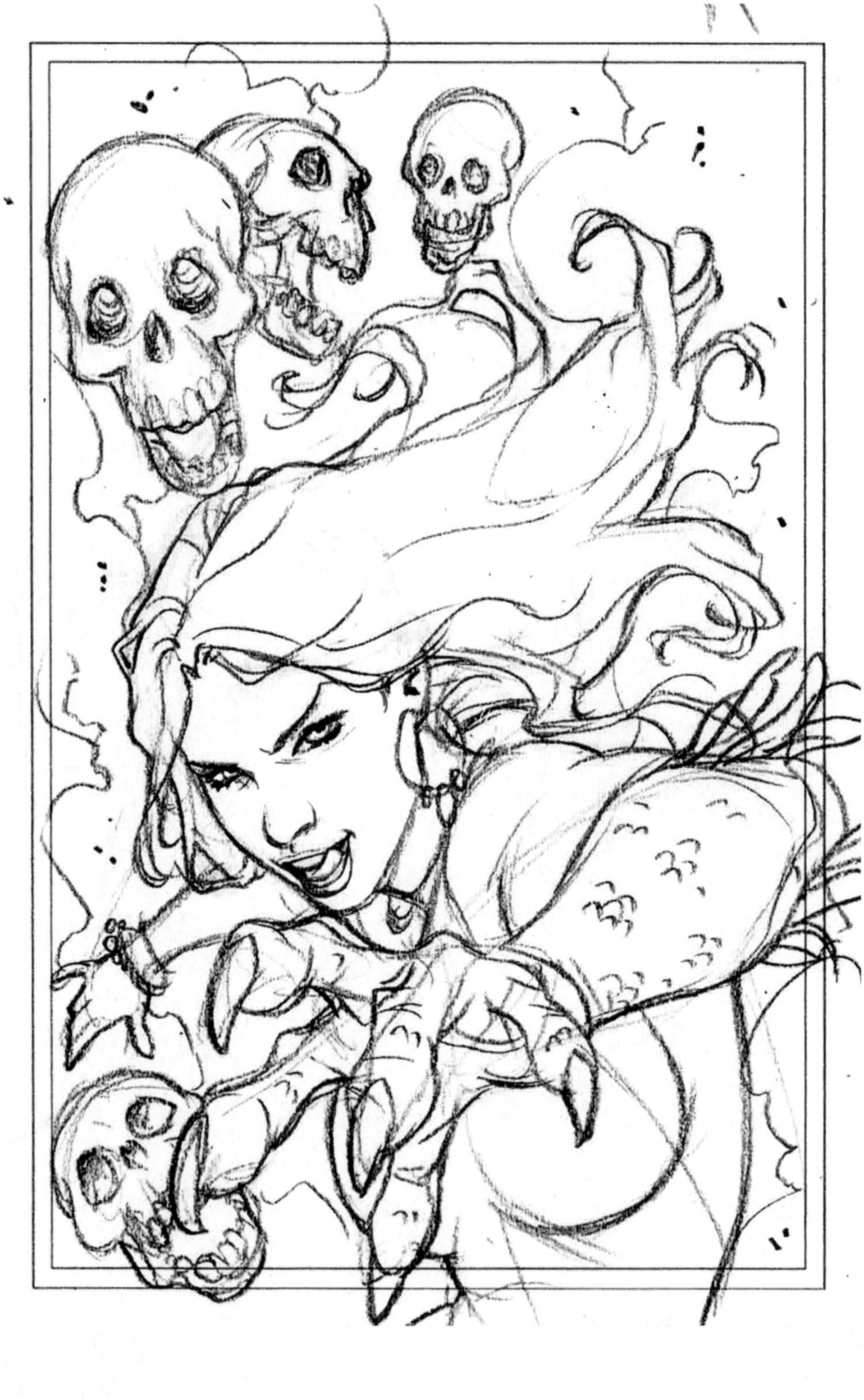

VOODOO

UNUSED COVER BY SAMI BASRI

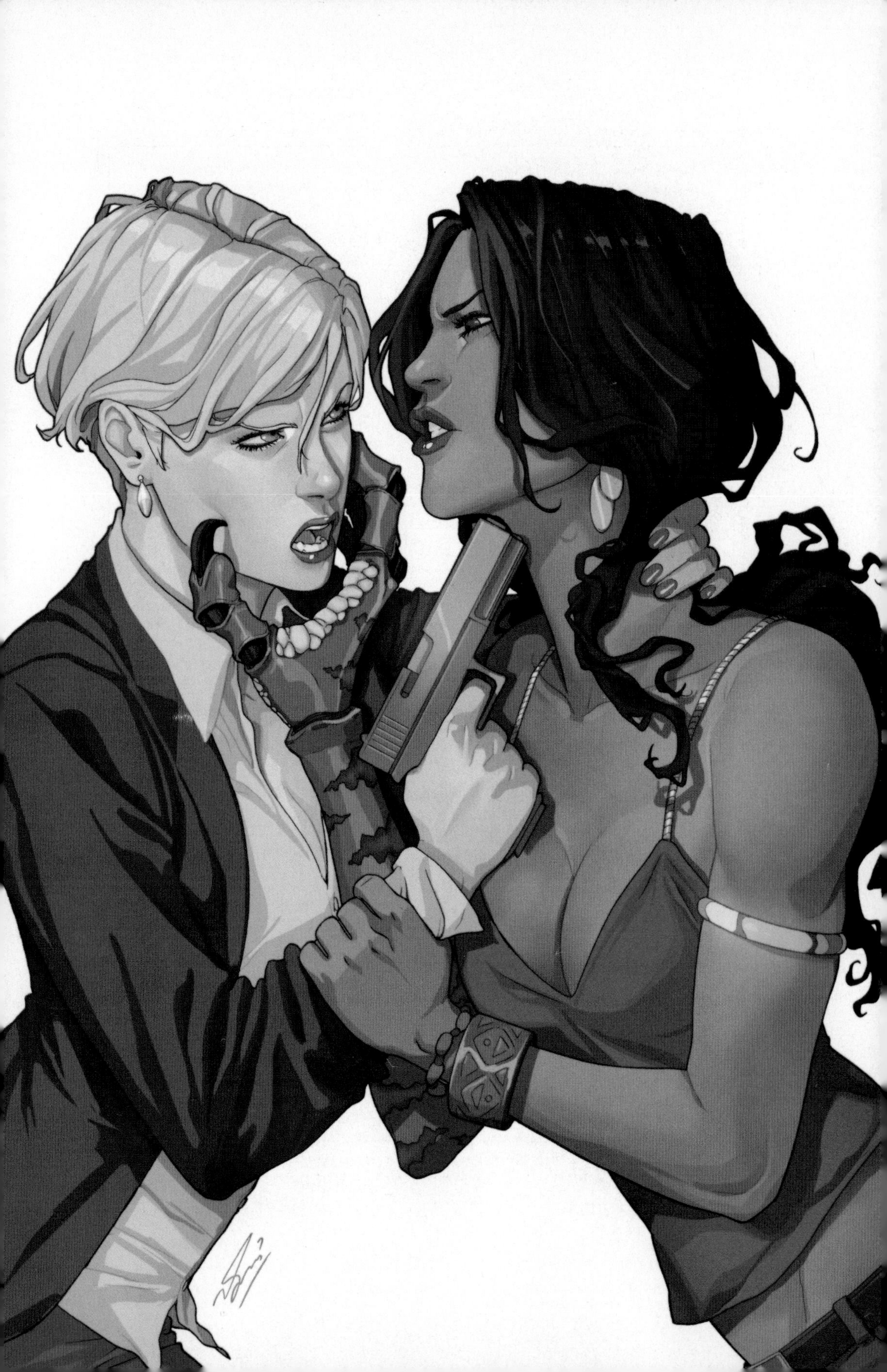

THE NEW 52!
JUSTICE LEAGUE
VOLUME 1 ORIGIN
GEOFF JOHNS JIM LEE SCOTT WILLIAMS

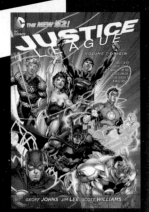

DC COMICS–THE NEW 52!

GRAPHIC NOVELS RELEASE SCHEDULE

MAY
- Animal Man Vol 1: The Hunt
- Batman Vol 1: The Court of Owls
- Catwoman Vol 1: The Game
- Green Arrow Vol 1: The Midas Touch
- Green Lantern Vol 1: Sinestro
- Justice League International Vol 1: The Signal Masters
- Justice League Vol 1: Origin
- Stormwatch Vol 1: The Dark Side
- Wonder Woman Vol 1: Blood

JUNE
- Batman: Detective Comics Vol 1: Faces of Death
- Batwoman Vol 1: Hydrology
- Frankenstein Agent of S.H.A.D.E. Vol 1: War of The Monsters
- Legion of Super-Heroes Vol 1: Hostile World
- Mister Terrific Vol 1: Mind Games
- Red Lanterns Vol 1: Blood and Rage
- Static Shock Vol 1: Supercharged

JULY
- Batgirl Vol 1: The Darkest Reflection
- Batwing Vol 1: The Lost Kingdom
- Batman and Robin Vol 1: Born to Kill
- Demon Knights Vol 1: Seven Against the Dark
- Grifter Vol 1: Most Wanted
- Men of War Vol 1: Uneasy Company
- Suicide Squad Vol 1: Kicked in the Teeth

AUGUST
- Deathstroke Vol 1: Legacy
- Hawk and Dove Vol 1: First Strikes
- O.M.A.C. Vol 1: Omactivate!
- Resurrection Man Vol 1: Dead Again
- Superman: Action Comics Vol 1: Superman and The Men of Steel
- Superboy Vol 1: Incubation
- Swamp Thing Vol 1: Raise Them Bones

SEPTEMBER
- Aquaman Vol 1: The Trench
- Birds of Prey Vol 1: Trouble in Mind
- The Fury of Firestorm: The Nuclear Men Vol 1: God Particle
- Green Lantern Corps Vol 1: Fearsome
- Legion Lost Vol 1: Run from Tomorrow
- Teen Titans Vol 1: It's Our Right to Fight
- Voodoo Vol 1: What Lies Beneath

OCTOBER
- All-Star Western Vol 1: Guns and Gotham
- Batman: The Dark Knight Vol 1: Knight Terrors
- Green Lantern: New Guardians Vol 1: The Ring Bearer
- I, Vampire Vol 1: Tainted Love
- Justice League Dark Vol 1: In the Dark
- Nightwing Vol 1: Traps and Trapezes
- The Savage Hawkman Vol 1: Darkness Rising
- Supergirl Vol 1: The Last Daughter of Krypton

THE NEW 52!
GREEN LANTERN
GEOFF JOHNS DOUG MAHNKE

THE NEW 52!
BATMAN
SCOTT SNYDER GREG CAPULLO JONATHAN GLAPION

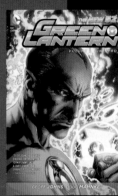

NOVEMBER
- Blackhawks Vol 1: The Great Leap Forward
- Blue Beetle Vol 1: Metamorphosis
- Captain Atom Vol 1: Evolution
- DC Universe Presents Vol 1 Featuring Deadman & Challengers of the Unknown
- The Flash Vol 1: Move Forward
- Red Hood and The Outlaws Vol 1: Redemption
- Superman Vol 1: What Price Tomorrow?

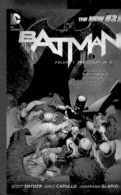

The First Volumes of the Decade's Biggest Comics Event

DCCOMICS.COM

DC COMICS